At the same time, the study challenges the contextual significance of empirical research: the relationship between listeners' expectations and preaching, the hopes that preaching connects to everyday existence, and that preaching in some sense mediates God's word, may even be considered to be transcultural. The study thus invites one to see preaching as a "catholic" feature of the worldwide church, both for preachers and listeners.

Theo Pleizier, PhD
Assistant Professor of Practical Theology,
Protestant Theological University, Groningen, Netherlands

Sermon Listening

A New Approach Based on Congregational Studies and Rhetoric

Enoh Šeba

© 2021 Enoh Šeba

Published 2021 by Langham Academic (Previously Langham Monographs)
An imprint of Langham Publishing
www.langhampublishing.org

Langham Publishing and its imprints are a ministry of Langham Partnership

Langham Partnership
PO Box 296, Carlisle, Cumbria, CA3 9WZ, UK
www.langham.org

ISBNs:
978-1-83973-221-8 Print
978-1-83973-481-6 ePub
978-1-83973-483-0 PDF

Enoh Šeba has asserted his right under the Copyright, Designs and Patents Act, 1988 to be identified as the Author of this work.

All rights reserved. No part of this publication may be reproduced, stored in a retrieval system or transmitted, in any form or by any means, electronic, mechanical, photocopying, recording or otherwise, without the prior written permission of the publisher or the Copyright Licensing Agency.

Requests to reuse content from Langham Publishing are processed through PLSclear. Please visit www.plsclear.com to complete your request.

Unless otherwise stated, Scripture quotations are from the New Revised Standard Version Bible, copyright © 1989 National Council of the Churches of Christ in the United States of America. Used by permission. All rights reserved.

British Library Cataloguing-in-Publication Data
A catalogue record for this book is available from the British Library

ISBN: 978-1-83973-221-8

Cover & Book Design: projectluz.com

Langham Partnership actively supports theological dialogue and an author's right to publish but does not necessarily endorse the views and opinions set forth here or in works referenced within this publication, nor can we guarantee technical and grammatical correctness. Langham Partnership does not accept any responsibility or liability to persons or property as a consequence of the reading, use or interpretation of its published content.

Contents

Abstract xi

Chapter 1 1
Introduction
    1.1 Context 1
    1.2 Problem and Significance 2
    1.3 Response 3

Chapter 2 5
Contemporary "Turn to the Listener" in Homiletics
    2.1 Communication Theory 7
    2.2 Literary Criticism and Philosophy 9
    2.3 Collaborative Approaches 13
    2.4 Conversational Approaches 15

Chapter 3 21
Rhetoric and Homiletics
    3.1 Classical Rhetoric 21
        3.1.1 Aristotle 22
        3.1.2. Cicero 25
        3.1.3 Quintilian 28
    3.2 Rhetoric and Homiletics – Story of the Intense Relationship 30
        3.2.1 Augustine 31
        3.2.2 Middle Ages and Reformation 35
        3.2.3 Enlightenment and Modern Era 36
    3.3 The Contemporary Revival, or How Homiletics Revisits
    Rhetoric 40
        3.3.1 Lucy Lind Hogan and Robert Reid 42
        3.3.2 Robin Meyers 46
        3.3.3 Craig Loscalzo 50

Chapter 4 57
Congregational Studies and Homiletics
    4.1 A Brief History of Congregational Studies 57
    4.2 A Closer Look: Three Classics 62
        4.2.1 James F. Hopewell 62
        4.2.2 Don S. Browning 65
        4.2.3 *Studying Congregations: A New Handbook* 67

    4.3 Homiletical Approaches Informed by Congregational
        Studies: Two Examples..72
        4.3.1 *Preaching as Local Theology and Folk Art*............................73
        4.3.2 *One Gospel, Many Ears* 78

Chapter 5 85
    Existing Empirical Studies in Preaching
    5.1 *Presence in the Pulpit*...85
        5.1.1 The Dimension of Security...86
        5.1.2 The Dimension of Deliverance 88
        5.1.3 The Dimension of Understanding.....................................89
        5.1.4 Further Observations..90
    5.2 *The Great American Sermon Survey*.....................................91
        5.2.1 Similarities and Differences 92
        5.2.2 Lessons for Listeners 94
        5.2.3 Lessons for Preachers...95
    5.3. *Listening to Listeners*..97
        5.3.1 Key Premises and Major Findings 98
        5.3.2 Listening Settings 99
        5.3.3 Twelve Features of Inviting Preaching............................103
        5.3.4 Concluding Observations...107

Chapter 6 111
    Croatian Baptists and Their Homiletical Practice
    6.1 History of Croatian Baptists..111
    6.2 The Existing Homiletical Literature.......................................118
    6.3 The Homiletical Practice of Croatian Baptists.....................122
    6.4 The Need for the Research 126

Chapter 7 129
    Presentation of Methodology
    7.1 Personal Motivation and Involvement 129
    7.2 Description and Details of the Research 131
    7.3 Research Strategy and Procedures 134

Chapter 8 139
    Data Presentation
    8.1 Ethos...141
        8.1.1 Communal Dimension...141
        8.1.2 Authentic Life of a Preacher...145
        8.1.3 Internal Ethos...147
    8.2 Logos 151
        8.2.1 Role of the Bible...151

    8.2.2 Authority 153
    8.2.3 Sermon Content 155
    8.2.4 God in the Sermon..158
  8.3 Pathos 161
    8.3.1 Congregational Emotions...162
    8.3.2 Listener's Emotions 164
  8.4 (Dis)connected 172
    8.4.1 Connections 173
    8.4.2 Disconnections 176

Chapter 9 185
Data Interpretation: Listeners' Expectations and Receptiveness

  9.1 General Expectations 185
    9.1.1 High Hopes of Preaching 185
    9.1.2 (Somewhat) Rough Reality 187
  9.2 Specific Expectations: When Sermons Are Actually Heard 191
    9.2.1 Understanding the Bible – Finding Guidance for
         Everyday Life..192
    9.2.2 Getting to Know God and Maintaining a
         Private Devotion...194
    9.2.3 Spiritual Battery Charging and Identity Affirmation........196
    9.2.4 Challenge to Change 198
  9.3 Are Expectations Sufficient? 199
  9.4 Responsibility: Backing Up Expectations......................................202
    9.4.1 Passive Responsibility 202
    9.4.2 Active Responsibility..206

Chapter 10.. 209
Theological and Theoretical Reflection

  10.1 Theological Framing 211
    10.1.1 *Imago Dei* and Formation of Character............................211
    10.1.2 Incarnation and Building the Community of Faith........219
    10.1.3 Priesthood of All Believers and the Relation of
          Community Identity to the Culture..................................225
  10.2 Final Reflections 230
  10.3 . . . and Some Personal Thoughts..233

Chapter 11.. 235
Suggestions for Improving the Practice of Preaching

  11.1 Suggestions to Preachers 236
    11.1.1 Understand Your Expectations...236
    11.1.2 They Want to Hear – Help Them! 237

        11.1.3 Never Underestimate their Commitment 238
        11.1.4 Appreciate the Diversity of the Audience 239
        11.1.5 If You Can't Listen, You Can't Preach – So
             Listen . . . and Repeat 240
        11.1.6 Do Not Persuade – Identify with Them Instead 241
        11.1.7 Actively Seek Critical Feedback 243
        11.1.8 Do Not Be Afraid of Losing Control 245
        11.1.9 Go Slowly 246
    11.2 Suggestions to the Listeners 248
        11.2.1 Come to Listen and Come to Hear 248
        11.2.2 Become a Constructive Contributor 249
        11.2.3 Take Your Share of Responsibility 250

Chapter 12 253
    Conclusion
    12.1 Limitations 253
    12.2 Research Objectives 257
        12.2.1 Expectations 257
        12.2.2. (Dis)engaging Factors 258
    12.3 Contribution to Knowledge 259
    12.4 Further Research Suggestions 264
        12.4.1 Preachers' Perspective 264
        12.4.2 Female Listeners' Perspective 265
        12.4.3 Perceptions from the Margin 265
        12.4.4 Passive Responsibility and Cultural Conditioning 266
        12.4.5 Identification Techniques and Strategies 267
    12.5 "Amen to That!" 267

Appendix 269
    Interview Questions

Bibliography 271

Abstract

The recent homiletical literature reveals the "turn to the listener" as a widespread trend of attempting to minimize the gap between the pulpit and the pew and indicates the increase in the reappropriation of various rhetorical contributions. At the same time, the development of congregational studies has encouraged practical theologians to conduct empirical studies in order to explore the highly contextual nature of sermon listeners' involvement in the practice of preaching. The investigation of my immediate context, however, proves that preaching holds a precious place in the theology and life of Croatian Baptist churches, but also identifies the absence of empirical research that probes their preaching practice from the hearers' perspective. These are the reasons why this study is motivated by the following research question: What are the real expectations and receptiveness of Croatian Baptists as sermon listeners, and how can these findings be utilised to improve the quality of preaching? To articulate dependable answers, I conducted a qualitative field study based on a phenomenological approach, using semi-structured interviews with eighteen members of five local Baptist congregations located in four Croatian towns. The feedback was interpreted by means of three rhetorical modes of appeal (logos, ethos, and pathos) which served a purpose of identifying their actual expectations and (dis)engaging factors that direct their listening participation and sermon reception. The same data was submitted to critical theological reflection, aiming at the theological warrants for constructive suggestions for the transformation of preaching practice. The findings from the research demonstrate that participants tend to hold a high view of preaching, and yet many of them report unmet expectations which may lead to lowering their expectations. Among the most prominent interviewees' expectations are: hope that the sermon will provide direction in their everyday life, desire to meet God during the sermon and to have their devotional reading of the Bible enhanced by sermon listening, a longing to have their spiritual batteries recharged, and anticipation that preaching should question their status quo and challenge them to change. Also, the study indicates that triggering the listeners' identification boosts their reception of the message and promotes their engagement. Although these particular findings are not generalisable, they nevertheless point to the possibility of an important implication: backing up the listeners' expectations with their active responsibility for the preaching may transform the entire practice into a constructive enterprise that bridges the gap between hearers and preachers. The specific suggestions, based on the study findings, to preachers and listeners in Croatian Baptist churches may serve both as an illustration of how preaching can be reestablished as a truly congregational practice and as an impetus for further studies in different contexts.

CHAPTER 1

Introduction

"When I am at church, I usually feel actively insulted by the rubbish I get to hear there most times."[1]

This sentence, written by a friend of mine who wished to remain anonymous, as a reflection on his experience of listening to sermons in various churches, illustrates the enigma that initially propelled this thesis. Preaching is typically an integral part of almost every church service – and for some Christian traditions, it is the focal point of their public worship and ecclesial identity. As such, its purpose has always been to communicate in order to edify, encourage, and enlarge the positive effects of congregating together as a people of God. Why, then, is the subjective perception of the listeners sometimes so different, if not completely opposite (an "active insult") from its intended goals? This inconsistency is intensified by its relative invisibility – the congregants attend the service Sunday after Sunday, and as they bring their expectations, they listen to sermons that create impressions and evoke responses that are not easily expressed, especially if they are not positive.

1.1 Context

Over the later part of the twentieth century, homileticians have increasingly addressed this and related problems by turning their attention to the listeners and their role in the preaching process. They have accurately identified the lack of dialogue and the inferior position of the listeners as the root of

---

1. Email to the author, 19 June 2015.

sermon inefficiency, experientially and repeatedly detected by both preachers and hearers in various contexts. Their own homiletical reconstructions have often been consolidated by insights from other disciplines, such as human communication theory, psychology, or literary criticism. Some of these contributions have effectively helped to build a new paradigm for preaching, one that respects the listeners by creating inductive movement in sermons, by incorporating dialogical principles, or by placing a stronger emphasis on acquiring a thick understanding of the actual listeners' world. It also has become clear that in taking this turn, homiletics can not only still learn from its ancient ally, rhetoric, but also receive valuable lessons from younger disciplines, such as congregational studies.

However, the prospects of closing the gap between preachers and their hearers can improve only insofar as the hearers are allowed to voice their concerns, convictions, and perspectives by themselves. As the researchers began to conduct empirical studies focused on those on the receiving end of sermonic communication, it has become evident that the preaching practice can experience qualitative transformation only when input from listeners is earnestly taken into account within its particular context. In light of these developments, a new trend is being developed that expects contemporary homiletics to precede its normative theological dimension with a descriptive approach that focuses on a particular *Sitz im Leben* of the preaching practice in question.

This is the wider context within which this thesis is located. So, in chapters 2–5, I will try to explicate more extensively four areas necessary for understanding this context. I will begin by focusing on the contemporary homiletical turn to the listener and move on to an account of the close relationship between rhetoric and homiletics in the past. A chapter on the development of congregational studies and their significance for homiletics follows. The fifth chapter will be dedicated to a presentation of three existing empirical studies on preaching from the listeners' perspective.

1.2 Problem and Significance

The awareness of this larger context directed my attention to a more immediate setting and helped me identify the crux of the problem. On the one hand, both theology and the history of the Croatian Baptists reserve a special place for preaching. On the other hand, its dynamics and underlying presumptions are typically never subjected to any serious evaluation. More specifically, preaching is both supposed to meet very high requirements and taken for granted without ever taking care to check the actual expectations, convictions, and needs entangled with the listeners' regular participation in sermon listening. Therefore, this entire sphere represents uncharted territory for Croatian Baptists and this thesis will be my attempt to articulate some responses to these concerns.

There are several reasons why a more profound comprehension of this problem can be so critical. First, hearing the listeners' side of the story will mean the development of prerequisites for dialogue will become part of the preaching practice. Opening a dialogue may allow all the participants to identify the real obstacles and address them properly. Such a dialogue could also pave the way for a continuous evaluation of preaching based on hard facts gathered from all involved parties. Secondly, the inclusion of listeners could also unlock a spectrum of chances for their involvement that is otherwise limited to a relatively inert mode of contribution. Thirdly, since the hearers stand for the congregational body present at the sermon, and it is these same hearers for whom the sermon is intended, their turning into active agents may lead to the unleashing of a fuller potential of the preaching practice in the life of the entire congregation. Finally, if this redefinition of the listeners' role can be supported by substantial theological and scriptural authentication, the whole practice of preaching might be reinvented as a vital dimension of congregational life, with formidable unifying and formative potentials.

1.3 Response

I now state how this research will be shaped to adequately address the issues described above. I will begin by formulating the research question: *What are the real expectations and receptiveness of Croatian Baptists as sermon listeners, and how can these findings be used to improve the quality of preaching?* The very nature of this question necessitates a qualitative field study rather than a quantitative study. The gradual development of my thesis demonstrated there was not enough naturally occurring data that could help me work out valid and trustworthy answers (this conclusion will be accounted for in chapter 6, after setting out a concise historical portrayal of Croatian Baptists with a special emphasis on their preaching practice). Thus, I had to decide upon a collection method that would generate the necessary type of data. A semi-structured individual interview proved to be the best choice. A more extensive explanation of these two decisions together with other methodological details will be offered in chapter 7.

As chapters 8 and 9 are entirely dedicated to the presentation and interpretation of the research data, I also need to mention the research integrity issues. Although I will further expand on these in chapter 7, my dual perspective of listener and preacher and the double role of insider and outsider should be acknowledged here and later considered while assessing my analysis and data interpretation alongside other personal motives that may affect my approach and involvement that could bear upon the process of data gathering and analysis.

Moving on from the interpretive stage of the research, I will also be shifting from a phenomenological approach to this qualitative study to a theological reflection that will help me understand whether there are sound theological grounds for envisioning a preaching practice focusing on the listeners' participation. Learning from the feedback of interviewees in this study, I will also ask about the potential benefits and possible repercussions for the entire congregation and its existence and identity. Dealing with these matters will be a main concern in chapter 10.

In chapter 11 I will articulate an answer to the latter part of the research question, which will take shape in a dozen tentative but contextually conditioned suggestions, for both preachers and listeners in Croatian Baptist congregations. Yet my hope is that they might elicit a certain degree of recognition among the readers (both preachers and listeners) from different backgrounds and instil further thinking through their preaching practice that can lead to the incremental development of more faithful expressions and dynamics of preaching within their respective situations.

My last chapter will serve as a conclusion. I will recount the methodological limitations of my study and sum up the deficiencies I observed during the research process. I will proceed with revisiting my research question and objectives and enumerate the unique contributions of my approach to this field. The chapter will conclude by giving an account of those subject matters that deserve further investigation but fell beyond the scope of the present study.

Before focusing attention on the specifics of my field study, I will start with a literature review section in the next five chapters beginning with contemporary homiletics and its take on the role of listeners in the preaching event.

CHAPTER 2

Contemporary "Turn to the Listener" in Homiletics

This chapter describes the homiletical trend that has been called the "turn to the listener" and that has significantly shaped various homiletical contributions in the latter part of the previous century. I will identify the major pieces of evidence and milestones of this trend, and concisely discuss the homiletics of several contemporary scholars. For reasons of space, I will not address the awareness of the importance of the listeners' part in the preaching process that existed before the twentieth century. Instead, I will proceed from the proposition that even though the listeners' role in preaching has never been a prominent concern, still there were historical periods during which preachers were more conscious of a demand to make their communication more easily apprehended by their specific listeners.[1] What follows is an exploration of the rediscovery of a dormant awareness of the importance of the listeners' part in the preaching process.

To start with, a brief recapitulation of the effects of Karl Barth's confrontation with the theological liberalism of the nineteenth century is necessary. In his theology the movement of God's self-revelation, and especially the incarnation and the second coming, prescribe the contents of preaching and set its boundaries. Thus, the word of God comes only from above and cannot arise from below: "Revelation is a closed system in which God is a subject,

---

1. For instance, Beverly Zink-Sawyer provides an early example, by mentioning Augustine and his "calling preachers to give deliberate attention to their mediation of the sacred space between the word of God and faithful listeners." Zink-Sawyer, "Word Purely Preached," 344.

the object, and the middle term."[2] Within this system, a preacher faithfully reproduces the word he hears, but there is no place for invention since ". . . it [the word of God] owes nothing to man's ingenuity; he can only bear witness to it."[3] The proclamation of God's truth does not require "vain images" or "outpourings of sentimental eloquence" on the preacher's part.[4] Preaching cannot be seen as "a joint action by two collaborators. It is the exercise of sovereign power on the part of God and obedience on the part of man."[5] The sole purpose of preaching is to confess the word of God.

However, the larger part of the twentieth century witnessed the overall decline of preaching's effectiveness and relevance, which led many preachers to reexamine the otherwise dominant Barthian standpoint; and their regular practice convinced them that such a clean, fully theological approach to preaching was impossible because sermons are always and inevitably embodied. Thomas Long suggests that at this stage many preachers have rediscovered the argument that Emil Brunner used in his dispute with Barth – he believed that the gospel can meet a human being only in his or her particularity and in specific situations.[6] Reaching that point requires preachers to get to know their listeners as they are in real life. Ronald Allen summarizes this requisite well: "The preacher who has a sense of the patterns of thought, feeling, and behaviours in the congregation can develop the sermon to have an optimum opportunity to communicate with the congregation."[7]

But how can this sense be obtained? How can the sermon be designed to take actual listeners seriously in all their human complexity? And have there been impacts other than the preachers' poor performance that stimulated and reinforced the homileticians' movement toward the hearers? Actually, there are many such stimuli and several ways of taking heed of listeners. For the sake of clarity, I will in some degree borrow from Allen's categorisation

---

2. Barth, *Preaching of Gospel*, 12.
3. Barth, 82.
4. Barth, 12–13.
5. Barth, 16.
6. Long, "And How Shall They," 174–179.
7. Allen, "Turn to Listener," 168.

of various stimuli and approaches to listeners,[8] although other systematic presentations can also be helpful.[9]

2.1 Communication Theory

The first stimulus to consider is the development of contemporary communication theory which began after World War II. It demonstrated some shortcomings of the linear model of communication which consisted of three elements: the sender/speaker, the message, and the recipient/hearer. In that model, a communication occurs when the sender forms his or her message and delivers it to the receiver who receives it. This understanding of communication is rather static and presupposes that communication traffic is a one-way process. When applied to homiletics, it became apparent both that traditional communication theory cannot account for all intricacies of preaching and that new developing theories can provide much more productive impulses for the redefinition of the preaching practice. Given a growing awareness that there is less and less evidence of substantial change in individuals and community as a result of the preaching ministry, it comes as no surprise that some homileticians turned to communication theory for help.

As early as the 1960s, Clyde H. Reid[10] undertook a study of the sermon as a form of communication and reached several conclusions: (1) the origin of the problem with preaching is in its communicative limitations; (2) the sermon usually takes on a monologic shape and as such represents a form of mass communication and is therefore unsuitable for the persuasion of listeners concerning controversial issues (to produce their comprehension of the preacher's message, its acceptance and resulting action, two-way communication is essential); (3) the sermon in itself is inadequate for the communication of the gospel unless it is supported by more elaborate "dialogue structures" which presuppose a more active involvement of the laity (sermon listeners).

At about the same time, Reuel Howe conducted one of the first investigations on preaching.[11] He observed that preaching is too often perceived as min-

---

8. Allen, 170–195.
9. For example, see Riegert, "What Is Authoritative," 5–14; Graves, "Deeply Dialogical," 24–31.
10. Reid, *Empty Pulpit*.
11. Howe, *Partners in Preaching*. Although he does not report extensively on his methodology, his book is mainly derived from a series of discussions with and among various

isterial performance which makes the audience passive and nonresponsive. His findings convinced him that the "lack of feedback strengthens all the stereotypes which people entertain about preaching." He also observed that the practice of preaching without feedback is an "irresponsible communication,"[12] unknown in other fields of human endeavour. Thus, he proposed the necessity of introducing dialogue in preaching, and he made a distinction between dialogue as a method and dialogue as a principle. The dialogical principle is a concern that prompts the preacher to care for and be sensitive to his listeners' experiences and perceptions, which in turn inspires them to come to grips with their own meaning after they have heard the preacher's meaning. Naturally, such dialogical preaching must be inclusive, meaning that it must make good use of contexts and practices which the congregation can recognize and identify with. At the same time, he calls for reflective listening from the congregation – "If the preaching of the gospel is urgent, so also is the hearing of the gospel, and an urgent hearer can make an urgent speaker. Each needs the other."[13] Therefore, for Howe, the problems with the failure of preaching are to be dealt with through the replacement of unsatisfactory communication principles, and this primarily means a stronger engagement on the recipient's side of the communication process.

Another development should be mentioned. Cultural studies in the 1960s pointed to the differences between oral and print cultures, showing that different mediums used for the transmission of the message possess different logic and shape different knowledge. The most often quoted statement of that period is Marshall McLuhan's line: "The medium is the message." The straightforward implication for homiletics was that the sermon as an oral communication is not to be composed and delivered using deductive and linear logic dictated by print logic. Instead, a new modus operandi is required which would allow the preacher's spoken words to become something more congenial to the oral-aural ways of communication and thus more easily establish contact with her hearers.

---

groups of clergy and laity, usually taking place after the church service and exchanging views on the sermon just heard.

12. Howe, 36.
13. Howe, 91.

In the following decades, a number of scholars continued to use empirical socio-scientific research based on contemporary communication theory in order to discuss the process of homiletical communication,[14] to suggest various ways in which preaching could be transformed to appreciate the circular and simultaneous nature of the communication process, and to elevate listeners above the role of mere consumers of religious entertainment. However, from the perspective of my subject matter, it is suitable to take note of Ronald Allen's remark that although much of communication theory draws from empirical research, such research has rarely been undertaken among congregations and their members as regular sermon listeners. Besides, the interest in communication theory has gradually diminished over time, which is not the case with other disciplines that are instrumental in the homiletical turn to the listener.[15]

2.2 Literary Criticism and Philosophy

Another impulse for making preaching more oriented toward listeners can be found in the philosophy of language and literary criticism. In his historical overview of the development of the New Homiletic – probably the most important homiletical paradigm shift of the twentieth century – O. Wesley Allen points out that although some preachers and homileticians have prefigured its emergence, it was really other academic disciplines which provided the strongest momentum for the rise of the New Homiletic.[16]

In the "linguistic turn" initiated by philosophers Ludwig Wittgenstein, Martin Heidegger, and others who maintained that the function of the language is not to name the reality, but to construct it, O. W. Allen recognizes the starting point of the trajectory that led to the New Homiletic. Following the work of Rudolf Bultmann, Ernst Fuchs and Gerhard Ebeling have founded a school of the New Hermeneutic which had a profound effect on Bible interpretation and preaching. The Bible has ceased to be a storehouse of eternal truths which can be unlocked only by the scientific approach or the source of the faith content which is to be discovered by asking the right questions.

---

14. A helpful overview of these efforts can be found in Allen, "Turn to Listener," 173–176.
15. Allen, 196.
16. Allen, 5.

Rather, it is a "word event" and its proper interpretation requires the existential involvement and willingness to allow its text "to ask questions of the interpreter." In this view, preaching is primarily an event whose goal is to help hearers to experience an encounter with the word of God. This encounter can, in turn, put some life-transforming decisions before the hearers.

At least equally influential was the work of Hans-Georg Gadamer. His concept of understanding as a process of negotiation and dialogue or as he puts it, of "fusion of horizons" had implications both for reading the Bible and for sermonic communication. As conversation always takes place in a language that does not reflect reality representationally, it is the language that creates this event of human experience of reality. A language represents a medium of our engagement with the world, but it inevitably and always involves other people.[17]

Roland Barthes' essay *The Death of an Author* stands for a paradigmatic contribution of critics who argued that the authorial intentions and their biographical data are usually unknowable and irrelevant for interpretation of their writing.[18] Instead, the readers turn into more active participants who construct the text's meanings rather than just consume them. Notions like this were representative of reader-response theory that focuses on the readers and it is their experience of a written work that guides their interpretation and completes the meaning of the text. This theory signified "the birth of the reader" and together with other ideas mentioned above, in the coming decades it significantly modified the perception of human communication, the roles of participants in communication, and the processes of literary interpretation.

This new understanding of language and literature was perhaps first fully applied to homiletics in David James Randolph's *The Renewal of Preaching*.[19] The definition he proposes is: "Preaching is the event in which the biblical text is interpreted in order that its meaning will come to expression in the concrete situation of the hearers."[20] The goal of a sermon is a ". . . *concretion*

---

17. Possibly Gadamer's most representative volume is *Truth and Method* (London: Bloomsbury Publishing, 2013).

18. Laura Seymour, *Roland Barthes's The Death of the Author* (Macat International Limited, 2018).

19. Randolph, *Renewal of Preaching*. The subtitle of this volume, *A New Homiletic Based on the New Hermeneutic,* mentions the term Randolph invented several years before to name a new, emerging approach to preaching.

20. Randolph, *Renewal of Preaching*, 1.

by bringing the meaning of the text to the expression in the situation of the hearers, rather than abstraction by merely exhibiting the text against its own background."[21] To accomplish this expression, the sermon must be concerned with the effect on the listeners, that is, with its function. He holds that the form of the biblical text may be suggestive for the sermon form, because then preaching will be more likely to do the same for contemporary hearers as the text did for the original readers or audience. Randolph also encourages preachers to employ their listening skills, primarily during their pastoral counselling ministry, to get a better understanding of how their preaching affects their listeners.

There is a unanimous agreement among scholars that the publishing of Fred B. Craddock's *As One Without Authority* in 1971 was a major milestone for homiletics of the last century.[22] In this book, all the impulses described so far culminated in the sense that Craddock not only fully recognizes the need for preaching that will be oriented toward listeners but also provides an extensive argument for such preaching. He was convinced the sermons of that era were simply not communicating, giving two reasons: (1) the increasing secularization of society and other rapid changes (technology, mass media . . .) have undermined the authority of the preacher and of the Scripture in a sense that it is not taken for granted anymore, and this reality requires a new relationship between the preacher and the listeners; and (2) old preaching forms do not accommodate well to new situations, especially because homiletics has previously allowed a separation between the form and the content. As a response, he suggested a twofold motion. First, this new relationship must entail more dialogue between the preacher and the listeners because they no longer consent to be just passive recipients, or in Craddock's own term, "javelin catchers."[23] Second, what needs to be revived is an awareness that the method of preaching itself represents a message. He goes as far as to say that the method of preaching can better disclose the preacher's theology than the content of his preaching.

He suggests that the prevalent type of sermon is determined by deductive movement and is effective in communicating only to the listeners who are

---

21. Randolph, 21.
22. Craddock, *As One*.
23. Craddock, 55.

ready to receive conclusions stated at the beginning of the sermon and then in the course of the sermon applied to their lives. However, Craddock is positive that a movement incorporating these observed needs is required. For a start, the inductive sermon must move from the particulars of experience shared by the listeners to the conclusion. This seemingly simple reversal means that if the particulars of experience provide a sermon's starting point, then there is a need for some shared ground which requires the preacher's identification with the listeners, so that they can later identify with her sermon. Since the preacher does not begin with the conclusion of her inductive study that took place during the preparation, she preaches in a way that opens a possibility for listeners to take the same road of inductive investigation and then to reach their own conclusions (which may differ from the preacher's). Finally, if the listeners manage to travel their own trip toward the conclusion, their own internalisation of the message will be highly personal and particular.

In that respect, the sermon can be best described as an "event" and its goal as a transformative experience for the listeners. This transformation is feasible because the inductive movement expects that listeners to fill in the gaps with their meanings, decisions, and ideas. Furthermore, using Heidegger's hermeneutics, Craddock demonstrates the radically different nature of the interpretative process: "[O]ne listens to the Word hopeful that it will shed light on our own situation which is obscure. The word of God is not interpreted; it interprets."[24]

In short, Craddock formulated an inductive theory of preaching out of his concern for the listeners. Keeping the monological form, he encouraged preachers to set up a specific dialogical principle which requires a capability to anticipate the listeners' response, and a capability to shape the sermon to the challenge of that response. Craddock himself became a leading figure of the New Homiletic, an outstanding but somewhat diffuse and diversified homiletical paradigm. Yet the common denominator of the movement's understanding of the listeners' role can be summarized in this way: listeners become active partners; they must be allowed to make sense of a homiletical event and to freely complete the sermon for themselves (even if this completion

---

24. Craddock, 42.

means the rejection of the sermon's message); and the sermon must appeal not only to the listeners' belief but to their experience and perception, too.[25]

Another notable change must be observed. During the 1960s and 1970s the eminence of the historical-critical analysis began to recede, and the Scriptures were increasingly read and interpreted as a work of literature. This trend resulted in a profounder understanding of the narrative dimension of the Bible and in the development of narrative theology. Consequently, in the 1980s both literary criticism and narrative theology inspired preaching to focus on the narrative dimension of both human experience and scriptural literature. The narrative character of God's saving story, in which believers participate, shed light on narrativity as a valid basis for the sermonic form and content, and redirected attention to the literary form of the biblical texts. Almost simultaneously, previous achievements of literary criticism affirmed the legitimacy of a plurality of interpretations. All these developments taken together signalled a need to redefine the role of listeners in the preaching process.

2.3 Collaborative Approaches

A different avenue toward listeners and their stronger participation in the homiletical event has been taken by some preachers and homileticians. When describing examples of this approach, Allen suggests that all of them are based on the process of listeners feeding forward into the sermon.[26] The primary undergirding idea is to get the listeners involved in the course of sermon preparation. This has two indisputable advantages: on the one hand, listeners are included even *before* the moment of preaching – moreover, they actively participate in the hermeneutical process. On the other hand, the preacher not only increasingly becomes aware of their perceptions of the biblical text, but he also begins to understand some of their questions, ideas, aspirations, and life struggles. Thus, the sermon preached from the pulpit is no longer the result of one person's labour or the act of oral communication delivered from a single perspective, but the fruit of collaboration between listeners and preacher.

---

25. An excellent contemporary reevaluation of the New Homiletic, written by some of its key protagonists, can be found in O. W. Allen, *The Renewed Homiletic*.

26. Allen, "Turn to Listener," 170–173.

The first to propose such an approach was Dietrich Ritschl in the early 1960s.[27] He believed that the entire congregation needed to be engaged in proclamation, a belief inspired by the doctrine of the priesthood of all believers. He suggested that in the early phase of sermon preparation, the preacher and a certain number of church members have to spend time reading and listening to the biblical text which they have selected together. The preacher then proceeds with the preparation by himself and the delivery is still monological, but his responsibility in shaping the sermon will be different after he has been assisted by the initial input from the congregation.

At about the same time, Browne Barr reported on his "sermon seminars," which were mid-week meetings when he would introduce the biblical text with a short exegesis, followed by a discussion in small groups about the relation of this text to the listeners' everyday life. There was no strict structure for these discussions, but they would conclude with plenary sessions when the groups' conclusions would be presented. The seminar would then close with a prayer time. The input collected at such sessions provided the preacher with insights into the listeners' authentic experiences and a clear sense of direction concerning the development of the sermon. Nevertheless, it was still up to the preacher to complete the process, draw up and deliver a sermon on Sunday, although her listeners had previously invested something of themselves into this process.

Probably the most elaborated and sophisticated implementation of this approach has been offered by John S. McClure in what he calls "collaborative preaching."[28] He employs an image of a "sermon roundtable" to indicate a preparatory session in which up to ten church members and visitors meet with the preacher. Before turning to the next Sunday's biblical text, the members discuss whether last Sunday's sermon mirrored their previous conversation in an adequate way. Then a brainstorming process begins in which group members deliberately engage with the voice of Scripture through a mutual conversation while the preacher serves as a facilitator. Afterwards he is the one who prepares the final form of the sermon which must remain faithful to

---

27. Ritschl, *Theology of Proclamation*, 117–134, 149–157, quoted in Allen, *Homiletic of All Believers*, 7.

28. McClure's homiletical conceptions span several of his books, but most relevant are *Roundtable Pulpit* and *Other-Wise Preaching*.

the dynamics of that roundtable discussion, meaning that the group's experience of the gospel must be either described or imitated. In a way, the group conversation *becomes* a sermon.

Even though McClure significantly redefines the hermeneutical task and envisions it as a shared responsibility of preacher and listeners, it is his insistence on diversity and the appreciation of differences as conversation starters that clearly distinguishes his collaborative preaching. Simultaneously, his abiding emphasis on the concept of "otherness" functions as a safeguard that keeps us from presuming a "symmetry of experience" between preacher and congregation, and as something that surpasses the reaching of consensus. "The goal of collaborative preaching is neither a like-minded community of obedient clones, nor a tolerant community of insightful individuals. The goal is a learning community of deeply engaged strangers."[29] In this way, he establishes his correlation with the other three homileticians who have yet to be mentioned here. Their contributions, though, fall under a slightly different category.

2.4 Conversational Approaches

This other set of approaches can be labelled as "conversational preaching." Its dominant characteristic is conversation as a metaphor, meaning that the preaching does not include the literal conversation but still aims at creating a sermon in which multiple conversation partners can recognize their voices.

In this manner, Lucy Atkinson Rose understands preaching as having two intrinsic presuppositions.[30] First, there is a fundamental connectedness between preacher and congregation. They belong to the same community of faith. They are interdependent, and both preacher and congregation are neither sender nor receiver of the message. The gap between preacher and listeners, so typical for more traditional homiletical theories, is obliterated, and they ". . . stand together as explorers, while a text, meaning or a mystery lies on the other side or confronts us as Other." What follows is that the hierarchical relationship between preacher and hearers is abolished, and this opens up the possibility for a truly conversational nature of preaching. Second, the

---

29. McClure, *Roundtable Pulpit*, 54.
30. Rose, *Sharing Word*, 89–91.

language used in preaching, just as all language, is "biased and limited" and "never innocent or unambiguous."

So when Rose says that the purpose of preaching is to gather God's people around the word, she means preaching as a conversation which "fosters and refocuses the church's central conversations."[31] These include dialoguing with God, but also with a range of human partners – people in the congregation, other communities of faith, marginal and excluded voices, and the world. The primary function of preaching is to edify the community of faith and to encourage members to corporately grow into the priesthood of all believers. However, due to serious limitations of language, this purpose can be accomplished only through careful evocative preaching which will not offer any fixed meaning but rather some specific experiences and tentative interpretations that will stimulate the listeners to create their own multiple meanings. The content of preaching remains particular and provisional and is always open to the test of further conversations within the community. Finally, the sermon Rose envisions does not include any actual interaction – it remains monologic in its outlook – but it must promote the communal search for meanings and the creation of the atmosphere of solidarity in which "[t]he preacher and the congregation gather symbolically at a round table where there is no head and no foot, where labels like clergy and laity blur, and where believing or wanting to believe is all that matters."[32]

Another proponent of conversational preaching is Ronald J. Allen.[33] For him, the conversation consists of establishing a "mutual critical correlation between claims of Christian tradition from the past (or from the other communities in the present) and the congregation in its present time, place, and social-intellectual-theological location."[34] It begins in the mind of the preacher as he prepares the sermon, it continues during its embodiment, and extends to the time after the sermon when the listeners continue to ponder and discuss. He develops his notion from Paul Tillich's concept of correlation, and from David Tracy's later correction of that concept. Basically, this is a two-way conversation in which the current situation receives corrections and answers

---

31. Rose, 94.

32. Rose, "Conversational Preaching," 26–30.

33. Ronald J. Allen is a prolific writer, but the best insight into his contributions can be acquired by reading *Interpreting Gospel* and "Preaching Mutual Critical Correlation," 1–22.

34. Allen, "Preaching Mutual Critical Correlation," 8.

from the tradition **and** the Christian tradition can be criticized from the standpoint of present-day experiences and knowledge of the congregation. This means there are several conversation partners: God, tradition, the Bible, the congregation, the life experience of the preacher, the wider Christian community, and the world. The ultimate purpose of preaching is to get closer to the "theologically adequate interpretation of the world" and to reevaluate the congregation's interpretation of the gospel.

After identifying the focus of a particular sermon (typically, this is a biblical passage, a doctrine or Christian practice), the preacher must recognize both hers and the congregation's existing preunderstandings of that focus. Only then is she to engage in conversation with her partners which will lead to the stage when the interpretative possibilities will be acknowledged, and actual mutual critical correlation established. But in this final stage some normative guidance is required, and Allen proposes the application of three norms, which he borrows from Clark Williamson – appropriateness to the gospel, intelligibility, and moral plausibility.[35] However, the interpretation reached at the end of this process is not to be considered as final or fixed. In Allen's understanding, each human expression of faith is partially determined by the interpretation, which is inevitably attached to assumptions typical for that historical period, so this particular interpretation as offered in the sermon should be open for future conversation and reevaluation.

Although it is certainly true that these conversational approaches shift some of the weight of authority and responsibility from the preacher toward the listeners and bridge the gap between the biblical text and hearers, it is also correct, as O. W. Allen observes, that in these models there are no real conversations in which hearers actively participate, that conversation is experienced much more by the preacher than by the hearers, and finally, that the sermon often appears as the beginning of every conversation within the congregation, as if there would be no other conversation if it were not for preaching.[36]

This brings us to the last scholar in this overview of recent homiletical contributions which have inaugurated "turn to the listener" in a critical way. O. W. Allen builds on the work of Rose, McClure, and Allen (among others)

---

35. For a more extensive description of these criteria, see Allen, *Interpreting Gospel*, 82–88.
36. Allen, *Homiletic of All Believers*, 14.

and begins with a careful definition of the term "conversation," since many scholars use that term or similar terms only as "passing metaphors." For him, the significant distinctiveness of conversation is that its goal is conversion and not persuasion which distinguishes it from the debate or argument. But the real novelty of his approach is reflected in his assertion that homiletical practice must not be ruled by the doctrine of the word of God, but by the doctrine of God's omnipresence. There are at least two indirect consequences of this theological statement.

First, this allows him to shift "the locus of the conversation from the preacher and the sermon to the congregation itself." Hence the "sermon ceases to be the starting point or the centre of the conversation and becomes a significant contributing factor to the ongoing conversations owned by the community."[37] In that respect, the purpose of the preaching is to contribute to the general matrix of the church's conversations as a "privileged" and "specialized voice" in this "give-and-take proclamation of the church." Preaching needs to be associated with the omnipresence of God which is discernible in all of the church's conversations and which must be proclaimed (but not exclusively through preaching). O. W. Allen is convinced that this is not a degradation of the role of preaching, but rather a restoration to its proper place.

Second, this also modifies the role and authority of the preacher. She is not responsible for the transferring of God's presence to those in the pews anymore. What is expected of a preacher, instead, is to refer to God's presence which is persistently experienced by individual believers and by the community as a body. Again, it may sound like an understatement of the preachers' role, but he maintains that their training and knowledge of how to recognize and proclaim God's presence sets them apart and serves as a reason why congregations will vest them with authority. Moreover, after making a historical survey of the linguistic turn which I have mentioned above, he demonstrates that the creative power of language as explicated by Heidegger, New Hermeneutic, and New Homiletic has smoothly blended with the Reformers' identification of the sermon as the word of God. Therefore preachers today should be viewed as "language teachers who offer the 'vocabulary' of Christian traditions to their congregations to use to shape, define, and create reality; that

---

37. Allen, 14–15.

is, to make meaning of God, self, and the world."[38] It is crucial to keep in mind that the reappropriation of this old "vocabulary" can happen only as a part of the slow process of speaking this language – and there is no speaking without listening. In that respect a conversational homiletic must not concentrate so much on an individual sermon, but on the cumulative effect that preaching week after week has on the ongoing conversations of the congregation.

By this time, an attentive reader would perhaps raise the question of the theological dimension of this critical homiletical shift. Of course, this is a fully legitimate question, but I will deal with it properly in chapter 10 by looking at the arguments that promise to prove that more active participation of listeners is not without its theological warrants. At this point, it will be sufficient to disclose that these arguments will depend on the treatment of three respective Christian doctrines: *imago Dei*, the incarnation and the priesthood of all believers.

In the previous section I tried to demonstrate that the contemporary turn to the listener in homiletics has not happened in isolation from other (nontheological) forces within the wider cultural sphere. From literary theory and communication theories, preachers have discovered that their audiences think, hear, and learn in many different ways. As more attention has been given to the listeners, various marginal groups that have never before been fully included in the life of the congregation emerged as potentially important conversation partners. And yet, there are still other disciplines that have an impact on homiletics today and will be examined in the following chapters. The first of these is rhetoric.

---

38. Allen, 54.

CHAPTER 3

Rhetoric and Homiletics

Over the course of its long history the term "rhetoric" has assumed multiple meanings. Contemporary societies all over the world frequently use that word in a pejorative sense – either it presupposes some sort of manipulation or misleading insincerity on the part of the speaker and implies "communication that trades on emotional appeal (and perhaps deception) in the absence of serious reasoning,"[1] or it signifies that there is not much content in the uttered words. This unfavourable usage only serves to echo the controversies that have surrounded this term since its very origins and to point to other, more subtle and profound levels of meaning which surpass the colloquial modes of expression.

This chapter will present a brief outline of historical development of this art until the present day, including the recent rebirth of interest in rhetoric. In addition, it will be shown how the practice of Christian preaching became entangled with rhetoric in a rather complex and ambiguous relationship. Finally, I will provide a concise account of a few contemporary homiletical reappropriations of various rhetorical theories.

3.1 Classical Rhetoric

In the fifth and fourth centuries BC the term τέχνη λόγον ("the art of speech, words, or discourse")[2] was being used for a number of rhetorical techniques that were already present in Greek society and literature. Their common

---
1. Murphy, *Reasoning and Rhetoric*, 57.
2. Kennedy, "Historical Survey of Rhetoric," 3.

characteristic was a persuasiveness of speech; George A. Kennedy describes the social context within which they developed as "the administrative and legal system of constitutional governments, which required individual citizens to be able to speak on their own behalf, often before large audiences."[3] Thus the purpose of the first written work on rhetoric, composed probably in the second quarter of the fifth century BC by Corax from Syracuse, was to equip citizens to argue their cases in court trials.

The invention of the term "rhetoric" is traditionally attributed to Plato (429–347 BC), although this coinage was incited by his disregard for the widespread practice of many Sophist philosophers, such as Gorgias (483–375 BC). He believed rhetoric is intrinsically shallow and seeks only the speaker's instant self-interest – and as such represents the opposite of a search for the truth through dialectic.[4] In his view, it was a simulation of justice and mere "pandering."[5] Rhetoric, Plato believed, should be considered a skill of practice, void of knowledge, and therefore inappropriate to be called an art or a subject of true philosophy.

Nevertheless, orators of the fifth and fourth centuries BC used and adjusted various Greek oral traditions of speech, and rhetoric was regularly taught in oratorical schools. However, Plato's account of Sophists' rhetoric pointed out what could constitute a valid art of rhetoric and provided the solid cornerstone on which a rhetorical theory will be built in the centuries to come.

3.1.1 Aristotle

Scholars are practically unanimous in considering Aristotle the most prominent figure in the history of rhetoric and in taking his theory as the most influential rhetorical contribution to the development of Western civilisation. In his book *On Rhetoric*, he works out a full rhetorical system with its rules of composition and technical frame of reference. What follows here is a short overview of his unique contributions.

---

3. Kennedy, 7.
4. Agnew, "Classical Period," 9.
5. Plato, *Gorgias*, 463a; 463d–465.

3.1.1.1 Relation to the Dialectic and Logical Reasoning

Aristotle's dealings with rhetoric reflect his awareness of numerous situations when demonstrative reasoning with its truthful premises and corresponding conclusion is not applicable. In such cases, non-logical factors such as probabilities have to be taken into account instead. Thus, he considered rhetoric to be only a knowledge of speech, ". . . a certain kind of offshoot *[paraphues]* of dialectic and of ethical studies (which it is just to call politics)."[6] Yet, he admitted that rhetoric still has some similarities with dialectic and shares with it specific logical elements.[7] This approval allowed him to turn rhetoric into a practical art, albeit contextually bound to monological oration performed as a civic discourse, concerned with reaching a verdict or enacting a policy. Such an art seeks after plausible arguments which will be presented so that the rhetor's listeners are persuaded in the end.

3.1.1.2 Three Genres of Rhetoric

Another important contribution of Aristotle was his categorisation of different species of rhetoric which can be differentiated according to the character of speech, the time it refers to, and the goal it seeks to achieve. A *deliberative* rhetoric is used in democratic assemblies where future decisions are being discussed and its goal can be either exhortation or dissuasion of listeners. Another genre is *judicial* rhetoric which is typical of law courts, concerned with accusations or indictments against somebody. Obviously, the goal of such speech is to prosecute or to defend. Finally, there is an *epideictic* rhetoric when the speaker refers to the past in his effort to praise or reproach somebody or something.[8] In all three instances, an audience needs to make a judgement, so the speaker must know how to craft persuasive arguments.

3.1.1.3 Means of Persuasion

However, rhetoric cannot be unrestrained in its search for the means of persuasion, and Aristotle makes a sharp distinction between those "nonartistic" means which already exist independently of a speaker and of his speech

---

6. Aristotle, *On Rhetoric*, 1.2.7.
7. Aristotle, 1.2.7.
8. The initial division is presented in Aristotle, *On Rhetoric*, 1.3. The more elaborate treatment follows in 1.4. – 1.15.

and those "artistic" means which the speaker must invent by a method. Consequently, he singles out three artistic means of persuasion or modes of appeal: logos, ethos, and pathos.[9] Obviously, the use of valid logical argument according to the exposition of Aristotle's rhetorical theory will make a rational appeal to hearers, but they inevitably make their decisions on the basis of other factors, too.

Listeners, in general, are attentive to the ethical dimension because they do not want to listen to someone who is either deceived himself, or liable to mislead them. In other words, Aristotle argues that on issues where there is no conclusive knowledge, listeners are more likely to believe a fair-minded person. The credibility of a speaker's character will result in his persuasiveness insofar as listeners perceive him as a person with practical wisdom, virtue, and goodwill. But Aristotle also suggests that any speech must be adapted to the character of the group of listeners – that is, the speaker's character must suit the presumed character of people who belong to the specific group defined by their age and fortune. He himself appeared to be so convinced of the sway of ethos that at one point he practically assigned to it primacy over other means of persuasion: ". . . character is almost, so to speak, the controlling factor in persuasion."[10]

As for pathos, Aristotle counsels the speaker to fashion his speech in a way that arouses such emotions among his audience that they become more inclined toward a specific judgement. However, before becoming capable of such undertaking, the speaker must make sure that he knows his listeners' state of mind when this particular emotion is felt, the object of their emotion (toward whom it is directed), and the reasons for that emotion. In order to help speakers master this skill, Aristotle effectively submits an exhaustive catalogue of emotions and their opposite counterparts,[11] together with suggestions on how to use them in one's address – depending on whether the speaker's goal is to win the approval of his audience or to discredit his opponent's arguments.

---

9. Aristotle, 1.2.2. – 1.2.3.

10. Aristotle, 1.2.4. For a more extensive examination of character, see 2.1.1. – 2.1.7., and on topics related to character, see. 2.2. – 2.17.

11. Aristotle, 2.2. – 2.11.

In summary, Aristotle's notions of rhetoric would prove to have a long-lasting effect in the centuries to come and to maintain "a consistent presence in the subsequent development of rhetoric, both through their elaboration in Latin rhetorical treatises and through their appropriation in the work of twentieth-century rhetoricians."[12]

3.1.2. Cicero

The transmission of rhetoric from Greek to Latin culture was a major development with consequences for rhetoric's identity and its function in society. The person who takes the most credit for this reappropriation of rhetoric in such a different political, sociological, and cultural environment is Marcus Tullius Cicero (106–43 BC).[13]

His famous quote, "I think that wisdom without eloquence is but of little advantage to states, but that eloquence without wisdom is often most mischievous, and is never advantageous"[14] comes from his earliest volume, *De Inventione* (ca. 89 BC), but it is the development of five "canons of rhetoric" that represents his most significant contribution (although it is sometimes attributed to Quintilian). According to this scheme, the process of preparation and delivery of a speech consists of invention (the discovery of information and construction of arguments), arrangement (placing arguments into a particular order based on the speaker's intention), style (choosing the language and putting the thoughts into sentences and figures of speech), memory (the employment of the mnemonic system which secures the oratory in the speaker's mind), and delivery (the process of oral expression and gesturing). In his most elaborate treatise on rhetoric, *De Oratore*, written at a more mature age (ca. 55 BC), he discusses the nature of rhetoric and builds on Aristotle's thought. Several distinctive features of his perspective deserve a special mention.

3.1.2.1 The Role of Rhetoric

Cicero insists on rhetoric's proximity to philosophy and believes it should not or could not be confined to the courts or political arenas. But even if it

---

12. Agnew, "Classical Period," 9.
13. For a detailed account of this transition and of Cicero's significance and unique contributions, see Fantham, *Roman World*.
14. "Treatise on Rhetorical Invention," IV, 241–380 (1.1).

were so, he was convinced that "... without extensive handling of all public business, without a mastery of ordinances, customs and general law, without a knowledge of human nature and character, he [the orator] cannot engage, with the requisite cleverness and skill, even in these restricted activities."[15] Therefore, a comprehensive education is an inevitable prerequisite for every orator,[16] and the ideal rhetor needs to be a laborious student of history, politics, law, and literature. However, in order to prevent the misuse of rhetoric, an advanced ethical attitude is also expected. In other words, eloquence has to be joined with wisdom so that rhetoric can escape the accusations that have been launched against it since the Greek era.

3.1.2.2 *The Prominence of Style – Three Styles of Speech*

Cicero follows the Aristotelian concept of a threefold means of persuasion, but for him, the excellence of persuasion is not elicited by an orator who knows how to incorporate these three means into the best argument, but by "one who knows how to move, teach, and please an audience while doing that."[17] This is to say that in Cicero's rhetoric, stylistic matters take up a distinguished persuasive function because the content and the form are inseparable, thus making persuasion highly dependent on the forms in which the arguments are presented.

Depending on the goal, Cicero suggests three different styles of speech. First, there is a plain or low style. It is appropriate for teaching the audience and for the transfer of information, and primarily appeals to the intellect. Its tone remains emotionally neutral. Second, there is a tempered or middle style. It combines the rational and emotional means of persuasion and aims at audiences' delight. Finally, there is an ornate or high style which is designed to move hearers, requiring the engagement of the orator's emotions and awakening of the hearers' passions. However, the use of style must be contingent on the predisposition of hearers, which is why Cicero indicates that the advocate must work to discern their emotions, thoughts, judgments, and anticipation, with the idea of predicting "... the direction in which they

---

15. Cicero, *De Oratore*, 1.48.

16. An extensive presentation of an educational plan for Roman orators can be found in *De Oratore* 1.113. – 1.204.

17. Hogan and Reid, *Connecting with Congregation*, 30.

seem likely to be led away most easily by eloquence."[18] Yet Cicero seems to be convinced that without stirring the hearers' emotions, it is impossible for the speaker to accomplish the goal of persuasion. Thus, the high style needs to be used to some degree in every speech.

3.1.2.3 The Correlation of Ethos and Pathos

The specific context of the Roman rhetorical situation prompted Cicero to reexamine the use of ethos and pathos and their correlation. Fantham observes, "Cicero was conscious that the Roman practice of entrusting one's defence to an advocate muddied the distinction between the favourable self-presentation of the defendant or litigant that was Aristotle's ethos, and the rousing of benevolent emotions (pathe) in the audience."[19] This means that ethos now includes the character of other involved parties, and not only of the orator. Thus he speaks of a need ". . . for the characters, principles, conduct and course of life, both of those who are to plead cases and of their clients, to be approved" by hearers, and points out that their emotions can be "won over by a man's merit, achievements or reputable life."[20] He then brings in his stylistic concerns and proposes the use of "gentle language" because the appropriate use of language also shapes the speaker's character for his audience. But stirring the hearers' emotions requires the employment of a more passionate tone distinguished by the speaker's authentic emotions. In Cicero's own words, "For just as there is no substance so ready to take fire, as to be capable of generating flame without the application of a spark, so also there is no mind ready to absorb an orator's influence, as to be inflammable when the assailing speaker is not himself aglow with passion."[21]

In a nutshell, the significance of Cicero's contribution to the development of rhetoric is well summed up by De Koster who declares that the vital element of Cicero's idea of rhetoric is that authentic speech "has its origins in passionate conviction, focused upon a precisely envisioned oratorial objective,

---

18. Cicero, *De Oratore*, 2.186.
19. Fantham, 76.
20. Cicero, *De Oratore*, 2.182.
21. Cicero, 2.189–190.

moulded by a 'style' that obliges every syllable and every gesture to pursue the predetermined end."[22]

3.1.3 Quintilian

The next crucial figure in the history of rhetoric is Quintilian (AD 35–96). By his time the era of the Roman Republic was long gone, having been replaced by the Roman Empire, and rhetoric gradually claimed its prominent position. In AD 71, Quintilian himself was the first person appointed by the Roman emperor to a chair in rhetoric.[23] Paradoxically, all these changes in the political and social climate led to the major loss of rhetoric's relevance. It was no longer needed to create political arguments or to influence the public decision-making process. Among the three species of rhetoric, only epideictic oratory retained its potency and prevailed in Roman schools.

Quintilian passionately studied rhetoric and considered Cicero to be the indispensable authority. He applied Cicero's ethical emphases to the educational system of the Roman Empire. His *Institutio Oratoria* (ca. AD 95) represents the most exhaustive extant account of classical rhetoric and the scholars tell us that when its intact version was discovered during the Middle Ages, it soon became "a major source on both education and rhetoric for the Renaissance and early modern period."[24] Here I will identify two hallmarks of his work.

3.1.3.1 The "Ethical" Goal of Rhetoric

Quintilian's primary goal is "the education of a perfect orator."[25] However, contrary to Aristotelian understanding that a speaker must be able to *present* himself as someone who is worthy of his listeners' trust, Quintilian's orator must *be* a good person and exhibit a virtuous character, not only in "possession of exceptional gifts of speech, but of all the excellences of character as well."[26] Furthermore, both goodness of character and skilful speaking must be "perfected by instruction." In this way, the continuous moral formation and

---

22. De Koster, "Preacher as Rhetorician," 311.
23. Kennedy, "Historical Survey of Rhetoric," 19.
24. Kennedy, 32.
25. Quintilian, *Institutio Oratoria*, 1.9.
26. Quintilian, 1.9.

extensive study of "just and honourable" knowledge go hand in hand.[27] An important consequence is this: a speaker's ethos is not limited to the time of speech anymore and it can be argued that the process of persuasion begins *before* the speech and extends into the time *after* the speech, especially if the life of the speaker is evident to his listeners. In that light, it is easy to understand why Quintilian sees rhetoric as the "science of speaking well" which "includes all the virtues of oratory and the character of the orator as well, since no man can speak well who is not good himself."[28]

3.1.3.2 The Importance of Style

Similarly to Cicero, Quintilian pays special attention to stylistic matters. He is convinced that style must occupy a higher position among the rhetor's duties, and he feels that Aristotle preferred invention at the expense of other rhetorical canons. To begin with, he recognizes the need for three different styles of oratory – the plain style is suitable for instruction, the forcible style aims at moving hearers to action, while the intermediate intends to "charm and conciliate" the audience. But, unlike Cicero, he recognizes there are many more variations, distinguished only by "shades of difference."[29] Resisting the superfluous style of his contemporaries, he advocates a style reminiscent of Cicero's, marked more by clarity and simplicity than by embellishment, excessive ornamentation, far-fetched affection, and "meretricious finery"[30] and explains it by saying: "[t]he usual result of over-attention to the niceties of style is the deterioration of our eloquence."[31] For him, eloquence is a critical indication of the orator's mastery of language and this is why without stylistic concerns all other components of the rhetorical process remain ineffective.

At least two repercussions of Quintilian's approach must be noted. Firstly, the strength and credibility of an argument no longer rest solely on invention and arrangement. Quintilian shows that the rhetor's style shares in that responsibility, too. Secondly, contrary to the older rhetorical conventions, three means of persuasion – logos, ethos, and pathos – are not to (and cannot) be

---

27. Quintilian, 12.2.1.
28. Quintilian, 2.15.34.
29. Quintilian, *Institutio Oratoria*, 12.10.58–70.
30. Quintilian, 8.1.26.
31. Quintilian, 8.1.22.

retained for the exclusive purposes of the invention canon. *Pathos* and ethos can be particularly instrumental and needful in other stages of the orator's task, especially in the development of style.

After this short review of the history of classical rhetoric, the origins of linkage between rhetoric and homiletics must be submitted to closer scrutiny. During this process, several insights will emerge which will both shed a light on this puzzling relationship and render material to be taken advantage of in later parts of this thesis.

3.2 Rhetoric and Homiletics – Story of the Intense Relationship

At the very outset of Christianity, rhetoric and proclamation of the gospel engaged in a peculiar relationship. The early church generally perceived the art of persuasive speech as incompatible with its preaching practice. Some church leaders may have been former teachers of rhetoric and their conversion experience implied keeping a distance from a previous secular lifestyle. But there was another, probably stronger, reason: they were convinced that "preaching *truth* and making *plausible arguments* were incompatible tasks"! For them, preaching was akin to a logical demonstration of proof. Scripture was perceived as final truth, and "it was the Spirit that bore witness to the *truth* of God's word, not the opinion of persuaded audience members."[32] On the other hand, the most common audiences were not Jewish, but Greco-Roman, which naturally meant their expectations were heavily conditioned by predominant principles of rhetorical training and practice which were the preeminent preparation for and requirement of any discourse of civic life in the Roman Empire. Thus, early Christian preaching was at least influenced by rhetorical techniques and strategies and indirect evidence of this can be found in works of a number of scholars who discovered traces of rhetorical facets in New Testament writings, particularly in the Pauline corpus.[33]

However, the status of this relationship changed seriously soon after the Constantinian shift in the fourth century. Christianity became a major factor in the public arena and one of the first challenges was how to preserve the

---

32. Hogan and Reid, *Connecting with Congregation*, 34.
33. See, for instance, Warner, *Bible as Rhetoric*.

earlier practice of preaching in the face of the dominant discipline of rhetoric. Once semi-private homilies in house gatherings, the sermons turned into discourses spoken in front of large audiences. This change signified a much wider issue, that of the correlation between the divine and human element in preaching. The person who undertook to resolve this unsettled relationship is Augustine of Hippo.

3.2.1 Augustine

As a former teacher of rhetoric, Augustine (354–430) retrieved the goal and focus of classical rhetoric and implemented it for Christian use. His four-volume *De Doctrina Christiana*[34] (the last book in particular) represents a full-blown account of applied rhetoric and is usually considered a first homiletical textbook. His project of appropriation and application of rhetoric requires a further consideration.

3.2.1.1 Apology for Rhetoric

Augustine realistically observes that teachers of false doctrines are well versed in presenting their cases in a way which is pleasing, easily understood, and believable. He also sees that preaching does not accomplish the desired effects. In fact, sermon listeners are often bored, their understanding is "clouded," and their desire to believe "stifled."[35] However, he believes that this "faculty of eloquence"[36] is equally accessible to both Christians and their opponents and equally capable of serving their causes – therefore, it would be foolish for Christians not to use it against false teaching or for preaching the truth in an engaging and believable way that would make their listeners more disposed to accepting their speech. In fact, he claims, there are some preachers who follow the rules of rhetoric, simply because they are eloquent speakers and not because they intentionally pursue their eloquence.[37] He is also convinced that rhetoric is useful not only for apologetic purposes but for inducing believers to pursue holiness in everyday life.

---

34. Augustine, *On Christian Teaching*.
35. Augustine, *On Christian Teaching*, 4.4.
36. Augustine, 4.5.
37. Augustine, 4.11.

3.2.1.2 The Christian Application

In matters of style, Augustine does not depart from his Roman rhetorical models. He agrees that three styles of speaking are fitting for preaching – the restrained, mixed, and grand style – and he specifies three goals of a sermon: "So the speaker who is endeavouring to give conviction to something that is good should despise none of these three aims – of instructing, delighting, and moving his hearers – and should make it his prayerful aim to be listened to with understanding, with pleasure, and with obedience . . ."[38] But he claims there is a delicate interconnectedness of instructing, delighting, and moving the audience at work. Hence, he proposes that these three styles should be used interchangeably while three aims of preaching are being pursued. In other words, there is no aim that is designed for a particular style.[39]

Yet, in the specific context of preaching, the speaker most often aims at the particular action of his listeners and thus he should typically intend to reach all three goals of speaking, ". . . when advocating something to be acted on the Christian orator should not only teach his listeners so as to impart instruction, and delight them so as to hold their attention, but also move them so as to conquer their minds."[40] Augustine is also concerned about the possible abuse of eloquence and suggests a specifically Christian antidote – instead of the wide education and fostering of general human goodness, he prescribes wisdom that is attained only as the preacher grows in understanding of the scriptures.[41] In a similar fashion, he attributes the preacher's eloquence to divine inspiration and states that both preachers and listeners should seek God's guidance in receiving the "right" message, because ". . . who can know what it is expedient for us to say or to our audience to hear at a particular moment but the one who sees the hearts of all?"[42]

Keeping in mind that rhetoric is seen here from a strictly Christian perspective, there is no doubt that Augustine perceives scripture as the starting point for all five rhetorical stages, especially since Books 2 and 3 of *De Doctrina Christiana* are almost entirely dedicated to careful interpretation

---

38. Augustine, 4.96.
39. Augustine, 4.145.
40. Augustine, 4.79.
41. Augustine, 4.19–20.
42. Augustine, 4.88.

of biblical writings from the rhetorical perspective. In Book 1 the summary of Christian doctrines is presented as a treasury of elementary arguments, which leads Don H. Compier to conclude that the invention stage depends considerably on the basic core of doctrinal teaching, on exegetically informed use of biblical quotes, and on following the hermeneutics of biblical orators which then guides the application of biblical passages.[43]

3.2.1.3 Communication and Listeners

Augustine's propositions to Christian orators reveal his awareness of the importance of the hearers' reception. Therefore, a preacher needs to adjust his rhetorical devices and style in a way that assures his message has the best chance of getting communicated to the audience. His aim is, of course, to persuade, but in accomplishing this aim, the preacher should use colloquial language, the speech of uneducated, especially if clarity of speech is impossible to reach through the refined language: "What is the use of correct speech if it does not meet with the listener's understanding? There is no point in speaking at all if our words are not understood by the people to whose understanding our words are directed."[44]

Being conscious of the monological nature of preaching, he advises preachers to do their best not to raise any obstacles by their style or performance. These efforts toward intelligibility are even more important because there is no opportunity for asking questions or for the two-way exchange of opinions and Augustine urges, "[T]he speaker's sensitivity must come to the aid of the silent listener."[45] Likewise, he shows the appreciation of nonverbal communication occurring during the sermon and counsels preachers to be attentive to movements and other signals during the sermon to determine whether the audience reached an understanding of their argument.[46]

In the background of all these recommendations is a basic yet profound idea: the orator should not take for granted that his communication is successful because he is done with his speech. Only after he is understood can he be sure that communication took place. The confirmation of understanding

---

43. Compier, *What Is Rhetorical Theology?*, 12.
44. Augustine, 4.66.
45. Augustine, 4.67.
46. Augustine, 4.68.

cannot be provided by the preacher himself, which is why the role of the listeners is so vital.

3.2.1.4 Preacher's Ethos

Probably the most important of Augustine's modifications of classical rhetoric is the conviction that Christian orators are not after crafting plausible arguments on disputed matters; they are to persuade others in the *truth* of the gospel. A notable consequence of this conviction is his emphatic insistence on the primacy of ethos, both in the sense of the preacher's ethos, and in the sense of development of listeners' ethos as a result of preaching. When discussing the significance of the first sense, he maintains that "[m]ore important than any amount of grandeur of style to those of us who seek to be listened to with obedience is the life of the speaker."[47] At one point Augustine refers back to his model of preacher who incorporates both wisdom and eloquence and underscores the ethical dimension once again by depicting a lifestyle of a person who may lack eloquence of words, but can still possess an eloquence of life:

> If he is not even capable of this [speaking eloquently and wisely], he should seek to live in such a way that he not only gains a reward for himself but also gives an example to others, so that his way of life becomes, in a sense, an abundant source of eloquence.[48]

Expressing the same idea in more negative terms, he goes even further and claims that preachers whose speech is in conflict with their behaviour are like forgers and thieves since they do not own the words they preach, which, in turn means it is not them who preach.[49]

There is a consensus that Augustine's appropriation of rhetoric remained an unquestioned authority in the homiletical field for more than a thousand years, at least in Western churches. Over the centuries the formal rhetoric of homiletics developed from Augustine's legacy, a process made easier as Christendom gradually merged with the secular culture and rhetoric was

---

47. Augustine, 4.151.
48. Augustine, 4.158–159.
49. Augustine, 4.161.

no longer perceived as a secular art. However, its prominence in nurturing Christian life slowly but steadily began to lose ground during the early Middle Ages.

3.2.2 Middle Ages and Reformation

Hughes Oliphant Old simply describes this situation: "For centuries other forms of devotion had eclipsed preaching, and it became more and more obvious that the Church suffered from the lack of a preaching ministry."[50] However, the major revival came about in the thirteenth and fourteenth centuries and its main agents were Franciscans and Dominicans, two newly established orders whose members lived as mendicants in the early years. Their preaching introduced several novelties. Even though today there are only a few extant sermon manuscripts written in vernacular languages, it is almost certain that these preachers used languages which people could understand. And while they still relied heavily on four senses of the biblical text (the literal, the allegorical, the tropological, and the anagogical), they also ushered in thematic preaching. Under this style "scripture was increasingly examined not as text, *but for* texts which the preacher might thematically amplify."[51] In addition, they reintroduced a more formal structure based on the employment of various rhetorical tools to create catalogues of commonplaces and themes suitable for this sort of preaching. The textbooks they used are commonly called *Artes praedicandi* while the most important homiletical aid invented during this era are *exampla*, the collections of illustrations.[52] At least equally important was a return of doctrinal and ethical catechesis which was sorely missing in previous centuries. After being "almost embalmed, almost fossilized"[53] for a long time, preaching had been revived by friars who knew how to creatively employ their rhetorical devices and offered their lives as a means of persuasion through personal and communal ethos. On the whole, their contribution signalled the onset of the strongest bond between rhetoric and homiletics as the latter becomes heavily discussed following the "taxonomic" approach known from the ancient rhetorical traditions (and

---

50. Old, *Reading and Preaching*, 342.
51. Hogan and Reid, *Connecting with Congregation*, 36.
52. Edwards, *History of Preaching*, 224–231.
53. Old, *Medieval Church*, 408.

developed in typically scholastic commentaries), because at that point *truth* needed help from the art of persuasion in order to convince multitudes in churches of the need for ethical behaviour.[54] The striking paradox, though, is hidden in the fact that this consistent application of rhetoric, as prescribed by Augustine and perpetuated by scholasticism, led to a dismemberment of rhetoric, since practically speaking only the categories of delivery and style remain.

The next epoch in the relationship between homiletics and rhetoric was the Renaissance. Its humanism and the re-creation of interest in classical works of literature and their physical rediscovery meant that preachers also turned to Greek and Roman rhetoricians in a quest for argumentation which would support the validity of revelatory truth as contained in the Bible. It reintroduced logical argumentation and forcefully reclaimed the rhetorical logos as a central notion of Christian preaching. The Reformation period served to further advance this trend because the preaching of Reformers favoured the argumentative form due to their disputes with Rome. In effect, the literal sense begins to dominate in preaching. On the other hand, the invention of printing thoroughly changed the perception of sermons. In the Guttenberg era, written texts became more accessible than ever, and their logical structure and clarity emerged as a new standard to which other forms of communication must adapt. Thus, sermons had to compete for the attention of their listeners, and preachers began to imitate the linear structure and other features of written material.

3.2.3 Enlightenment and Modern Era

The period of the Enlightenment and later modernity could be roughly described as the dark age of rhetoric. There are at least three important moments which can help to explain this. Firstly, the transition from early modernity reached the point in the second half of the eighteenth century when the Enlightenment set itself up as "a culture of print." Rhetoric, firmly grounded in the oral nature of communication and based on face-to-face discourse, could not stand that attack.[55] Secondly, in the age of reason and the explosion of scientific investigation, "transparency" and "neutrality" emerged as the

---

54. Hogan and Reid, *Connecting with Congregation*, 36.
55. Bender and Wellbery, "Rhetoricality," 15.

leading values of theoretical and practical discourse. In other words, the communication became "derhetoricized" – there is no need for an audience to be persuaded anymore, since "the reader is addressed as the potential observer of what the writer recounts as having himself observed."[56] Thirdly, literature was transformed into an autonomous field of discourse defined by the concept of authorship as a source of text and by the individual expression which binds imaginative discourse to the area of subjectivity. The consequence was that literature became predominantly concerned with meaning, rather than with its function and results, but also that the study of literature receded to the academic fields and retreated from everyday life. As Compier observes, the only remaining function of rhetoric was to occasionally potter about issues of style and delivery trying to present the results of the procedures of the search for the objective truth in a verbally more attractive form.[57]

Strangely enough, the detachment of homiletics from rhetoric did not follow at once. A number of influential homileticians of the nineteenth century believed that rhetoric could still serve the cause of Christian preaching. A brief account of the contribution of John A. Broadus (1827–1895) will be sufficient to argue in favour of these claims. Broadus' textbook entitled *On the Preparation and Delivery of Sermons* (1870) was perhaps the most influential book on homiletics after Augustine's *De Doctrina Christiana*.

To begin with, he understands homiletics to be "simply the adaptation of rhetoric to the particular ends and demands of preaching."[58] In the second edition of his book, there is a definition of eloquence: ". . . speaking as not merely to convince the judgement, to kindle the imagination, to move the feelings, but to give powerful impulse to the will in the direction of truth's requirement,"[59] which echoes aims of classical rhetoric together with Augustinian ethical outcome. For him, the invention rests on the biblical text and the results of its interpretation, and Broadus' famous concept is the idea of a proposition which he understands to be "the gist of the sermon." This is a single claim, grounded in the text and warranted by the principles

---

56. Bender and Wellbery, 10.
57. Compier, *What Is Rhetorical Theology?*, 13.
58. Broadus, *On Preparation*, 10–11.
59. Broadus, *Treatise on Preparation*, 4–5.

of proper interpretation[60] which is an impact of logical reasoning that has always been crucial for the persuasive appeal of logos. Broadus strongly believes in reasoning and the pivotal role of arguments: "[P]reaching and all public speaking ought to be largely composed of argument, for even the most ignorant people constantly practise it themselves and always feel its force when properly presented."[61]

However, Broadus holds that other appeals have their place, too. The final part, conclusion, is particularly suitable for emotional appeal, partly because the conclusion is the most critical part of the sermon – rhetorically, psychologically, and spiritually – and partly because this is the point when preaching must address the hearers' wills and emotions. He understands that application or direct appeal cannot be delivered without the participation of the preacher's authentic emotions or without inducing proper emotions in his hearers – without appealing through ethos, there is no affecting the will.

Expectedly, Broadus firmly insists on the preacher's personal piety that corresponds with the preacher's external ethos – echoing Quintilian's and Augustine's understanding of the ethical dimension which transcends the boundaries of public discourse. Broadus specifies that a lifestyle of devotion, investment in one's knowledge and talents, and dependence on the Holy Spirit must be embodied in a delivery which reveals that the preacher is "possessed with the subject," convinced and influenced by the importance of what he is about to say.[62] In Broadus' view, this interplay of logos and ethos actually surpasses the significance of "technical" elements of delivery, such as gesticulation, vocalization or articulation.

The relationship between homiletics and rhetoric was profound, even at the close of the nineteenth century. Nevertheless, it is possible to see in retrospect how their relationship facilitated the submission of Protestant preaching to the prevailing rationalism. The prevalent "culture of print" forced sermons into competition for the attention of churchgoers. In order to keep their chances of winning, Craddock observes, sermons ". . . competed for attention by seeking to possess the qualities of a written text: logical development, clear argument, thorough and conclusive treatment. In other words, the sermon

---

60. Broadus, *On Preparation*, 45–48.
61. Broadus, xxii.
62. Broadus, 14–17, 264.

carried the entire burden; the listener accepted or rejected the conclusions."[63] In the process, the excessively rationalistic argumentation began to occupy the field of sermon invention and arrangement while gradually edging out other rhetorical means of persuasion. The growing priority of textual issues and the continuous search for the right interpretation of the *text*, meant that preaching did not consider potential rhetorical concerns and goals of *oral* discourses which were the major way of transmission of divine revelation for most of history. Consequently, the expected outcome of preaching came down to a mental consent to the set of information provided by the preacher.

Related to this was the urgency of reconciling modernity's worldview with the Christian tradition. Christian theology, and preaching in particular, needed to explain (and sometimes to explain away) the "irrational" and experiential elements of its tradition by means of rational argumentation. However, since the language of preaching communicated less and less effectively to modern listeners, Barbara Brown Taylor maintains that preachers resorted "to language that substitutes explanation for experience."[64] And this need was best met by propositional preaching, as outlined by Broadus and his followers.

By now, I think, it is safe to claim that throughout this long period from Augustine until the middle of the twentieth century, rhetoric's level of influence on homiletics has been constant, but uneven and variable. The nature of their mutual bond is perhaps best expressed in this diagnostic sentence of Mary Lyons: "Any claims made for either rhetoric's total dominance or homiletics' complete independence from it miss the point, verified by history, of their enduring symbiosis."[65]

And yet, this symbiosis was seriously questioned in the second half of the last century. This disapproval was largely inspired by Karl Barth's theology of the Word.[66] In accordance with his understanding of preaching already

---

63. Craddock, *As One*, 30.
64. Taylor, "Preaching the Body," 209.
65. Lyons, "Homiletics and Rhetoric," 3.
66. However, it can be argued that this separation was also caused by homileticians who wrongly assumed that contemporary rhetoric is still stuck in the rationalism of the nineteenth century. Thus, Hogan and Reid claim that homiletics during the third quarter of the twentieth century was rejecting a rhetoric that was already a "petrified artefact!" Hogan and Reid, *Connecting with Congregation*, 42.

referred to,[67] Barth openly attacks the Augustinian endorsement of rhetoric and its subsequent turning of homiletics into merely "sacred rhetoric" during the long centuries which followed tis initial adoption. Preaching does not need to persuade; it simply proclaims and exposes. The proclamatory physical embodiment in the preacher is mostly irrelevant and it must not stand in the way of the preaching of the gospel. Preaching does belong to the church, but it does not grow out of its current experience and is not to be crafted or delivered with the believers' emotional disposition or other potential points of contact in mind. Barth even goes so far as to say, "It is dangerous even to address a specific congregational situation or experience in terms of a specific text."[68] As a result, the congregation's role in preaching is reduced to that of a passive addressee and its situation turned into irrelevant circumstances with no bearing on the sermon's goal, methods or form.

In conclusion, it may be said that the combined effect of overwhelming modernist rationalism and a strong theology of the Word as exemplified in the theological system of Karl Barth gradually ruled rhetoric out of homiletical theory and practice.[69] Nevertheless, another change was in sight.

3.3 The Contemporary Revival, or How Homiletics Revisits Rhetoric

During the late twentieth century a substantial rebirth of interest in rhetoric took place, and its effects are still in force today. Yet it would be a mistake to assume that the present-day regard for rhetoric entails a simple replication of rhetorical concerns which were predominant in previous epochs. With so many profound changes taking place during the twentieth century, it is impossible to imagine that rhetoric would once again capture the attention of scholars and remain unaltered. For instance, Bender and Wellbery argue that this return to rhetoric should be understood as "an alteration that renders

---

67. See Chapter 2.
68. Karl Barth, *Homiletics*, 50.
69. André Resner points out that after Barth, homileticians were generally left with two choices – they either followed him and tended toward a "homiletical Docetism" (preaching is disconnected from its physical embodiment) or they dismissed his understanding and subscribed to a "homiletical Donatism" ("the efficacy of the preached word is dependent in some way on the person of the preacher"). However, a majority in one way or another espoused Barth's theology of the Word, especially within Protestantism. Resner, *Preacher and Cross*, 62.

the second version of rhetoric, its modernist-postmodernist redaction, a new form of cultural practice and mode of analysis."[70] This version is not a unified discipline but rather "a transdisciplinary field of practice and intellectual concern."

As a result, during the second half of the previous century rhetoric permeated various academic disciplines, such as anthropology, communication, economics, law, literary studies, management, marketing, philosophy, psychology, theatre, and women's and gender studies. This also meant that an exceptionally diverse rhetoric scholarship flourished creating manifold intersections of rhetoric and other academic fields.[71] More importantly, it contributed to the evolution of awareness that rhetorical figures of speech are not to be studied within an isolated, linguistic domain; they belong to the province of everyday communication. It means that rhetoric is relocated into the sphere of everyday life where it continues to display both continuity and discontinuity with the rhetorical heritage of earlier centuries.[72] This is what Bender and Wellbery isolate as major elements of discontinuity:

> We are dealing no longer with a specialized technique of instrumental communication, but with a general condition of human experience and action . . . [Also], there can be no single contemporary rhetorical theory . . . Modernist (and postmodernist) rhetorical study is irreducibly multidisciplinary.[73]

Having that in mind it becomes clear that, technically speaking, it is infeasible to study rhetoric as such. At the same time, there are a number of disciplinary variants of rhetoric which can be mutually reinforcing. Furthermore, there are areas of scholarly research yet to be explored from this perspective.[74]

---

70. Bender and Wellbery, *Rhetoricality*, 4.

71. Krista Ratcliffe offers a helpful "snapshot" of research areas and corresponding bibliographies in rhetorical studies in her essay "Twentieth and Twenty-First Centuries."

72. Bender and Wellbery list several areas where this dynamic is evident. For instance, when discussing mass media communication, they observe, "The collation of image and sound in the mechanical media, even where oral language is concerned, *recalls* but does not *reconstitute* the face-to-face speech and physiognomic and gestural performances of classical rhetoric." Bender and Wellbery, 32 (emphasis mine).

73. Bender and Wellbery, *Rhetoricality*, 38.

74. Particularly interesting for my purposes here is Ratcliffe's suggestion of "rereading theories and cultures to identify silence and listening as rhetorical arts" as one of those areas. Ratcliffe, "Twentieth and Twenty-First Centuries," 187.

In light of my research interests, this is the proper moment to turn to several examples of more recent homiletical attempts to reformulate of the preaching task bolstered by contemporary rhetorical contributions. The choice of these examples is intentionally selective, arbitrary, and not exhaustive. My purpose is to offer a glimpse of the breadth of contemporary homiletical pursuits and to display the fruitfulness of the current interplay of rhetoric and homiletics.

3.3.1 Lucy Lind Hogan and Robert Reid

In their book *Connecting with the Congregation*, Hogan and Reid summon preachers to take a "rhetorical stance." Drawing from multiple contemporary rhetoricians, they propose that the weight of the preaching task should be placed not only on the three legs of a classical means of persuasion (logos, pathos, and ethos), but also on arrangement and style. Since these two can be shown to "represent "ways of knowing," they also function as means of persuasion.[75] What are some of their valuable insights derived from these basic propositions?

In their treatment of ethos they point out that the relationship between the external ethos (created by the development of character and the investment in education and reading, and constituted by external credentials given by a congregation or denomination) and the internal ethos as developed during the sermon, could very well be the most urgent issue for preachers.[76] They compare the internal ethos to the development of specific persona or the role during the sermon which takes place irrespective of the preacher's conscious contribution. Observing that preachers more often than not rely on their external ethos, Hogan and Reid suggest that they should also place an "intentional emphasis" on character as projected during the sermon. Therefore, the next challenge in the informed use of ethos is that of correspondence "between the persona developed within the sermon and the person of the preacher who meets them [believers] every day."[77] This correspondence highlights the concern for the authenticity of a preacher. In order to be perceived as authentic, Hogan and Reid argue (and here they borrow from Bernard J. F.

---

75. Hogan and Reid, *Connecting with Congregation*, 158.
76. Hogan and Reid, 52–53.
77. Hogan and Reid, 62.

Lonergan) that preachers must be capable of exhibiting certain characteristics different from classical rhetoric: attentiveness, intelligence, reasonableness, and responsibility. These will supply them with authority because authority as a legitimate power "grounds its source of power in cooperation, and the carrier of power is the community."[78]

The discussion on pathos starts off with theological support: emotions are a constitutive part of our belief because our faith "is ultimately grounded in the love of God who calls forth faith from us."[79] To preach about this God is possible only with a balance of reason and emotions. On the other hand, it also means that there is no response to preaching which does not entail some affective reaction of the listeners. Again, these facts should prompt preachers to shape the emotional appeal of their sermons with deliberation. To do so, they need to keep two important goals in mind: to create a sense of presence through identification and to establish a real connection between the assumed audience and the actual audience.

As for the first, Hogan and Reid assume that listeners need to care first in order to be moved, and that caring comes only after the "preacher gains control of the imaginative ability to create presence for bringing a matter before the consciousness of listeners."[80] Here they are building on Kenneth Burke's concept of persuasion as the art of creating identification. The closer to the matter listeners feel they are, the more likely they will be to identify with and care about it. And the next stage will be a tendency to unconsciously persuade themselves. This approach should not be viewed as a shrewd technique, but as an intersection of ethos and pathos. A preacher's ethos as a projection of her character and persona includes the passions; as a result, she not only cares about what she is saying, but is willing to make her concern evident so her listeners will get involved and care about the same matter.[81]

Yet the preacher must constantly be reminded that there is "a distinction between the concrete audience that listens to a speech and the audience the speech constructs by its assumptions about the listeners. The former is outside

---

78. Hogan and Reid, 63–64.
79. Hogan and Reid, 73.
80. Hogan and Reid, 77.
81. Hogan and Reid, 79.

the text while the latter is inside."[82] The gospel may be universal, but it still must be preached in a way that particular listeners will be able to truly hear it and the preacher's knowledge of them can come about only through listening. To foster this knowledge, Hogan and Reid recommend adoption and development of two sets of interpersonal communication skills: empathetic listening and dialogical listening – one is focused on gathering opinions from members of the congregation, and the other is directed at engaging church members in the process of "'collaborative' meaning making."[83] Thus, the persuasive potential of pathos depends heavily on the connection between a preacher and her audience, and it can be fulfilled only insofar as the preacher becomes a continual listener of listeners, before and beyond the preaching event.

Turning to logos, after the affirmation that arguments and persuasion are integral elements of virtually every human conversation, and thus inevitable components of preaching, these two authors spell out a vital claim: "The real question may have more to do with how overt versus how collaborative our approach to persuasion will be, since the role of persuasion in preaching is always one of degree, rather than kind."[84] It reveals that although persuasion is still critical for the task of preaching, its pursuit may need to involve more sensitivity for the listeners and for the creation of meaning through conversation. They find endorsement for this view in Aristotle's concept of practical reasoning (*phronêsis*). It is context-based and directed toward a particular audience with the purpose of obtaining their agreement. It usually omits one of the premises which calls forth the involvement of listeners who by intuition supply the missing part of the argument. Along the way, listeners identify with the content and claims of the orator's speech.

However, this procedure presumes that certain assumptions are shared between listeners and speaker. Hogan and Reid describe a possible outcome in the contexts where this homogeneity is not present by referring to another contemporary rhetorician's model. Stephen Toulmin suggests that a claim (argument) a speaker makes is supported by the data and backed up by warrants. However, warrants are usually only implicit, and they may become responsible for the listeners' disagreement with a speaker – because they may not share

---

82. Hogan and Reid, 81.
83. Hogan and Reid, 82–83.
84. Hogan and Reid, 93.

the assumption which for the speaker functions as a warrant. It follows that the preacher depends on his listeners to supply the warrants, and if he is unaware of those warrants, he may easily lose his listeners. The consequence for preachers is that they must not assume the argument that would persuade themselves would undoubtedly persuade their listeners. Instead, they should submit their arguments to closer scrutiny and look more mindfully for the assumptions behind these arguments.[85]

It is also noteworthy that Hogan and Reid under the heading of invention introduce the notion of conversation partners.[86] They recognize the communal nature of rhetorical argumentation and suggest that the process of invention should involve a conversation with sermon listeners, theologians, church tradition, and various marginalised voices. This will make the preacher more aware of influences which may have already been shaping his sermons. At the same time, engaging in the conversation during the process of invention will reveal that the preacher and the congregation have changed since the last sermon, along with the situation. All of this points to the conclusion that even arguments and reasons possess the contextual nature, that logos has its *Sitz im Leben* which is why it would be wrong for preachers to presuppose it is some fixed or unchanging reality which can easily be "copy-pasted" from one sermon to another.

Hogan and Reid also have an engaging chapter on *arrangement*.[87] Building on the general consensus in contemporary rhetorical theories, they commence with the understanding that organizing strategies are perceived as an inherent facet of the argument. Far more than just merely organizing the content, the arrangement serves to advocate a cause and to engage the listeners. Specifically, there are certain types of responses which the speaker may want to thereby elicit from listeners. When applied to the field of homiletics, this means that preachers should, after completing their exegetical work, consider what kind of response they would like to obtain from their listeners, and then choose an appropriate way of structuring the sermon. According to Hogan and Reid, the arrangement can be guided by four different preaching intentions – "to provide an explanation, facilitate an encounter, create an

---

85. Hogan and Reid, 97–99.
86. Hogan and Reid, 105–107.
87. Hogan and Reid, 113–136.

experience of meaning, or explore the possibilities of engagement through the formative language of faith." This attentiveness to arrangement is more valuable if we recognise that form is never really neutral; even an uncritical and arbitrary choice of form in which the sermon's content will be rendered still operates as "the active ingredient fundamental to both its [sermon's] experience and the way in which it enacts the faith of its listeners."

3.3.2 Robin Meyers

Another approach which deserves our attention here is Meyers' model of preaching as self-persuasion which represents a unique appropriation of the rhetorical strategies and various findings of human communication theories and research. Let me explore the main hallmarks of his homiletics.

Meyers' proposal is focused on building an authentic sermonic passion that represents not only a certain state of mind but also a particular methodology.[88] This passion needs to permeate a sermon and must be born out of the preacher's honest struggle with a biblical text. He says, ". . . just as there was passion and inspiration involved in getting the words of Scripture *onto* the page, so must there be passion and inspiration in getting them *off* the page."[89] But to become passionate, the preacher cannot deal with the Bible as if it is a reference tool or a resource for proof-texting. The biblical text has to be approached as a conversation partner; this requires intentional effort to refuse to be satisfied with delivering sermons resembling "fortune cookies (fits everyone, applies to no one)." The passion will come as a result of a specific posture, elsewhere described by Craddock as *overhearing*, by Meyers as listening emphatically through exegesis (although he advises reading the scriptural text and listening to it even before using the exegetical tools in preparation in order to hear it as believers will hear it the next Sunday morning).[90] This passion, though, will not be induced only by conversing with the biblical text. The preacher will do her best if she engages in "empathetic imagination" even before she meets with the biblical text[91] in order to begin to listen to her listeners. Thus the preacher becomes capable of maintaining a healthy balance

---

88. Meyers, *With Ears to Hear*, 5.
89. Meyers, 62.
90. Meyers, 38–39.
91. Craddock, *Preaching*, 95–98.

between distance and intimacy toward the biblical text and the reality of the experiences of her congregation.

At the point of uttering the sermon, the preacher is still not exempt from listening. He needs to simultaneously speak and listen to himself speaking. Why? There are two reasons. Listening to the words spoken in front of listeners allows the preacher to intervene, to correct or to change his expressions: "The speaking brings a new hearing and effects subsequent speech . . . A sermon not spawned by the ear may be stillborn on the tongue. Listen, then speak, then listen to yourself speaking."[92] Even more importantly, listening while speaking models the behaviour which he wishes for his audience: "The harder the congregation listens, the harder the preacher listens. The harder the preacher listens, the harder it is for the congregation not to."[93]

The real aim here is to achieve identification. As the preacher listens to the text and to her listeners, she establishes a pattern of behaviour, hoping it will become "contagious" so that listeners will eventually identify with it. However, this identification needs to be triggered by the listeners' emotional arousal which is possible because of human empathy. This arousal Meyers terms as "vicarious identification with the emotional state of others."[94] The preacher's role here is crucial since his disclosure and wrestling with the text must be genuine so that listeners can identify and begin to shape their own messages. What happens in the process is that listeners may realize that they are "preached for rather than preached at"[95] simply because they feel this sermon is for all of them (preacher not excluded!).

Meyers is firmly assured of the bond between the form and the content, and submits some elaborate suggestions concerning the language and style of preaching. The preacher's preparation needs to be governed by the question "What would be the most appropriate listeners' response to the experience of the sermon?", and at the very core of that experience is *evocation*. His emphasis is clearly on the primacy of pathos, since edification ". . . comes after examining the meaning of what has been evoked, for what has not been

---

92. Meyers, *With Ears to Hear*, 43–44.
93. Meyers, 127.
94. Meyers, 118.
95. Meyers, 65.

stored in the heart is soon erased by time."[96] This is also a key reason why he advocates language more akin to private discourse, expressions which are appealing to the senses, the dominance of present tense and active voice, and description instead of explanation.

Even more specifically, Meyers signalises that narrative is the most potent rhetorical form for enticing listeners into self-persuasion. "In self-persuasion, stories are indispensable because they place the listener in the posture of overhearing. This is the posture of the preacher with regard to the text, and both the listener and the preacher with regard to the sermon . . . Stories invite participation precisely because they do not demand it."[97] At the same time, the narrative form resembles the form of our lives, and besides *saying* something, it also *does* something.

Finally, he also advises that the preacher should intentionally leave some things unsaid and some images incomplete ("the aesthetic of restraint"), while building an atmosphere of anticipation. This will give rise to the dramatic dimension of the sermon. Consequently, the audience is never directly addressed, and listeners enter this drama vicariously. Such participation on the part of listeners is essential since there is a growing body of evidence in the social sciences confirming the change of attitudes is usually accomplished through vicarious experience.[98]

Given the conversational nature of the sermon preparation, it is unsurprising that Meyers insists on the inclusion of dialectical principles in the creation of sermon experience. There are two chief reasons for that. The first is that the dialectical relationship between the preacher and the text is responsible for the existence of the sermon in the first place, and the dialogue between these two that takes place in front of the audience is the very incentive for the listeners to identify with the preacher. Secondly, the self-persuasion of listeners and potential changes of their attitudes and behaviour is tightly linked with the dialectical dynamics. Meyers says, "People are not ultimately persuaded by accepting or rejecting the truth that others have discovered and are now peddling; rather, they are persuaded by their *involvement* in the dialectic of

---

96. Meyers, 73.
97. Meyers, 89–90.
98. Meyers, 122.

truth-finding."⁹⁹ He looks to psychology and the notion of "cognitive schemata" to affirm that human attitudes are not easily changed, especially not by coercion. Thus, it is required for the sermon to possess a dialogical nature in which listeners will recognize themselves and want to join in the conversation. This non-coercive and yet alluring quality is best described as a sermon which "asks to be invited by not demanding to be invited in."[100]

In a sense, Meyers' entire *modus operandi* rests on the conclusion of various studies showing that the messages we create for ourselves are more authoritative than any others. Contemporary active participation theories reveal that listeners are not passive, message-manipulated recipients, but active participants in the exchange of messages who "talk to themselves" as they create their own meanings. And this is what propels his decision to make self-persuasion a pivotal property of preaching and to state that the goal of the speech is "to elicit a kind of authoritative *intrapersonal* conversation in the listener." This causes a noticeable shift to happen because it "locates persuasion at the ear of the listener, not at the mouth of the rhetor."[101]

At the same time, self-persuasion presupposes that faith is something to be constantly renewed, reinvigorated, and negotiated. A preacher's open declaration of imperfection and the incompleteness of her faith made public in the sermon puts her in the position of her listeners and grants her an opportunity to preach "side-by-side" with the congregation. This entitles Meyers to describe his approach as a listener-centred homiletics. Even though a preacher's self-persuasion is the necessary first stage, and he "still sets the scene and directs the rhetorical drama," and while the message, the style, and delivery still must be carefully shaped, it is the *listener* who is in the end responsible for the persuasive outcome. All of this makes Meyers' approach unmistakably rhetorical, but his peculiar take on persuasion makes it distinctive, if not somewhat controversial.

---

99. Meyers, 98.
100. Meyers, 103, 102.
101. Meyers, 12, 13, 49.

3.3.3 Craig Loscalzo

The central intention of Loscalzo's book[102] is to lend his expertise to preachers interested in establishing better contact with listeners in their sermons. In short, he offers a homiletical interpretation of Kenneth Burke's rhetoric concentrated around the idea of identification. According to his observations, there are two notable reasons why preaching should be empowered by a preacher's intentional identification with his listeners. One is that only preachers who take enough care to get to know their audiences are able to deliver sermons that connect with the audience and produce passion, and another is that the time for "rhetoric of authority" is gone, especially when a growing gap between this type of preaching and the actual ethical standards of some preachers is publicly observable.[103] Since the goal of preaching is always to draw forth listeners' response to the good news, provoke their deliberate action and the change of their conduct, the identification serves here as a means for persuading them toward that goal. In Burke's terminology, this identification takes place as the speaker talks his listeners' language by speech, gesture, tonality, order, image, attitude, idea; identifies [his] ways with theirs; or manages to show that his cause can be identified with specific behaviours they approve.[104] Loscalzo concludes that in terms of persuasion nothing really compares with the effects of identification: "All the logical arguments in the world will not persuade as effectively as the reality that you truly have identified with the lives of your hearers"[105]; but he adds that in this process there must be no trace of manipulation since that would be "antithetical to the gospel."

There is a sense in which identification grows out of human differences – their recognition is a necessary precondition for identification and each set of differences represent a potential opportunity for developing identification. The Bible often endorses the unity in diversity; the apostle Paul, for instance, advocates identification among believers as the body of Christ but acknowledges existing differences as well. Believers can also notice the internal divisions whenever they admit the gap between their beliefs and practice.

---

102. Loscalzo, *Preaching Sermons That Connect*.
103. Loscalzo, 15–17.
104. Burke, *Rhetoric of Motives*, 55.
105. Loscalzo, *Preaching Sermons That Connect*, 21.

Because of that, a removal of "*harmful* division" through the process of identification represents a way to real unity. Loscalzo puts it this way, "Persuasive preaching using identification emphasizes what we have in common with our hearers and minimizes our differences."[106] This selective focus on the points of agreement is a crucial principle of identification. Starting from there, for a preacher to identify with her listeners may include a number of things: to empathize with them, to have compassion for them, to preach with passion, and to embody the good news for them and among them. Taken together, it seems plausible to conclude that these actions demonstrate identification is found at the intersection of logos, ethos, and pathos.

Loscalzo proceeds to explain the nature of identification. It is, above all else, a deliberate act, but it must be performed without any hidden agenda and grow out of a genuine relationship with hearers that requires time and sensitivity to their needs and real-life circumstances. This is an ongoing process where the preacher must be observant of and reflect on changes in his congregation. There is a mutuality involved, meaning it will be a two-way learning process in which a preacher must use empathetic imagination, too. Yet it is also a growing process in the sense that over time conversations with listeners must reach deeper and deeper levels of human experience.[107]

There are more than a few biblical characters (Moses, Amos, Ezekiel, Paul, or Jesus) whose personal example can both exemplify and sustain the idea of identification. Loscalzo here sketches a helpful résumé of instances where their life and ministry reveal the persuasive effects this approach can cause. Expectedly, he points to the incarnation as "the quintessential model" of identification. This claim is later expanded by his assertion that ". . . proclaiming the gospel completely and authentically to our listeners means becoming one with them. When we identify with them, we follow the model of Christ."[108]

Since the identification is made possible through a specific relationship between a preacher and members of a congregation, Loscalzo naturally focuses on the preacher's personality and traits. From a rhetorical standpoint, he reminds us that at the moment of preaching what matters is the listeners' perception of who the preacher is, which can greatly influence the reception

---

106. Loscalzo, 23.
107. Loscalzo, 25–30.
108. Loscalzo, 55, 58.

of the sermon's content. Therefore, the preacher needs to help hearers to perceive her as she really is.

In order to make this more applicable, Loscalzo lists several characteristics which can facilitate identification.[109] Preachers should keep on guarding and communicating their moral integrity, which includes careful handling and fulfilling of given promises. At the same time, preachers need to be open and honest about their own struggles while maintaining their integrity in sermon preparation. Another important characteristic is an authenticity; preachers need to be real persons, able to recognize their humanity and limitations while accepting God's divinity. Loscalzo here gracefully comments, "As you recognize your humanity, you give your hearers permission to recognize theirs."[110] An authentic preacher will be confident in showing her weakness, but approachable and accessible for her congregants, too. The third requirement is that preaching should emerge out of "a genuine growing faith" which stands for the substance of a preacher's ministry. The fourth characteristic is competence in ministry. There is an expectation of a certain quality and authority in preaching, but the retention of this competence obliges preachers to invest in lifelong learning and to consider it part of their ministry. Finally, an authentic concern for people is also required and should be mirrored in a passionate approach to everything related to preaching. Loscalzo specifically advises preachers to prudently construct their language in preaching and suggests the use of inclusive language and the avoidance of theological jargon.

However, for identification to happen much more is necessary. The preacher must be engaged in a continual congregational analysis. Loscalzo tries to make this task comprehensible by relying on Burke's terminology; a preacher needs to get to know his "preaching scene" simply because communication is always "circumstantially founded."[111] To properly understand and engage this situation, they must adequately evaluate their scene by getting to know the contexts in which listeners live. He specifically suggests that for homiletical purposes preachers must analyse the world scene, the cultural scene, the religious scene, and then the congregational scene. Just the same, he admits

---

109. Loscalzo, 62–79.
110. Loscalzo, 72.
111. Burke, *Permanence and Change*, 183, quoted in Loscalzo, *Preaching Sermons That Connect*, 83.

that preachers cannot be professional analysts of the first three scenes but insists they can make this sort of analysis a part of their lives and interpret events, changes, and situations in the world and society as they would hermeneutically interpret biblical texts.

Yet, they can be far more thorough at the congregational level. There they should realize that the congregation can be considered both a social unity and a collection of individuals. In the first case,[112] the preacher addresses the "social consciousness" of the congregation that is usually defined by what Burke calls "frames of acceptance" and "frames of rejection." These are norms of behaviour and experience which define acceptable and unacceptable patterns of conduct. They can be learned about either by intentional inquiry or by engaging in informal conversations. Loscalzo points out that preachers do not need to give consent to those frames as preaching often can serve as a "catalyst of change" of congregation's attitudes and behaviour, but they must invest effort to understand them. When addressing the personal needs of individuals, preachers will be aware of the existence of differences within the congregation; people may be at different positions on a "belief spectrum" or have differing interests or problems. There are also demographic varieties, gender-related differences, and people belong to different age groups. However, all such issues experienced personally are real issues the Bible addresses, and the preacher's responsibility is to call believers' attention to the connection between the Bible and the world of their problems.

Loscalzo closes his book by spelling out proposals of several strategies for identification. It is identification that enables the preacher to design the sermon as a specific response to a specific problem in a specific situation, bearing in mind particularities of his congregation and the individuals who belong to it. So, the strategy of attitude offers two possibilities: a sermon can either "comfort the afflicted or afflict the comfortable."[113] Identification will help the preacher, depending on the adopted attitude, to either reduce the opposition or destroy the apathy of listeners. Another strategy is that of interest. To preach an interesting sermon asks of the preacher to keep her listeners in mind from the very beginning of sermon preparation. The supporting material and stories should be related to what is close to them,

---

112. Loscalzo, *Preaching Sermons That Connect*, 98–100.
113. Loscalzo, 109–113.

should come from various sources (films, TV shows, music . . .), and should preferably be contemporary. But, Loscalzo warns, "Interest in preaching is never for interest's sake. It is always for the sake of identifying with the audience, saying to them that we have their best interests at heart and that our preaching is with them rather than at them."[114] When discussing the strategy of form, he maintains that different forms are suitable for different purposes. However, in the case of preaching out of passages, sermons should generally follow the form which is found in the text itself in order to *do* the same thing as the original text *did*.[115] When presenting the strategy of language, Loscalzo confirms that the language of preaching may easily be one of the most important factors for creating identification. Essentially, the language should resemble oral communication and use vocabulary with which the audience most easily identifies.

At the very end, Loscalzo picks up the question of delivery.[116] Addressing preachers, he strongly emphasises that the use of the body and the voice can either enhance or prevent identification. Because of that, all the elements of physical presence such as body posture, eye contact, and facial expression should be considered "as intentionally as you do the exegesis of the biblical text and the composition of the sermon."[117] Also, he encourages preaching without notes for two reasons: firstly, because "[a] sermon is something that is heard, not read. Preaching is an event created, not a document delivered," and secondly, because it allows for a much higher level of awareness of the listeners at the very moment of delivery, including the possibility to observe the changing reactions of his listeners, and provide impromptu adaptations to them.

The insights from three contemporary homiletical approaches described in this section can certainly suggest certain trends. First of all, the notion of persuasion as a primary goal of preaching has changed.[118] There is not only a

---

114. Loscalzo, 117.
115. Loscalzo, 117–118.
116. Loscalzo, 147–157.
117. Loscalzo, 150.
118. Naturally, there are also homileticians who have their doubts about persuasion as the valid goal of preaching. For instance, Robert Lischer believes that persuasion is not a theologically adequate concept – the gospel's character is a revelation and as such it destroys the existing linguistic moulds and refuses to be reduced to a mere "strategy of influence." Lischer,

strong awareness of the latent possibility of manipulation and coercion that conflicts with the essence of the gospel, but also the perception that the road toward persuasion is much more complex and requires both a far more active involvement of listeners and the preacher's engagement with them outside of the limits of the actual sermon. Secondly, the means of persuasion are not to be limited to logos, ethos, and pathos. The interaction among the five rhetorical canons is intensive and their borders are probably blurred more than ever. Persuasion can be accomplished only as a result of the careful, synergic engagement of all rhetorical stages implemented during the entire process of sermon preparation, which can no longer be comprehended as a one-time event. Instead, preaching is increasingly discovered to be an ongoing relationship in which preacher listeners still have different roles and responsibilities, but their positions are less defined by being on opposite sides of the pulpit. Finally, much of contemporary homiletics, appreciative of contemporary rhetorical contributions as much as of inputs from other disciplines, understands that speaking must be preceded by listening. Since preaching is a highly contextual form of human communication, an enormous need to investigate the immediate context of preaching is being detected. Inasmuch as preaching is an inherently communal event, the study of its congregational context is highly valuable and provides additional impulses for the further progress of homiletics. It is therefore befitting to devote my next chapter to the field of congregational studies.

"Why I Am Not Persuasive," 13–16. Yet others question persuasion's ethical validity – see, for example, McLaughlin, "Ethics of Persuasive Preaching," 93–106.

CHAPTER 4

Congregational Studies and Homiletics

As I move on to the third discipline (that is also the backdrop of my research), I will aim to accomplish several purposes in this chapter. First, I will describe the origins, purpose, methodology, and intended benefits of congregational studies. Secondly, I will illustrate these introductory insights in greater detail by looking at three influential books. Finally, I will turn to the intersections of congregational studies and homiletics to show how two selected homiletical approaches adopt or complement the procedures of inquiry and the goals of congregational studies. At the end of the chapter, I will show why and how congregational studies, together with the homiletical shift toward listeners and contemporary rhetoric, offer both a legitimate source of stimulation and a well-suited storehouse of guidelines for a qualitative study among Croatian Baptist believers who listen to sermons in the context of their congregations.

4.1 A Brief History of Congregational Studies

The supreme motive behind putting a local community of believers into the focus of a distinct study is an insight from a simple observation: there are no two identical congregations. Given the fact that all congregations represent believing communities in which Christian faith takes a particular form, it is impossible to extend the knowledge of the Christian religion without learning about Christian congregations. Since their individual expressions of faith are formed in distinct locations and times and imply distinct ways of doing things, any kind of generalization about churches is reductive and deprives us of the possibility of understanding them comprehensively. Carl Dudley explains why congregations have not been seriously treated until rather recently: "[c]ongregations may have suffered from a neglect bred by familiarity – a sense that what they do is obvious or unremarkable." He also provides a rather inclusive definition by stating that "[c]ongregational studies constitute those tools of research and reflection that examine congregations with the seriousness they deserve."[1] More specifically, he brings up the affinity with practical theology in the sense that both disciplines presume that the starting point of accounting for God's movement in this world can only be located in practice. However, since the variety of these tools and the diligence of reflection and research have been increasing over the decades, a brief historical overview is necessary in order to offer reasons for the prevalence of a multidisciplinary approach in congregational studies.

The origins of the study of congregations can be traced back to the turn of the twentieth century in the United States. Allison Stokes and David A. Roozen tell us that in spite of periods when the expansion of its scope was attempted (the 1920s and 1950s), it is only in the 1980s that "a named field of inquiry called "congregational studies" has emerged."[2] They argue that during these fifty or sixty years, most of this research has been conducted from the outside, in the context of demographic changes, and was faced with two challenges:

> One was the decline of establishment churches in the inner city and the development of new churches in emerging neighborhoods; the other, meeting the social and spiritual needs of the "new immigrants" to the inner city neighborhoods being abandoned by establishment churches.[3]

James Hopewell labels this set of approaches as *contextual studies*. They were directed against parochialism and spurred by ecumenical convictions. The intent behind those studies was to propose a different model for a local church within the secular context. Typically, they were designed and supported by experts in sociology and ethics. The anticipated missionary activity of the congregation was its participation "in the missio Dei, the all-encompassing act of God toward God's full creation."[4]

---

1. Dudley, "Giving Voice to Local Churches," 742.
2. Stokes and Roozen, "Unfolding Story," 183.
3. Stokes and Roozen, 185.
4. Hopewell, *Congregation*, 22.

Mathew Guest, Karin Tusting, and Linda Woodhead broadly categorize all types of congregational studies as either extrinsic or intrinsic. These earliest attempts fall under the extrinsic type, meaning that their goal implies "some broader good, such as a concern to assess the role of congregations in the generation of social capital, or a desire to enrich theological reflection with 'congregational voices.'"[5] In the case of the United Kingdom, these earliest, *communal* studies were largely motivated by concern over the growing individualisation of Western society and by the hope that Christian churches can provide focal points of fellowship which would strengthen the communal dimension of the society at large.

By the 1970s, a wider cultural shift occurred, and social idealism was replaced by the desire for self-fulfilment. At that point, Stokes and Roozen argue, ". . . contextual studies of the congregation gave way to examining the local churches from within. 'Renewal, became the new metaphor, and researchers began to view a congregation's challenges as issues of internal *process* and *program*."[6] Hopewell sees this as a shift by which the focus on the vitality of the congregation is reestablished. The various approaches which he classifies as *mechanistic* concentrate on the effectiveness of programs. They operate primarily in compliance with rational principles, and the most faithful representation of their hopes is the *church-growth movement*. It is largely concerned with the size of congregations and the salvation of individual souls. This is why the help of organizational studies is employed; exact formulas and efficient methods are critically required because, in the perception of the movement's leaders, churches are in great need of "the rationalization of congregational process and the animation of social will to achieve results."[7] The sway of the church-growth movement was and still is the strongest among American evangelicals.

Guest, Tusting, and Woodhead observe that with the increasing influence of organizational studies, since the 1980s more and more congregational studies "generally derive from university departments of management science or applied social science,"[8] and not from churchmen. However, this is

---

5. Guest, Tusting, and Woodhead, "Congregational Studies," 2.
6. Stokes and Roozen, "Unfolding Story," 186.
7. Hopewell, *Congregation*, 26.
8. Guest, Tusting and Woodhead, "Congregational Studies," 6.

not a universal rule, especially not after the emergence of the *church-health* approach. From its very beginnings, the famous experiment with Wiltshire Church[9] included a wide collaboration between experts in congregational studies, church-growth experts, and those involved in local church ministry. This approach has been further developed in the *Handbook for Congregational Studies* and its revised and renewed version entitled *Studying Congregations: A New Handbook*.[10] The latter will be presented in the next section. However, here it is sufficient to say that it represents a truly interdisciplinary project with a full-blown theological dimension and is conceived to be an entirely practical tool for church health analysis and improvement. It also conveniently illustrates the advantages of the church-health approach because it turns congregational studies into a pragmatic discipline, accessible both to laity and ministers, as well as experts in various fields. In Hopewell's terminology, this and similar approaches are called *organic*. These approaches consider the congregation as a whole which is greater than the sum of its parts and is usually called "community." In that respect, the local church is regarded as a growing organism, but its growth aims toward communal maturity, and is not measured by the increase in size or efficiency.

Another category of congregational studies is urged by the development of practical theology; its starting point is an exploration of the doctrine from the ground level of the lived experience (instead of enforcing doctrine on experience). Practical theology helps to build a climate conducive to congregational studies by stressing that the congregation is a locus of experience. The exemplary work of this approach is *A Fundamental Practical Theology* (1991) by Don S. Browning. As will be discussed more extensively in the next section, its major original contribution is a theological method whose departing point is a description of a congregation in its immediate situation. It then investigates and consults theological traditions and engages these two in conversation. Finally, it reverts to practice and suggests possible routes for transformation in the areas of congregational care, worship, preaching, education, social service, and church development.

---

9. This research was conducted as several scholars and experts visited the respective church on a particular Sunday in 1981. Dudley, *Building Effective Ministry*, 1983.

10. Carroll and Dudley, *Handbook for Congregational Studies*; Ammerman, Dudley, Carroll, and McKinney, *Studying Congregations*.

The remaining types of congregational studies, according to Guest, Tusting, and Woodhead, fall under *intrinsic* studies. These are studies conducted entirely for the sake of congregations and their better understanding. One of the most influential books on congregational studies, Hopewell's *Congregation: Stories and Structures* (which I will treat in more detail later on), they understand to represent a *self-contained* study, because "[h]is approach is to treat the congregation as a self-contained entity, rather than attempt to relate it to wider contexts."[11] His "symbolic" or "cultural" approach stems from his conviction that every congregation has its own, peculiar meaning which is conveyed in a story.

Another category of congregational studies mentioned by Guest, Tusting, and Woodhead is a *typologizing* study. Put simply, this is a study which simultaneously deals with several congregations which then, in turn, allows for proposing a new typology to be useful as a tool for further congregational analysis. The last type to be mentioned here is *contextualizing* intrinsic studies. Their aim is to establish a relationship between congregations and their social and cultural context but without any other motivation.

What, then, are the potential rewards for a congregation willing to submit to this discipline of self-reflection? Dudley's observations are helpful here. First, he states that congregations have been traditionally "regarded as consumers of the creative work done by others – branch office outlets for a faith that is determined by some distant, more powerful source," the sources he has in mind being seminaries and denominations. But as congregational studies over the later decades of the last century refocused from the outer cultural context to the internal issues of a congregation, local church leaders begin to see them as more relevant and far more constructive in getting to know the identity and "personality" of their congregations. Furthermore, as congregational studies provided tools to gather manifold stories told by individual believers about their congregation, the leaders understood them as opportunities to discover a unique "mind of the congregation" and make the congregation more aware of and sensitive to its own feelings, beliefs, convictions, and loyalties.[12]

---

11. Guest, Tusting, and Woodhead, *Congregational Studies*, 10.
12. Dudley, "Giving Voice to Local Churches," 743–744.

Therefore, the process of learning theology can be reversed: if seminary students visit congregations not to practice what they already learned, but to observe and learn from congregations, then "local churches can identify and share the way they experience faith in the trenches, while seminaries can set faith in a conceptual and historical context."[13] This would certainly transform congregations into more eloquent partners in theological dialogue and refine theological education.

4.2 A Closer Look: Three Classics

4.2.1 James F. Hopewell

James Hopewell's only book, *Congregation: Stories and Structures*, may easily represent a milestone in the field of congregational studies. In the overview which follows, I will isolate the chief features of this book which made his views unavoidable for all subsequent developments in congregational studies.

The essence of his theory of congregations is probably best summarized in this sentence: "congregational culture is not an accidental accumulation of symbolic elements but a coherent system whose structural logic is *narrative*."[14] This theory originates from a year during which Hopewell observed and studied two small local churches in Georgia. At the close of that period, he concluded that

> ... a group of people cannot regularly gather for what they feel to be religious purposes without developing a complex network of signals and symbols and conventions – in short, a subculture – that gains its own logic and then functions in a way peculiar to that group.[15]

This means that the congregation develops its own peculiar language, or "idiom," which consists of words, gestures, and artifacts. Its function is twofold: it not only represents an identity marker which differentiates the congregation from all other congregations, but it is also "a deep current of narrative interpretation and representation by which people give sense and order to

---

13. Dudley, "Giving Voice to Local Churches," 745–746.
14. Hopewell, *Congregation*, xii.
15. Hopewell, 5.

their lives." Even if this current runs on an unconscious level, says Hopewell, it is partially reinforced by images which belong to humanity's common search for meaning. Even more, this proves that a "congregation is held together by much more than creeds, governing structures, and programs."[16]

Hopewell goes on to explain that every idiom is comprised of both verbal and nonverbal elements, but what largely constitutes it as a unique system of signs is the mixture of symbols and signals. Signals are signs "that convey a message significant to the corporate life of the congregation," while symbols "refer to a signal that commands markedly higher recognition and respect from members as an element essential to parish life." What is particularly remarkable is that both signals and symbols can originate from all kinds of sources rooted in the experience of congregation's members, meaning that Christian congregations inevitably derive their idioms from their "complex heritage of Christian and non-Christian sources."[17]

Hopewell establishes a clear connection between the congregation's idiom and its identity and sees three reasons why believers should become more aware of the idiomatic, local manifestation of ecclesial life. Firstly, a better understanding of the idiom would help them to see their congregation's potential. Secondly, it would intensify their aptitude for the proclamation of and listening to the gospel. Finally, the understanding that their congregation uses the cultural forms common to other human communities can teach them a substantial lesson about solidarity. From the standpoint of researchers and church leaders, instead of being deemed an organization which a priori needs to be revised or adjusted, a congregation can now, through the appreciation of its language, be held "as a structure of social communication within which God's work in some ways already occurs."[18]

Yet, the full grasp of the nature of congregational life cannot be attained without comprehension of narrative's function. This is where, according to Hopewell, symbolic approach to congregational studies has precedence over other approaches: "Only narrative is sufficiently sensitive to amplify the unique accents of a congregation's idiom, sufficiently intricate to explain the congregation's constitutive power, and sufficiently comprehensive to link

---

16. Hopewell, 5.
17. Hopewell, 8.
18. Hopewell, 11.

congregational events and meanings."[19] On that account, the narrative fulfils a threefold role in the life of the congregation:
1. The congregation's self-perception is primarily narrative in form.
2. The congregation's communication among its members is primarily by a story.
3. By its own congregating, the congregation participates in narrative structures of the world's societies.[20]

Although Hopewell mostly focuses on presenting the tools used in the identification of congregational worldview,[21] he also articulates some proposals aimed at the betterment and renewal of congregations. For instance, he claims that every congregation has three latent ministries in their story.

The ministry of *evocation* has the potential to correct the wrong assumption, perpetuated by the image of the church being defined by programs and statistical numbers, which sees individuals as "essentially private contributors to the church who volunteer their presence, time, funds, and energy to constitute its being." The corporate story portrays believers instead "as agents in a drama, not donors to a program." The narrative, thus, establishes the communal sense of being, and its main goal is "the formulation of a larger setting for the self, one that situates the individual as part of the society and a world."[22]

The ministry of *characterization* has the task of pronouncing and shaping a congregation's distinct character – the set of values and inclinations by which this congregation can be told apart from other entities. This process is imperative when a congregation has no sense of its corporate identity because then it is usually assumed that this identity simply equals the sum total of personal stories of its well-known members – more often than not, pastors.

The last ministry Hopewell mentions is a ministry of *confession*. Within its narrative framework, the congregation can recognize that in the midst of the plot of its story it is possible not only to take responsibility for its past and present but also, "in the light of God's story for all humankind," to decide "to claim a transformed future."[23] In essence, this is a ministry of hope,

---

19. Hopewell, 50–51.
20. Hopewell, 46.
21. Hopewell, 67–100.
22. Hopewell, 194.
23. Hopewell, 197.

of confessing that the congregation's particular story is somehow situated in God's wider, all-encompassing narrative in which the entire humanity's transformation will be a final resolution.

4.2.2 Don S. Browning

Browning's *A Fundamental Practical Theology: Descriptive and Strategic Proposals* technically does not fall under congregational studies. His goal is at the same time both modest and grandiose: at one point he claims he did not intend to create a new genre of theology but rather to broaden or redefine what has been called *practical theology*. Yet, very soon he declares that what he proposes is a model for theology as such! All theology should be practical in the sense that all disciplines should be subspecialties of what he calls a "fundamental practical theology."[24] Given the breadth of his enterprise and the limited space in my thesis, I will focus only on those elements in Browning's book which either highlight the importance of studying congregational dynamics or demonstrate compatibility with my research in some other respect.

He begins his enterprise by asking about the possibility of reestablishing the stronger role of practical reason (or wisdom) since Western societies, in his analysis, suffer from not having "a clear idea of how practical reason and tradition relate to one another." What he intends to understand is how religious communities "make a difference in how practical reason works."[25] As he moves on to define the movement of his theology, Browning says that every approach to the theological task begins "with questions shaped by the secular and religious practices in which we are implicated . . . These practices are meaningful or theory-laden."[26] In his view, a theory is never detached from practices. Aware of them or not, theories are both behind the practices and embedded in them. From the perspective of congregations, the reflection on practices begins in the time of crisis. It includes their description and reexamination of the ideals and norms which govern them. Questions generated during this process are then brought into a dialogue with the sacred texts. As this conversation unfolds, new meanings within the texts get discovered, and practices change. Therefore, his fundamental practical theology follows this

---

24. Browning, *Fundamental Practical Theology*, ix, 7–8.
25. Browning, 4.
26. Browning, 5.

movement and can be divided into descriptive theology, historical theology, systematic theology, and strategic practical theology. This last one consists of the church disciplines of religious education, pastoral care, preaching, liturgy, social ministries, and others.

Finally, some of Browning's thoughts and conclusions on transformation are particularly relevant for my purposes. First of all, there are two basic attributes of transformation: it is always dialogical in nature, and God is the ultimate agent of transformation (in the theological perspective everyone else is viewed as one of the "metaphors of God's deeper transformative love"). Although in the end the transformation gets actualized at the stage of strategic practical theology, its roots are already present in descriptive theology.[27] This is because descriptive theology's task of shaping questions which will prompt new meanings within the congregational context is capable of transforming "our fundamental visions and narratives that provide the envelope for a practical reason." A descriptive theology is important because it tends to the basic human need to be understood and thus helps to "maintain a workable sense of self-esteem and self-cohesion."[28] If people feel misunderstood, the sense of identity of individuals or groups is under a threat, and people are unlikely to accept any change. This is why descriptive theology or "exegeting the congregation" (a concept I will describe very soon) is crucial from a homiletical perspective – which is, in its essence, a transformational perspective.

But Browning reminds more than once that the engagement in descriptive theology is not value-neutral – it is "an act of empathy expressed within the limits of a historically situated dialogue." It also has a rhetorical potential since it "helps discern the points of continuity between the witnessing initiators of transformation and the persons or groups addressed."[29] And if this is so, then a transformation is absolutely unthinkable without listening. And listening, of course, is not passive – it is the first stage of any dialogue, and it is practised with the goal of later description in mind. Listening may

---

27. Browning understands descriptive theology to be using human sciences within an overtly theological perspective. This means it must openly admit and assess its normative religious and ethical assumptions. The gist of transformation is thus already contained in descriptive theology's readiness to "appreciate and criticize" practices it attempts to understand. Browning, *Fundamental Practical Theology*, 93.

28. Browning, 279, 285, 284.

29. Browning, 284.

even be the most evident expression of love, and Browning calls it "an act of descriptive theology – an act that in itself witnesses to God's grace in creation and redemption," even though it is more readily associated with the practical ministerial disciplines, such as preaching, worship, or counselling.[30]

All of this reveals another truth: transformation is always mutual. Both the person who takes initiative and acts out in serving and the person who receives this service are transformed during the process. However, Browning predicts that in the future more and more congregations will need a broader, group-based practical reasoning, instead of leaders authorizing a complete process of reasoning for the congregation. He supports this with the claim that "[s]ome issues are so novel, so complex, and so delicate that we cannot expect any leader or group of leaders to master all exegetical, factual, and logical demands."[31] If true, this trend will only enlarge the dialogical nature of transformation, both of individuals and of congregations.

4.2.3 *Studying Congregations: A New Handbook*

The resourceful book *Studying Congregations: A New Handbook*, edited by Nancy Ammerman and others, is predicated on several key premises concerning the nature of a congregation and the meaning of the process of studying the congregation. These assumptions permeate the entire work, even if it is a joint project of eight scholars. First of all, the authors are deeply convinced that since congregations not only perpetuate and transmit the knowledge of faith traditions but also foster values which benefit communities on a wider scale, their worth is not limited to their members. On the other hand, given that they are based on the principle of voluntarism which "lends itself to social exclusiveness,"[32] they can cause as much harm as good and there is always a question mark on their ethical and theological justification. But the authors also believe that the search for this equilibrium "between gathering with one's own and remaining connected to a larger, more diverse community is at heart of what it means to congregate."[33] Also, it is their shared understanding that a congregation is best described as

---

30. Browning, 286.
31. Browning, 290.
32. Ammerman, Dudley, Carroll, and McKinney, *Studying Congregations*, 8.
33. Ammerman et al., 9.

> . . . a complex interplay of external and internal factors. Contextual forces act on congregations and call for adaptive responses, and internal meanings and capacities within congregations enable them to *choose* to shape their own lives and act on rather than always be *acted upon* by their environment.³⁴

The authors suggest there are at least three reasons why a systematic approach (as opposed to mere informal observation) to the study of the congregation has additional benefits. The formal approach can more easily get to the root of the problem, it provides the tools which enable the congregation "to step out of its everyday, taken-for-granted perceptions and reflect on key issues in a more systematic, precise, and analytic manner,"³⁵ and it requires a balance, a sense of proportion, and turns its results into a common property. Moreover, the very process of the study, as it happens, propels change in the congregation.

From a theological perspective, the congregational study reveals how the congregation understands faith at work. Since its self-perception and decisions about the future are both informed by the way it perceives God's activity and presence, the significance of the congregational study is particularly evident in the situation when the congregation needs to affirm its identity, or when it is necessary to initiate changes or make decisions concerning the future. And this is precisely the moment when theology should play a prominent role because "[a]ny response a congregation makes must be more than pragmatic or expedient if the congregation hopes to be faithful in its discipleship and consistent with the religious tradition it represents."³⁶

Given the connection between practical theology and congregational studies as discussed above, it is not surprising that the authors consider their model of congregational study to be an exercise in practical theology. Similar to Browning, they begin with a description of the situation, or more specifically, by "intentionally grounding their [congregations'] theological work in their current setting and its challenges."³⁷ In the next step, the researcher (or preferably, the researching committee made up of various members of

---

34. Ammerman et al., 169.
35. Ammerman et al., 197.
36. Ammerman et al., 25.
37. Ammerman et al., 26.

the congregation) explores stories, creeds, doctrines, and scriptures which, from a historical point of view, supply the congregation with the content of its faith tradition. Then a dialogue between these resources and the current situation follows; this is a theological reflection in which a knowledge of the congregational context is part of the theological process. Out of this encounter, a new action, or renewed practice of faith (a transformation, or a change) will be born.

So, although the methods and tools employed by the congregational studies come from various disciplines, its goal is unmistakably theological. But what exactly can congregational study discover through the exercise of practical theology? First, there are *explicit and implicit theologies* present. The explicit theologies are relatively easy to unveil as they are visibly existent in doctrines, creeds, confessions, liturgy, sermons, or a mission statement. However, the implicit theologies "are sometimes harder to name than [the] explicit, but they are crucial for understanding any congregation's life. These implicit theologies may often guide the congregation more surely than does its mission statement."[38] They may shed light on not so desirable truths, and yet, they are needed for a full theological profile of the congregation. They may be found, for instance, in or under the congregational stories, leadership styles, or in the way funds are managed.

Then, a study will seek to reveal *multiple theological perspectives*. A number of different experiences and various social locations will cause a number of dissimilar understandings. There might be differences in the theological perspectives of pastors and leaders and other members, differences which are a result of different roles in a congregation, or generational differences. All of these and many others can serve as a starting point for the inquiry into existing differences within the congregation but must be handled with utmost confidentiality and care.

And yet, it is possible that the most fruitful approach is to go after the congregation's *narratives*, *practices*, and *texts*. An entire range of questions concerning God, humanity, evil and sin, the congregation, and life can be asked, and the observed narratives, practices, and texts will suggest specific answers that in the end provide profound insights into *the theological content in congregational life*. For example, the *narratives* usually revolve around some

---

38. Ammerman et al., 32.

prominent individuals in the congregation, and they are commonly associated with a specific biblical story or event. They are "the stories that shape and transmit the memories of a congregation," and they represent a principal way of congregations' expression of their identities. As for the *practices*, they are depicted as "pathways . . . [that] take us from the memories of the past and steer us through the uncertainties of the present."[39] There are several areas of church life where a diligent researcher will detect much about what roles the congregation is expected to play, and they include: a congregation's physical space, patterns of worship and of gathering, and meetings on special occasions. And *texts* here stand for what the congregation has to say about itself, and normally represent the ideals, and not so much the present state. However, all the mission statements, educational curricula, and various promotional materials and slogans can be examined, not only for the formulations of explicit theology, but also for those things they do *not* say.

Then the study reaches the stage when the researcher can set the interaction between implicit and explicit theologies in motion. This is also the phase when the theologically educated members of a congregation can be useful as they will better understand the dimensions of explicit theology which may be unknown to others. The supreme idea is that this conversation between explicit traditions and implicit practices "will lead you toward the 'strategic' work of your practical theological process – the actions you take out of your new understanding of your faith."[40] Now, this is a process of doing theology during the congregational study. What is a particular novelty of this book is a set of perspectives or ways of looking at the information gathered through the study, called "frames" or "lenses." Four of them are proposed, but admittedly this list is by no means exhaustive.[41]

The first one is called the *ecological frame*. To view the congregation through this frame means to presume that all congregations are "open systems" in which an interaction is going on within the congregation as well as between the congregation and its environment. The ecological frame tells us how various social, political, religious, and economic forces in a congregation's

---

39. Ammerman et al., 33, 34.

40. Ammerman et al., 37.

41. The gender perspective could have easily been presented as another frame, but it has been integrated in all other frames instead. Ammerman et al., 37.

context influence the congregation, but also how the congregation affects these forces. The required activities include gathering demographic data, information about significant cultural groups or subcultures, and insights about the political power of various groups in a community. The growing awareness of a community's diversity may bring about conflicts, but this is not necessarily a negative phenomenon since "the only congregations that avoided conflict were those who refused to change, a refusal that would ultimately mean their demise. The only sure way for a congregation to die is for it to close itself off from its context."[42]

The *cultural frame* deals with the congregation's unique identity shaped over time. This is an anthropological approach that studies the congregation "as a group that has invented ways of being together that are uniquely its own,"[43] although these ways are subject to change. But this uniqueness is a mixture of influences from a congregation's religious traditions, the larger secular culture (especially the language), existing expectations of what a religious congregation should look like, patterns of social class and ethnicity, and so on. The exploration of this rich texture of communal fabric should focus on the study of activities, artifacts, and accounts. It is through the regular patterns of activity that the congregation communicates to itself and others what it is about; various material objects not only help the congregation to do what it wants to do, but also communicate its particular culture; and its myths and stories convey the particularities of both explicit and implicit theologies.[44]

The *process frame* considers an element of the congregational study which at the same time seems to be the most accessible and the most evasive. It studies "the ways in which a congregation plans and makes decisions, rewards and punishes its members, and fights and solves its problems."[45] To understand these dynamics, it is necessary to study both formal and informal processes. The formal processes "include practices, procedures, and policies that have openly been considered and officially accepted by the congregation." On the other hand, the informal process "refer[s] to the social interaction that occurs without guidelines or instruction – [which] just happens." Through activities

---

42. Ammerman et al., 76.
43. Ammerman et al., 15.
44. Ammerman et al., 84–101.
45. Ammerman et al., 105.

such as "congregational learning, group building, and conflict management," a researcher may discover a rather intriguing "dual guidance system of the congregation" where the "informal processes keep the congregation moving with the minimum effort" and prove to be stable and resilient, even under pressure (or particularly then!).[46]

Finally, there is the *resources frame*. It understands a congregation "as a collection of elements drawn out of a wider social and religious context that together have the potential to accomplish social and religious goals." It tries to understand what potential "capital" the congregation possesses and evaluate its limitations. Both tangible and abstract resources are specifically listed and examined: membership resources, commitment resources, capital resources, financial resources, physical and space resources. The preferred outcome of studying a congregation through this frame is an enhanced knowledge and eagerness on the behalf of the entire congregation to carefully build a good stewardship of its resources.

This volume brings an extensive technical presentation of various methods and tools to be used in congregational studies,[47] but the authors explicitly say that their application will not yield immediate answers to the problems and issues in any congregation. What it can do, though, is to equip people doing a study with the knowledge to draw on during the process of decision making, and thus make them more capable of a faithful and effective response.

4.3 Homiletical Approaches Informed by Congregational Studies: Two Examples

It is appropriate now to focus on some examples of how homileticians can make good use of congregational studies and incorporate their insights in the development of preaching strategies that are more listener-centred and more sensitive toward the communal nature of the environment in which preaching takes place.

---

46. Ammerman et al., 107, 109–125.
47. Ammerman et al., 196–239.

4.3.1 *Preaching as Local Theology and Folk Art*[48]

At the very heart of the homiletical proposal of Leonora Tubbs Tisdale are two underlying observations. The first insists that the fact that preachers regularly need to address their listeners who do not share their worldviews is simply irrebuttable and increasingly present. Her second remark is that the skill of "exegeting the congregation," as opposed to the exegesis of the biblical text, is largely underestimated and overlooked. Given that seminary education leaves to preachers' intuition to determine how to exegete their congregations, there are some common, recurring mistakes that exist in preaching ministries everywhere. Preachers tend to prepare generic sermons for generic hearers not embodied in a real-life of specific congregations, they paint too simplistic or generalised portraits of their hearers, or they end up projecting their own issues on the congregations.[49] Assuming that this "lack of contextual 'fit' between the sermon and the hearers" is a greater issue than the poor quality of preaching at the theological or communicational level, Tisdale poses two questions: How can preachers become better exegetes of local congregations and their subcultures? And what difference does such knowledge make for local preaching – both in its theology and in its art (language, illustrations, and form)?[50] She proceeds with answering these questions and building a case for contextual preaching "which not only aims toward greater "faithfulness" to the gospel of Jesus Christ, but which also aims toward greater "fittingness" (in content, form and style) for a particular congregational gathering of hearers."[51]

To begin with, Tisdale explicitly says that congregational studies (along with cross-cultural mission) offer the most constructive input toward answering the first question. She claims that the contextual dimension of congregational identity is the most viable way of helping preachers learn how to prepare sermons and preach them across the subcultures in the congregation. Yet, this contextuality needs a theological backing, and she finds this in conversations with Tillich, Calvin, and Brueggemann.[52] The contextuality helps to remove those obstacles to hearing the gospel which are not part of

---

48. Tisdale, *Preaching*.
49. Tisdale, 23.
50. Tisdale, xi.
51. Tisdale, 33.
52. Tisdale, 35–38.

its natural offensiveness, including theological jargon, complicated sermon structure, or images inappropriate for the embodiment of the gospel. Also, contextualized preaching follows the "accommodating way in which God has dealt with humanity in revelation," with the incarnation being God's ultimate act of accommodation to humanity. Finally, putting particular biblical texts and a particular congregational context side by side in the preacher's imagination can elicit new meanings and cause new hearings of the gospel.

Since Tisdale favours identity as the primary category for studying a congregation, it is not surprising that she supports symbolic congregational studies and urges preachers to become "amateur cultural anthropologists." Preachers are already involved in an informal congregational analysis, and since they naturally find themselves in the dual role of insider and outsider, participant observation is apparently the most expedient research method. By looking at various congregational "culture texts" which will disclose aspects of a congregation's identity, a preacher should also be able to locate particular symbols. Tisdale suggests a list of congregational symbols that most readily lend themselves to symbolic analysis: stories and interviews, archival materials, demographics, architecture and visual arts, rituals, events and activities, and people. The adopted methods and procedures of ethnographic analysis provide for her a basis on which she develops various sets of questions that can be used in approaching and observing these congregational symbols.[53] But this descriptive stage is not an end in itself; it must be followed by the analytical step. Relying on contributions from the field of anthropology, Tisdale discusses three elements of congregational identity (worldview, values, and ethos), and introduces seven lenses "through which pastors can approach congregational symbols and begin to make assessments – both anthropologically and theologically – regarding congregational worldview and values." These are views of God, humanity, nature, time, church, Christian mission, and the interrelations of the first six areas.[54]

How does this search for a fuller understanding of the congregation convert into the construction of theology for local preaching? Tisdale here uses the image of dance. The interpretive process of sermon preparation can be imagined as a dance in which the preacher is a key partner with freedom

---

53. Tisdale, 64–77.
54. Tisdale, 77–84.

"to attend to the various partners" which are Scripture, congregational context, and church doctrines and tradition. While dancing with the Bible, the preacher engages both in "priestly listening' ... on behalf of the congregation with its own distinctive subculture" and in "'priestly questioning,' asking questions and raising the issues that arise out of congregational life."[55] Partnering with the congregational context, on the other hand, will make sure "that the preacher will 'name God in the world.'" The third partner is the doctrinal traditions that connect sermon preparation with the larger Christian community which spans space and time and should go beyond the preacher's own denominational tradition or theologians he agrees with. Yet, every doctrine should be treated as local doctrine and not approached as an "ideology" (normative at all times and in all situations), but rather reinterpreted with due respect to both its original context and to the new context in which it is examined.[56]

The process of sermon preparation can thus be depicted as a "from con/text to the sermon" process. Contextuality in preaching requires more flexibility in the stage of text or topic selection, asking for the predominance of congregational concerns over the strict use of lectionary preaching or other previously set agendas. Tisdale supports the idea of a first naïve reading and backs it up from the congregational perspective: "[I]t is in this first reading that the preacher most closely approximates the congregation's own naïve hearing of the text when it is read aloud in worship."[57] This first contact with the text should not be rushed and should be allowed enough time for the biblical world and congregational world to come together at the very beginning of the preparation process.

At the stage of application of interpretation methods, though, Tisdale is concerned about the superficial and premature identification of the world of original listeners with the world of a congregation. Therefore, she advises preachers to supplement historical-critical methods with other, particularly sociological, methods although she welcomes other interpretive angles, too. For example, the literary and symbolic methods are precious for their attention to the poetic and narrative aspects of texts which in their present shape

---

55. Tisdale, 95.
56. Tisdale, 98.
57. Tisdale, 104. Cf. Craddock, *Preaching*, 105–107.

"provide deeper insight into the ways in which Scripture's own symbols, images, plots, and characterizations can work (and have worked) to reshape congregational imaginations."[58] The reader-response method highlights the truth that the Bible has not been interpreted by scholars alone, and points out the interpretation of local communities in a response to their contexts through the centuries. However, her major motivation is probably best summed up in this sentence: "If the room for sermon preparation . . . is . . . populated with those who interpret life and biblical texts in radically different and challenging ways, then the dance can become very interesting indeed – possibly even transformative!"[59]

But if we accept that Tisdale's definition of theological construction for preaching as local theology reads as "the engagement of the horizons of biblical texts and congregational context in a fitting and transformative way,"[60] what happens when the preacher begins to probe *"both the consonances and the dissonances that are created when the idiom, worldview, and ethos of the biblical text and the idiom, worldview, and ethos of the congregation meet?"*[61] Several possible correlations can be established and Tisdale suggests these as potential strategies useful to a preacher in a search of a theme for proclamation.[62] (1) Preaching can affirm what the congregation already believes, and confirm its values and practices, thus sanctifying its imagination. (2) Preaching can stretch the limits of the congregation's theological imagination, and in this manner extend "both comfort and challenge." (3) Preaching can turn the assumed ordering of the congregation's imagined worldview upside down, just like Jesus's parables usually did. (4) Preaching can challenge and judge the false imaginings of the congregational heart – idolatries and deceptions within the congregation's character which must be exposed. (5) Preaching can help congregations envision worlds they have not yet begun to imagine so that glimpses of the future world can induce the transformation of the present one.

---

58. Tisdale, *Preaching*, 107.
59. Tisdale, 110.
60. Tisdale, 90.
61. Tisdale, 111.
62. Tisdale, 111–121, and Tisdale, "Exegeting the Congregation," 84–85.

Tisdale is fully aware that congregational concerns are to be pressed not only in matters of sermon preparation but also in the questions of delivery and style. She does that first of all by affirming the artistic nature of preaching: "Preachers, like artists, are engaged in a vocation that requires them to express the inexpressible." Commenting on the closeness of preaching to the fine arts, she finds that the term "folk art" does more justice to her congregational emphasis. In her view, "the worldview and values assumed in contemporary or classical art and literature are far removed from the ordinary, everyday worldview of a particular faith community. Questions raised about life in a contemporary novel are not the congregation's questions." She also broadens the dance image by declaring that a preacher has a dual role: she is not only a dancer but a choreographer, too. The choreographer's task is to "enflesh the sermon's theology in language and form that are equally fitting and transformative for congregational imagination."[63] For a preacher willing to undertake this task, Tisdale has some guidelines concerning both language and form.

As for the use of language, it must fulfil a twofold function; it needs to revise the assumed world of the congregation taking into account the language and symbols of the Christian faith, and it also must reinterpret the ancient language of the Christian faith taking into account the world of the congregation. Therefore, preaching as folk art tends to use the conversational language of the congregation as it refutes the idea that the sacred is detached from the secularity of everyday life. Also, this kind of preaching will make every effort to locate its illustrations and examples in real-life situations, while images and metaphors will be local thus increasing the probability of an encounter of the biblical world with the congregational world.[64] With regard to sermon form, Tisdale grants that congregations are not monolithic when it comes to the ways of knowing. She is also aware that a congregation's subculture is not the only factor affecting hearers' sermon form preferences. Yet, she is convinced that within a particular congregation some sermon forms can thrive and be more willingly received than in another. For this reason, the diversity of forms is encouraged – and clues can be taken either from the biblical text or from the congregational context.

---

63. Tisdale, *Preaching*, 122, 124, 126.
64. Tisdale, 127–133.

In closing, her proposal can aptly be condensed by quoting her own expressive conclusion:

> By attending closely to congregations and their cultures, by identifying and removing false stumbling blocks to the hearing of the gospel, and by enfleshing the gospel in sermons which are – in their theology, language, and form – both more fitting and more transformative for local communities of faith, preachers encourage others to join the circle and to participate with their whole beings in the gospel's liberating dance.[65]

4.3.2 *One Gospel, Many Ears*

In their book *One Gospel, Many Ears*, Joseph R. Jeter, Jr. and Ronald J. Allen approach the problem of diversities within the congregation from the homiletical perspective. They start by noting the complex nature of the relationship between individuality and communality in the congregation:

> The congregation is embodied in individual Christians. Preaching intends, in part, to help form the congregation as community . . . The congregation as community is not intended to be a homogenous group. To the contrary, an integral part of the vocation of the church is to bring together people who manifest different qualities (e.g., race, ethnicity, gender, age, social class) to witness to the great reunion that God intends for all peoples.[66]

This future union, however, does not obliterate the present particularities by which they participate in the life of the congregation. These distinctive groups can be discerned along two different lines. There are "formally constituted groups" within the congregations such as prayer groups, small (cell) groups, or single persons' groups. Yet there are also other groups which are not formally constituted, but their members still share some common traits (groups defined by gender, age, ethnicity, personality types, or patterns of mental operation). What Jeter and Allen derive from this fact is that these groups are inevitably prone to the ways of thinking which are congruous to

---

65. Tisdale, 143.
66. Jeter and Allen, *One Gospel*, 183.

their distinctive traits. Even more important is that they also possess different listening tendencies. From a homiletical point of view, this sets before the preacher a demanding challenge, "to prepare sermons so that they have a good *opportunity* to be received and processed by the different kinds of listeners in the congregation."[67] To respond properly, a preacher needs to allow each of these groups access to the "speaking centre,"[68] or even better, to turn his preaching into the speaking and listening centre of the congregation. Jeter and Allen are confident this can become a reality if the preacher understands that giving voice to various groups also means "help[ing] them [to] have an optimum opportunity to hear and understand the gospel and one another." But to make that possible, a preacher must recognize and apprehend the characteristics of these distinct groups and pay heed to them during all stages of the preaching process.

Before we proceed to the specifics of several listening profiles, let us consider an additional factor that bears upon opportunities for various groups to hear the gospel and each other. Every preacher builds his or her peculiar style, which in itself is beneficial since it "helps to bring congruity between the preacher and the message." But if the preacher does not dare to leave the province of that style, it "can leave some listeners feeling that they have not been full participants in the preaching conversation." Due to the diversity of listening groups in every congregation, preachers have no choice but to intentionally transcend their preferred style of preaching and learn how to preach in other styles. This is also mandatory because different subject matters and situations may require different approaches, and preachers should not arbitrarily choose from a storehouse of predefined templates. An approach to a particular sermon should instead, in Jeter and Allen's words, emerge "from the encounter of the congregation (and the various subcongregations within it) and its various listener tendencies, the occasion (with its needs), the biblical text, the gospel, and the preacher."[69]

As they identify a variety of listening profiles, Jeter and Allen use six traits that can be isolated as controlling factors. Applying every respective trait, they

---

67. Jeter and Allen, 10.

68. The term is adapted from Nancy L. Eiesland, *The Disabled God: Toward a Liberatory Theology of Disability* (Nashville: Abingdon, 1994).

69. Jeter and Allen, *One Gospel*, 11, 13.

can differentiate diverse groups which then allows them to locate the points of correlation between the gospel and these particular groups. Then they detect places where the gospel presents a challenge for the groups' preferences. Finally, they focus on the issues of content and form in preaching which may foster or discourage communication for those groups.

The first trait is *age*.[70] As the primary concern of the book is congregations in the USA, authors distinguish four generations in American society (Builders, Silents, Boomers, and Generation 13) and subject them to the analytical procedure described above. They issue a warning, though. Preachers must be aware that none of these groups is monolithic: within each generation, there may be many divergences, and "characteristics of each generation are not frozen."

Several studies in social sciences prove that humans prefer some types of communication and are less receptive to other types. This is why Jeter and Allen present insights from three different pieces of research – faith development theory, Myers-Briggs Type Indicator, and Neuro Linguistic Programming theory – in order to demonstrate how preferences in learning and communicating (also called modes of perception) function as another trait.[71]

Gender is the second trait discussed in this insightful work.[72] Studies show that men and women use different metaphors when talking about knowledge. For example, men tend to use visual metaphors while women frequently employ vocal metaphors. These sets also refer to deeper qualities related to Christian knowledge of God and others; we need both intimate connectedness with God, other people, and the world (as implied by vocal metaphors), and yet we need to be able to rise above ourselves and critically observe and modify our perceptions and conduct (as implied by visual metaphors). Yet another study on gender differences in communication[73] reveals that men usually employ language to establish and maintain their status or to preserve their independence, while women most often use language in order to establish connections and nurture relationships. Jeter and Allen claim that

---

70. Jeter and Allen, 21–47.
71. Jeter and Allen, 50–77.
72. Jeter and Allen, 79–102.
73. Tannen, *You Just Don't Understand*.

"the language patterns of women are more congenial to the vision of life shaped by the reign of God," and yet, they normally speak less in public and in congregations. This is precisely why preachers should provide more space for female voices, and bring them, together with other marginalized voices, to the speaking centre.

In our contemporary world different cultures frequently exist in proximity and often mingle and merge, thus creating multicultural settings. Jeter and Allen convincingly argue that *culture*, therefore, presents another trait responsible for the existence of multiple listening patterns.[74] Moreover, one would do well to understand the term "multicultural setting" not only as a social context of people from more than one racial or ethnic group. By defining the culture as a "learned experience" composed of three components (what people think, what people do, and what material artifacts they produce), Jeter and Allen suggest to preachers four ways of addressing the multicultural nature of the congregation: they can teach the congregation about its multiple cultures, reflect critically and theologically on cultures present in the congregation, help the congregation to enact truly multicultural worship, and lead the congregation toward the launch of the multicultural mission.

Another class of people mentioned in the book is called *"the least of these"* and represents various groups usually found on the margins of the congregations, or even beyond them: the strangers, the general minority (older adults and children), the poor, and those who are physically or mentally disabled.[75] The authors observe that even though hospitality toward strangers is deeply embedded in the Christian faith, it is often simply overlooked. Facing a stranger is always a good reminder that the preacher is not in control of the preaching event since it is "a compound of text, Spirit, sermon, preacher, audience, occasion, and other factors." On the other hand, it is also a reminder of the need for singularity and immediacy in preaching. A particular sermon may be the last (or only) sermon the stranger will hear in her life. Also, preachers should truly respect strangers' effort to come to the church – by doing that, they "have opened the window to themselves by themselves" – and remember that the first idea communicate should always be a God's unconditional love.

---

74. Jeter and Allen, *One Gospel*, 103–128.
75. Jeter and Allen, 129–148.

When it comes to putting the elderly and children into the speaking centre of the congregation, the authors suggest that preachers keep in mind that their preaching could be "one of the few caring voices" these people will hear during the week. They also recommend the conscious effort of making themselves available to the experience of being old (or young) and remind preachers that both older adults and children have shorter attention spans and may lose their focus during the sermon.

After assuming that money could easily be the biggest obstacle in relationships between people in contemporary congregations, the authors reckon that poverty is the most visible manifestation of socioeconomics as a divisive factor in the church. Poor people often are not at the level of literacy which is assumed by worship liturgies or hymnbooks and preachers should take care to phrase their sermons in language these people can understand. They should also preach the corporate nature of faith instead of promoting individualistic or personalist faith which emphasises personal salvation that in turn can foster neglect of others, especially of those who are socially disadvantaged.

The last group of "the least of these" are people with mental and physical disabilities. They usually share the pain of other marginalized people – the sense of being excluded and not loved. In order to bring these people into the speaking centre, Jeter and Allen maintain, it is sometimes necessary to shape the preaching in a way which will address the merits of less visible gifts – such as the gift of listening, the gift of availability, or the gift of empathy – which frequently can be found among those who cannot take on other important and more prominent responsibilities. In cases of those who lose their memories and other mental abilities, a preacher can still approach them through remembering them as they were and imagining the way they will be after! It is possible to address them as they are at the present, but also to bring "both memory and hope to the speaking center."[76]

Listening patterns can be conditioned by *theological orientation*, too. One of the key responsibilities preachers have is related to helping congregations understand the sources of their perception of God. This duty is particularly urgent given the fact that congregants often quarrel over theological issues without comprehension of how the Bible, tradition, experience, and reason influence their standpoints. The honest preacher will make sure to disperse

---

76. Jeter and Allen, 147.

the impression that her sermon goes straight from the Bible to the present day and will carefully expose the impact of other sources on the sermon's content and meaning, including one of informal traditions. Also, through the honest, fair, and precise representation of multiple positions, preachers will display their trustworthiness, which is a road toward earning a hearing from all sides of the theological spectrum.

After the analysis of all six traits that may shape listening tendencies independently or in the combination, the question remains: What strategy can preachers implement to address their heterogeneous congregations? Jeter and Allen believe that a "pastoral exegesis of the congregation" or "pastoral listening" should sufficiently make them aware of predominant listening patterns and furnish them with information on how to prepare sermons which will correspond to those patterns. What they offer are four possible strategies:[77]

(1) A pastor develops a sermon (or a series of sermons) with a particular listening group in mind. That group is brought to the speaking and listening centre during the entire sermon. This approach is especially appropriate when there is a group with a specific pastoral need. Other groups can still receive something since listeners possess the inherent flexibility which allows them to "overhear" messages not directly addressed to them.

(2) A preacher can intentionally prepare a sermon which integrates several various features that increase the receptivity for different listening groups.

(3) Over a longer period, a preacher can combine elements of the first two approaches. By doing that, he may cover the full range of listening tendencies within the congregation. No single sermon will speak to everyone, but in the long run, no group will be left out.

(4) A preacher can also make his way through the sermon by initially focusing on the text and immediate occasion, and then build the sermon by taking different listening groups into account.

Jeter and Allen are deeply aware that sermonic communication sometimes evades the conventional homiletical rules and admit that no listeners can be limited by their listening traits – these are "not a straitjacket, but an indicator of probability."[78] People get changed over the course of time, and each person is a unique composite of listening traits. However, a preacher who

---

77. Jeter and Allen, 15–20.
78. Jeter and Allen, 18.

can establish a meaningful correlation between the congregational context and the content of the sermon will "often find people listening eagerly from across the various listening spectra."[79]

The authors list several benefits that may arise from their approach. By considering the differences in congregational perception, a preacher can shape sermons so they typify the oneness of the church. By preaching multidimensional sermons, preachers can also help the congregation to identify and face its own diversities. And by her inclusion of various groups and putting them in the speaking centre, a preacher can visibly demonstrate God's inclusiveness and love.[80]

Congregational studies, thus, constitute a pragmatic discipline that perfectly fits into a descriptive dimension of practical theology. The empirical research I am about to present is both justified and reinforced by its determination to access the doctrines and practices of a particular congregation at the ground level of experience. The approach of congregational studies can enhance our understanding of specific practices, such as preaching, and the discipline's multiple perspectives can facilitate a dialogue with congregational norms and sacred texts. And since its ultimate purpose is to promote transformation within a congregation, the accomplishment of that goal is inconceivable without mutual listening. At the same time, two examples of homiletical appropriation of congregational studies prove that contextuality of preaching is feasible when appropriate analysis and "exegesis of the congregation" isolate different listening tendencies and thus help a sermon to be heard across different groups. To consider these dynamics more closely, I now turn to the existing empirical studies that were designed to focus on listeners' experiences of preaching.

---

79. Jeter and Allen, 20.
80. Jeter and Allen, 18.

CHAPTER 5

Existing Empirical Studies in Preaching

Existing empirical studies in preaching are still not abundant, but I chose to present the goals and major findings of three which possess some level of correspondence with my intended purposes.[1] All of them propose a number of constructive suggestions concerning the development of a preaching practice more sensitive to the listeners' participation. Later, these will be juxtaposed to my own study findings and observations.

5.1 *Presence in the Pulpit*

Hans van der Geest, a Dutch pastor and psychologist, analysed more than 200 worship services within his work of supervising ministers undertaking Clinical Pastoral Education. These church services took place in a hospital chapel and sermons were preached by participants in the programme. The

---

1. My account is by no means exhaustive. In recent years, more research has been conducted than ever before. Yet, the actual numbers are still low. Although space does not allow for a detailed overview of all these studies, a useful guide can be found in David Rietveld, "A Survey of the Phenomenological Research of Listening to Preaching," *Homiletic* 38, no. 2 (2013), http://dx.doi.org/10.15695/hmltc.v38i2.3867. The geographical location of these studies is highly diverse. For example, one is done in Denmark: Marlene Ringgaard Lorensen, *Dialogical Preaching: Bakhtin, Otherness And Homiletics* (Göttingen: Vandenhoeck & Ruprecht, 2013); another in Madagascar: Hans Austnaberg, *Improving Preaching by Listening to Listeners Sunday Service Preaching in the Malagasy Lutheran Church* (New York: Peter Lang, 2012); a third one in Holland: Theo Pleizier, *Religious Involvement in Hearing Sermons: A Grounded Theory Study in Empirical Theology and Homiletics* (Delft: Eburon Academic Publishers, 2010); and yet another in the USA: John M. Martin, "Preaching for the Listener: Does Vineville Baptist Church in Macon, Georgia, Prefer Logos, Pathos, or Ethos in Connecting with Sermons?" (unpublished doctoral dissertation, Mercer University, 2011). Accessed 20 November 2015, <http://search.proquest.com/pqdt/docview/864740931/abstract/CEA9F964C1C24725PQ/1>.

listeners were other ministers and some lay people. After the sermon, a leader would gather a group of around ten participants and lead them to reflect on their experience. During that process, he or she would collect and systematise the feedback. Then the preacher would join the discussion, respond to the observations made by the listeners, and describe his or her personal background which affected the sermon. The final stage focused on the preacher's personal issues identified during the discussion, but this part would occur within a much smaller group, if not in a private conversation with a leader.[2]

Van der Geest's primary concern was to determine the short-term effect of a sermon. To do so, he argues that sermons must be analysed within their natural contexts, which includes participation in the worship service. Furthermore, the path toward discovering the sermon's effect leads through the listeners' spontaneous, natural reactions to the impetus of preaching, and these can be located exclusively in their feelings (although the listeners are inclined to offer their judgements instead). Van der Geest maintains, "The analysis is fruitful only when one succeeds in exactly identifying the two quantities: *cause* (in the sermon) *and feeling* (in the listener)."[3]

However, his research yields findings in the form of summaries of the three most frequent categories of statements: (1) the strongest need among listeners is for the sermon to be "personal," (2) the second most often expressed theme is an expectation that the sermon should offer deliverance or release, and (3) the remaining statements usually reflect the listeners' need for understanding or knowing, which will provide a sense of direction in their existential affairs of daily life.[4] Van der Geest cautions that listeners' feedback in itself cannot be taken as adequate grounds for homiletics, but is essential in order to build a homiletics which respects their expectations. He then proceeds to elaborate on three dimensions necessary for effectual, engaging preaching.

5.1.1 The Dimension of Security

There is an ultimate hope which churchgoers bring with them every time they attend a church service, a hope that their basic trust will be endorsed and

---

2. Van der Geest, *Presence in Pulpit*, 1–8.
3. Van der Geest, 20.
4. Van der Geest, 28–29.

renewed once again. This basic trust van der Geest describes as a child's initial affirmation of trust in life caused by the care given by its mother.[5] However, in the context of a church service, participants wish to reinforce this trust by experiencing security with God. He points out how crucial the proper recognition of this expectation is: ". . . we preachers are not aware enough of this hope. The analyses of sermons and worship services show clearly that we make our worst mistakes in this dimension."[6]

To avoid these mistakes, preachers should take note of "a parallelism between the love of God sought by the congregations and the way the preachers present themselves. Because the first quantity is very personal, the second should be, also." Listeners' responses in this research prove that their sense of security increases proportionally to the increase of personal components in a preacher's presentation. The first requirement for personal presentation is *sincerity*. It denotes the preacher's investment of personal beliefs and experiences in his proclamation which inevitably affects the physical aspect and nonverbal element of his presentation. Since every sermon is, by its own nature, an expression of a preacher's personality and thus subjective, a preacher should then offer an authentic version of himself. That, of course, entails a readiness for exposure and vulnerability. Another requirement, a social side which complements a more personal property of sincerity, is actually *speaking to people* characterised by a genuine concern for them. This demands that preachers preach without notes, using a dialect and a conversational language appropriate for oral communication. It also calls for preachers' determination to directly address listeners, but also asks for their wisdom in providing a space for listeners' freedom of choice. Here van der Geest points to the observed reality that pastors generally refrain from taking on the authoritative role, which is precisely what is necessary to fulfil the listeners' need for the security. Finally, among other conclusions stemming from the discussion on the dimension of security, he comes up with the following statement, "Feeling oneself spoken to by God and feeling oneself spoken to by the preacher are interdependent facts, and this requires that homiletics takes the preacher's personality more seriously than before."[7]

---

5. Van der Geest, 34.
6. Van der Geest, 38.
7. Van der Geest, 39, 64.

5.1.2 The Dimension of Deliverance

If the first dimension reflects the listeners' need for stability, the second echoes their expectations of change. They need to hear a message of rescue, a language of hope, words that break the spell of their present condition. Their search for confirmation in the old and familiar is thus matched with this longing for something which will open a future for them. If this polar tension is not present in preaching, van der Geest maintains, their expectations are not being met. This tension also corresponds fully with theology's dual proclamation of the cross and resurrection, of judgement and grace; of the law and gospel. As a matter of fact, van der Geest interprets his findings to mean that ". . . only a distinct proclamation of the law and gospel can awaken genuine hope . . . Only if the darkest darkness of the law and the brightest light of the gospel are proclaimed together do people feel spoken to and engaged." The deliverance brought about by the gospel can be experienced only after listeners are addressed in their anguish by preaching about the law.[8]

Yet this has additional consequences for the preacher's role and function. Her message must be "personally established" if this dual proclamation is to be recognised by the listeners. Van der Geest expresses it in the following way,

> The preacher's own discovery of where the Bible's relevance can be found is the only promising access at all to this book, since without this discovery, without this subjectivity the word is robbed of its humanity . . . it is the only access to the essentials, to the power of the transmitted tradition, to the authority of the gospel itself.[9]

Furthermore, she is to accept responsibility for the listeners, but without resorting to any sort of coercion or passing on some "universally accepted value system" since this has no persuasive power. Instead, whenever the preacher finds a biblical text to be relevant, she should act as the text's advocate over against listeners who are to be treated as mature persons. But at the same time, the preacher remains the listeners' advocate over against the text.[10]

---

8. Van der Geest, 97. It might be argued this is a typical instance when a researcher's personal theological and ecclesiological tradition (in this case, a Lutheran law/gospel dichotomy) may bear upon his interpretation process.

9. Van der Geest, 82.

10. Van der Geest, 86.

Finally, van der Geest points out that preaching with the dimension of deliverance in mind also has its limitations. Preachers should keep in mind that the sermon, being a form of mass communication, is primarily suitable for reinforcing already existent beliefs and convictions.[11] In that respect, a genuine change in behaviour or opinion is "possible in the monologue situation of the sermon only to the extent that the preacher succeeds in lending expression to a seeking or insecurity already present in the listeners."[12]

5.1.3 The Dimension of Understanding

This brings me to the last dimension of the experience of the sermon as presented by this research, the dimension of understanding. The life of a Christian believer is a matter of perpetual tension between certainty and uncertainty because faith is dealing with the realities distant from our immediate experience and senses. As the pendulum of believers' experience swings back and forth between these two extremes, people repeatedly come to the church service looking for and expecting the possibility of being persuaded, of getting hold of understanding, and of gaining security again. And yet they also carry with them an inner opposition, born out of insecurity. This attitude is then best described by van der Geest's claim that they are "so positively predispositioned for this surrender that they are disappointed if they do not get the opportunity to do so." But before one could assume that the only missing piece is a preacher presenting clear and logical arguments, he hastens to clarify that in this area of life logical argumentation makes a weak ally. "The truth sought again by the people in a worship service is not an objective one, but is rather an existential truth precipitating engagement and participation, not cool ascertainment . . . It's a truth giving a feeling of security."[13]

A solution to this problem brings us back to the relationship between preachers and their listeners. More precisely, preachers should become "the questioning listeners," capable of facing issues raised by the temptations of faith so that they may be recognised and identified by the congregation on its journey from uncertainty to certainty. But questions will not suffice; they

---

11. This follows Reid's evaluation of sermon as a means of human communication. Cf. Reid, *Empty Pulpit*, 82.

12. Van der Geest, *Presence in Pulpit*, 103.

13. Van der Geest, 117, 120.

also anticipate some sense of direction. In van der Geest's words, "They expect the preacher to have found a traversable path, otherwise he or she should not be preaching."[14]

What can preachers do to create a sermon which will elicit some sort of understanding on the part of the listeners? They can make good use of language that is rich in vivid expressions. Narratives and images are particularly recommended. Such language encourages the listeners' participation in the sermon which, in turn, generates a "subjective evidential experience" and the listener ". . . is not rationally persuaded, but rather existentially struck."[15] The narratives and images can prompt two types of process –identification (a process of recognising the similarity between the listener and the character in the story) and projection (a process by which a listener invests her own experiences into a narrative or image). Still, this graphic speech needs to be supplemented by conceptual language in order to name, summarize, and allow access to experiences aroused by a narrative or image. Van der Geest concludes, "Analyses of worship services and sermons have shown me that those in a worship service are quite willing to acquire knowledge and understanding, but their condition is that it [should] not be a rational understanding, but rather an understanding or recognition touching on the existential realm."[16]

5.1.4 Further Observations

Two more highly specific observations can be made on the basis of this study. First, the content of the sermon is far less in the focus of listeners when the real effects are considered. "Experiencing, sensing, and feeling are more important to them than insights and being persuaded. They are more concerned with the effect of what is said than with its meaning."[17] This again puts a spotlight on a preacher's role, which is why van der Geest argues that proclamation includes not only content and human language but ". . . also the preacher's whole capacity for communication or for disturbing communication." He goes on to say, "Homiletics is still too idealistic here and thus

---

14. Van der Geest, 126.
15. Van der Geest, 129.
16. Van der Geest, 142.
17. Van der Geest, 60.

even a bit docetic. The human element is even more human."[18] It naturally follows that a preacher's personality is so central – a fact which has been neglected by traditional homiletics, but not by congregations or even preachers' self-perceptions.[19]

Secondly, viewed from the perspective of listeners, a relationship between the preacher and the listeners adopts a new, almost sacred, dimension. At one point, van der Geest underscores it by reflecting on the triangle of biblical text, preacher, and listeners that seems to be drawn along different lines:

> What characterizes the text over against the preacher is its unlimited dependability and objectivity. But by the same token, the preacher has what the text lacks: the capacity to speak, to present oneself visibly, to be there live. The actual mystery of the encounter with God is perhaps more directly connected with the text than with the preacher, but the *place* the text comes to the congregation is the relationship to the preacher.[20]

5.2 *The Great American Sermon Survey*

Some twenty years later, another discerning study appeared, Lori Carrell's *The Great American Sermon Survey*.[21] Some introductory remarks will help in assessing its findings. First of all, they are based on a qualitative study conducted in the USA among both listeners and preachers. A thousand randomly selected preachers across the country were given an opportunity to take part in a survey and to include their listeners as well. In response, 102 preachers completed surveys and recruited listeners to do the same thing (479 of their listeners submitted surveys based on open-ended questions). In the final stage, sixty-four preachers agreed to an in-depth phone interview.

The feedback from surveys and interviews shaped the book in which Lori Carrell approaches the research from a communicative frame of reference, assuming that preachers and listeners necessarily interact and share

---

18. Van der Geest, 64.
19. Van der Geest, 153.
20. Van der Geest, 63.
21. Carrell, *Great American Sermon Survey*.

the responsibility for the "co-creation of meaning during the sermon."[22] Such assumption naturally "asserts that the meanings made in the minds of the listeners are just as valid as the words of the preachers' sermons."[23] And while preachers' words are normally audible every Sunday, the listeners' thoughts are either dismissed as irrelevant to the process of shaping the sermon's message or simply undiscoverable by the regular preaching practices in most Christian traditions. Yet, from the communicative perspective, Carrell suggests the acceptance of an important premise: "the perceptions of listeners are real, not wrong or right."[24] This is why the primary goal of her study is to compare the preacher and listeners' perceptions of preaching as a communicative act.

According to her observations, in an American society where communication mostly takes place in a virtual space, there is still one place which people regularly attend with an expectation of hearing a public speech, with a desire "to try to satisfy their craving for the early rhetorician's ideal – a good person speaking well about something that matters." This place is the church, claims Carrell. In spite of the domination of new technologies, the influence of the spoken word does not need to become extinct, she says. Yet, the biggest problem and challenge could be the "cycle of low expectation, which preachers and listeners can perpetuate," originally caused by the lack of meaningful, honest, and regular dialogue about preaching between preachers and listeners. To rectify this perpetuation, Carrell suggests that the silence between preachers and listeners must be explored because this very silence about preaching and the meaning of the sermon obviously communicates something. Carrell's book thus can be read as her attempt to probe this "ambiguous nature of silence" and to help both sides to eliminate this "lack of shared meaning" about that silence.[25]

5.2.1 Similarities and Differences

After compiling her results, Carrell presents some striking points of agreement and divergence between listeners and preachers. As for the similarities,

---

22. Carrell, 6.
23. Carrell, 9.
24. Carrell, 35.
25. Carrell, 21–22, 29, 58.

both groups agree on the ideal length of the sermon (20–22 minutes). They also share the same expectation that the sermon's content is not to be discussed either before or after the worship service by a preacher and his listeners. Listeners either do not perceive this feedback to be their responsibility, or they lack the time, or they feel preachers are doing so well that there is no real need for them to offer their feedback. On the other hand, only 9 percent of preachers confer with their listeners during sermon preparation and this always happens informally. During the sermon, preachers are normally able to get some nonverbal feedback but there are no formal processes of soliciting feedback from listeners after the sermon.

And this is where similarities end and discrepancies begin. First, most preachers are men, while most listeners are women. Carrell argues that so-called "disconfirmation" is a frequent phenomenon in preaching, implying that men preach as if women are not present in the congregation or in a way that trivializes them. Such a gender-based insensitivity reinforces the impression of sermon irrelevancy among female listeners.[26] Another major mismatch is discovered when the goal of preaching and sermon listening is analysed. 65 percent of listeners want inspiration or life application while 54 percent of preachers want to change the listeners (and only 17 percent of them see themselves as "translators" between the Bible and the life of listeners). Listeners generally want to hear the Scripture for the present week, while preachers are more concerned with moving their listeners to take a more active approach and initiative in their own personal lives. In addition, preachers often feel that listeners expect entertainment, but what they expressed as their demands are more relevant illustrations, passion, and stronger links with their experience.

There are other more subtle differences in perceptions. For instance, although listeners are quite correct in their evaluation of how much time preachers need to prepare their sermons, the preachers' common understanding is that listeners are disrespectful of sermon preparation time. At the same time, preachers' busyness seems to be the main reason why listeners feel they cannot approach them and initiate a conversation about the sermon. In a similar fashion, most listeners are convinced that their preachers feel nervous while preaching, and yet over 50 percent of preachers claim that they do not.

---

26. Carrell, 146.

The weight of these findings leads Carrell to reinforce her initial supposition: "The lack of dialogue is at the root of differences in other perceptions about the sermon."[27] And since the dialogue is missing, both parties become more and more entrenched in their unchallenged expectations. As a result, she says, "[t]he assumptions that preachers and listeners sometimes make about each other reveal that they may be generalizing, or even stereotyping, rather than actually knowing one another."[28]

5.2.2 Lessons for Listeners

Carrell proceeds by taking a step back and comparing preaching with teaching. Her pivotal question here is, "What are the communication characteristics of teachers who best facilitate learning?"[29] In answering this question, she observes the areas where communication education research may prove profitable for preaching practice and is once again led to suggest a move from monologue toward a dialogical concept of preaching. In the final chapters of her book, she articulates several clear-cut proposals for both listeners and preachers which are at the same time prompted by the results of her survey and sustained by her exploration of the educational field.

When it comes to her message for listeners, the first requirement is to overcome the understanding that the listener's role is passive and the premise which says that it is the preacher who is responsible for listeners' performance. Listeners can unleash the transformative effect by their competent listening, but it demands that they consciously focus on the immediate moment. This will trigger changes, regardless of preachers' attitudes. Carrell points out, "Even if our preachers are not treating us like partners, we can empower the sermon time by accepting our role as mutual meaning makers."[30]

Such an active listening obliges listeners to adopt a specific posture.[31] They need to deliberately become *attentive* to the verbal and non-verbal content of the particular sermon. To be able to *comprehend* the sermon, Carrell suggests that listeners would do well to choose a comprehending task or specific

---

27. Carrell, 141.
28. Carrell, 133–134.
29. Carrell, 168.
30. Carrell, 194.
31. Carrell, 193–205.

listening goal before every sermon. Furthermore, listening should be done with the desire to *remember*. The use of certain mnemonic tools during the listening may prove rather helpful in that respect. All these steps need to be accompanied by *analytical listening* – which is a recognition of a preacher's attempt at persuasion, investigation of her appeals, and making a conscious choice whether to be persuaded or not. This sort of listening attitude can lead listeners to reject preacher's persuasive discourse, but this refusal will happen only after listeners have "co-created a meaning" with the preacher. On the other hand, if this evaluation leads listeners to accept a preacher's persuasive appeals, then the outcomes may truly be transformative. Finally, active listening would not be rounded off without the *response* stage. Carrell is certain that the listeners' feedback must be allowed to flow back to preachers, and therefore she lists some practical recommendations for doing so.

Her recommendations are listed under three categories in relation to the time of providing the feedback: before, during, and after the sermon. Put briefly, she advocates for a planned approach to the process of sending feedback to preachers. Such an incentive is most efficiently created through regular "content-based sermon reflections," focused on the communicative effects of the sermon in question (instead of feedback being evaluative or plainly neutral). Yet another stimulating idea is the formation of a "pastoral care group" which should help pastors to respond to the practical and emotional needs of church members and thus put into practice the listeners' appreciation of preacher's preparation time.[32] This proposition reveals that Carrell is aware that breaking the silence between listeners and preachers may require profound changes in the structure of church life, and alteration of a pastor's job description. At the same time, it implies that establishing a dialogue can maximise the sermon's potential power and bring about far-reaching effects for the church as a whole.

5.2.3 Lessons for Preachers

Naturally, this research unfolds numerous opportunities for preachers to take in some worthy insights, too. Carrell is successful in linking preachers' and listeners' misguided expectations and buttressing these connections with input from the field of human communication. For instance, the message to

---

32. Carrell, 215, 213–216.

preachers gathered through the listeners' response in a survey is concisely spelt out in this way: "Provide a relevant message with clear ties to Scripture. Foster relationships with listeners. Work on your own spiritual life. Work on your organization. Work on your delivery. You are appreciated."[33] At the same time, she leaves no doubt on the matter of what should be the highest priority for preachers, if they are to turn the tide in their communication:

> *The Great American Sermon Survey* revealed that most of you preachers spend most of your sermon preparation time and effort studying the scriptural text. Nothing in this book suggests that you should diminish those efforts. Nearly everything in this book suggests that your efforts to study the "text" of your listeners do need to increase. Don't create a false dichotomy – spiritual truth versus listeners. Study both. You have two texts.[34]

In this plea, there is an ardent echo of Leonora Tubbs Tisdale's notion of exegeting the congregation and implicit accordance with assumptions of congregational studies. Listeners as another "text" simply stand as the only route toward the dialogue.

But she does offer some more specific hints which should help preachers to move their preaching closer to their listeners' expectations. For example, she detects a problem with preachers' reliance on literary style during sermon preparation. The survey reveals that 88 percent of preachers do not rehearse their sermons orally and when orality in preparation is missing, the delivery of an oral message is weakened. She warns against forgetting this most distinctive feature of the sermon as compared to other styles of communication: "While the media can exploit the visual modality, and technology can expand the size of the audience, the face-to-face sermon gains its power as it capitalizes on its strength – *its spoken nature* . . . The mental participation of the listeners is predicated on the oral style."[35]

Instead of trying to deliver a "relevant" sermon, Carrell claims, preachers should strive to "decentre" their sermons. What she means by this is a preacher's conscious effort to step out from the sermon's centre in order to

---

33. Carrell, 154.
34. Carrell, 209–210.
35. Carrell, 225 (emphasis mine).

take the position that evokes the listeners perspective. This move will be successful if a preacher manages to answer the crucial listeners' question: "How does this content resonate with what is already meaningful to us?"[36]

Toward the end of the book, Lori Carrell asks preachers to initiate at least one change upon reading her research.[37] Development of a "formal process by which to gather listeners' input for upcoming sermons" is called for. She suggests that preachers should announce the scriptural reading and sermon topics in advance, make a "Sermon Support" box available for collecting the listeners' ideas and questions, and most importantly, form a "listener support group" focused on sermonic content. This feed-forward group should be created through a rotational system of selecting the participants and involve no more than ten participants at once. Although it overwhelmingly resembles John S. McClure's "sermon roundtable," it affects the sermon preparation process in a different fashion. The group dynamics should propel the dialogue in which the preacher primarily participates as a listener to the listeners. This dialogue must begin early enough (six weeks before the actual sermon, suggests Carrell) so the preacher's preparation can be initiated and driven by the group conversation, and not vice versa. Carrell indicates that implementation of this model of preaching partnership will increase the transformative effect of preaching and also intensify the relational dimension of an entire congregation. In other words, the recovery of a preacher's listening capacities is not just a peripheral adjustment but the emergence of dialogue from which sweeping ecclesiological consequences may derive.

5.3. *Listening to Listeners*

A number of collaborators, including eight homiletical scholars on an advisory board, are responsible for what is likely the most extensive empirical study of sermon listeners to date. The project was started in 1999 by the Christian Theological Seminary in Indianapolis. The study has been conducted through interviews with 263 regular sermon listeners; 128 of them were interviewed individually while other participated in small group interviews. The participants belong to one of twenty-eight congregations of

---

36. Carrell, 219–220.
37. Carrell, 210–212.

long-established denominations, but still represent a wide denominational variety and diversity in their size and racial structure. These congregations also represent a variety of sociological backgrounds: urban, rural, and small town and suburban churches of various sizes.[38] The findings of this thorough study are published in four separate volumes.[39] On the following pages, I will try to recapitulate these results, their interpretations, and subsequent observations made by members of the research team.

5.3.1 Key Premises and Major Findings

At its very core, this study is founded on the conviction that, when asked, regular listeners can and will reveal insights on what facilitates and depresses their listening. Besides probing the listeners' individual listening orientations, the researchers are also interested in "how the congregation as community is affected by the sermon *and* by how the congregation as community affects the sermon and the preacher."[40] In other words, congregational culture is considered a critical factor in governing listeners' predispositions toward the sermon.

In order to analyse the diversity of responses, the researchers use Aristotle's threefold model of appeal. However, they redefine the three categories and add a fourth. For them, logos includes not only logical arguments with a persuasive agenda, but both inductive and deductive trains of thought, illustrations, and imaginative experience. Further, an ethos is perceived in a wider context of the congregational frame. As for pathos, it is not limited to stirring emotions among listeners, because the acceptance or rejection of sermonic ideas may be caused by emotional links whose origin is not found in the immediate preaching context and of which listeners themselves could be unaware. Finally, the additional dimension of "embodiment" is introduced to survey questions as well; its purpose is to allow listeners to describe how various elements of delivery (preacher's voice, face, gestures, eye contact, or movement) engage or disengage their proclivity for listening.

---

38. Allen, *Hearing the Sermon*, 144, n. 6.

39. Allen, *Hearing the Sermon*; Mulligan, Turner-Sharazz, and Wilhelm, *Believing in Preaching*; Mulligan and Allen, *Make Word Come Alive*; McClure et al., *Listening to Listeners*.

40. McClure et al., p. 8.

Regarding key findings of this study, these categories are found to function as "settings" through which listeners listen to sermons. To be more precise, for every listener, there is a primary setting which represents a port of entry to the sermon. But, "while the listener typically begins to listen through one setting, other settings (and the mix of settings) affect the ways the hearer responds to the appeals of the sermon."[41] So, while no setting is more important than others *per se*, and all settings influence the listening process to some extent, the individual listener is still inclined to process other settings from the outlook of the setting which serves as the primary channel. Thus, every listener hears and understands preaching through a unique interplay of settings, but with one setting being dominant over the others. Researchers report that about 20 percent of their participating congregants listen through pathos settings, and around 40 percent each listen through logos and ethos.[42]

5.3.2 Listening Settings

The designations and features described under each setting do not necessarily represent the listening pattern of *all* listeners who listen on that particular setting. There are no universally present experiences or themes, even for listeners who listen on the same setting. Yet, the frequency of certain concerns in the responses reveals a typical profile of individuals who enter the sermon by listening to the same channel.

5.3.2.1 Ethos Setting

People who initially receive sermons through the ethos setting share some common concerns. They are attentive to preachers' integrity – the correspondence between their words and deeds. They highly value preachers who appear to be "common" or "real persons," that is, they are drawn and not disturbed by their life. Allen puts it simply: "The preacher can attract many

---

41. Allen, *Hearing Sermon*, 145, n. 11.

42. Allen, *Hearing Sermon*, 148, n. 1. The study also shows that an embodiment does not function as a "setting" in a way comparable to the other three categories. However, other scholars demonstrate the significance of embodied communication in preaching. See, for example, Suzanne Scheiber Nawrocki, "Every Body Helps the Preacher: The Impact of Embodied Communication" (unpublished doctoral dissertation, Aquinas Institute of Theology, 2013). Accessed 10 September 2017
<https://search.proquest.com/docview/1426182389/abstract/9F020DB466814AB9PQ/1>. Her work specifically focuses on the gestures and their impact in homiletical delivery.

people who hear the sermon on ethos wavelengths into the world of the sermon by speaking about the preacher's own life and experience."[43] Also, if they perceive a preacher as being active in caring for people outside of her preaching tasks, their receptiveness to sermons will be fostered. Since they generally put a lot of emphasis on relationships, their grasp of a sermon's ethos is genuinely correlated with the nature of their congregation's culture. Allen outlines their mentality by saying that they

> . . . are concerned not only with the character of the preacher but also think of preaching as a relationship with the pastor and even see the purposes of preaching as an encouraging relationship. Such listeners most fully feel that they have heard a sermon when they feel a sense of relationship with the preacher and with other people in the congregation.[44]

Of course, listeners who hear through the ethos channel are sensitive to other settings as well. Therefore, there are points of intersection of ethos with logos and pathos. For instance, they are usually inclined to single out sermon themes related to a relationship with God and other people, or with service in the community. At the same time, as relationships typically include a discernible degree of feelings, pathos may have a notable meaning for these listeners. Allen proceeds to describe how,

> The ethos setting functions for this listener as a kind of lens through which pathos flows. The listener is "touched," but in a way that facilitates the relationship. The experience of pathos is not only an internal feeling for this listener but a source of power for expressing relationship with others.[45]

5.3.2.2 *Logos Setting*

The hearers who belong to this group highly value reasoning with a clear expression of significant content, clarity, consistency, and intellectual credibility. There is almost a unanimous agreement among them that the purpose of preaching is to convey information that will allow them to translate in

---

43. Allen, *Hearing the Sermon*, 38.
44. Allen, 18.
45. Allen, 40.

conceptual terms the biblical and gospel implications for their life. Typically, they appreciate solid organisation and want to see evidence of their preacher's preparedness (much more than their fellow listeners from the ethos and pathos groups). Along the same line, they also expect their ministers to invest in their continuous education and preparation time. Another trait found among the listeners from various theological orientations who approach sermon via the logos setting is a high esteem for the preacher's presentation of various possible interpretations and criteria for their mutual comparison. Finally, there is one concern virtually nonexistent among listeners who audit sermons on other settings; it is the notion that preaching is *the* most important part of the worship *and* that the rest of it is relatively insignificant. Some of these respondents claim they would not come to church if there was no sermon. Moreover, such conviction does not pertain only to listeners from churches where the worship is centred in the Word.

For these hearers, ethos concerns are present mostly insofar as a discernible and solid message is preached. For them, a message clearly takes priority over the messenger. They tend to "view relationships (or perception of relationships) from the perspective of understanding – both of how relationships help them understand the major ideas of the sermon and how the major ideas of the sermon inform their understanding of relationship."[46]

There are also various evaluations of pathos concerns when discerned from the perspective of the logos setting. Probably the most common phenomenon is the expectation of an intellectual interpretation of emotions encountered in sermons or in life in general; these hearers want to be able to properly name their feelings. Aside from that, for many of them, both feelings and stories have a "utilitarian character" and their function is to raise listeners' responsiveness to the central ideas, "to bring home the message" or to stir their thinking.[47] Intriguing, though, is a finding that some listeners do not notice emotional qualities of sermons and emotional responses of other listeners, while some hold that emotions are a way to excesses which impede the purpose of the sermon.

---

46. Allen, 61.
47. Allen, 67.

5.3.2.3 Pathos Setting

It is not surprising that the typical aspect of the evaluation of sermon on a pathos setting is the listeners' belief that God, specifically the Holy Spirit, works through feelings. However, this study reveals that for many listeners pathos is not only a mode of appeal known from classical rhetoric but also "a mode of knowledge that is activated by the sermon (and by associations evoked by the sermon)."[48] This explains why for these listeners even unpleasant feelings created by the sermon can be part of their ethos setting, provided they can trigger growth and initiate their self-examination. At the same time, feelings are often hidden from consciousness, but their disclosure is possible within the context of worship and sermons because preachers can provide a safe environment in which listeners will feel free to express their emotions. In doing that, preachers should help their listeners name their feelings in order to enable them to react and deal with them. Confessional preaching can be particularly conducive to this process. Those who enter sermons on the pathos setting are exceptionally receptive to stories, provided they are seen as true to life and have a ring of authenticity. But, according to the results of the study, there is another distinguishing mark of this cohort of listeners: a considerable number of them "speak with force and detail about the importance of embodiment reflecting and encouraging feeling." As inscrutable as this characteristic may be, Allen manages to offer the research team's conclusion that this embodiment is not actualized in a specific preaching style, but in "a quality with which the feeling in the listener resonates."[49] Eventually, we are reminded that the effects of the sermon for listeners in this listening group often do not come about instantly; the knowledge of a feeling induced by the sermon may require a longer period of time.

Again, listeners who are chiefly predisposed to listening on a pathos setting still hear preaching on the other two settings as well. What happens at those junctions? First, their impressions of a preacher's character and other ethos issues will be interpreted through the emotional effects they cause for them. For instance, if their feelings toward a particular preacher make them disappointed, they are likely to become disinclined to him. In a similar fashion, pathos-inclined listeners tend to consider some idea or proposition

---

48. Allen, 72.
49. Allen, 72, 84, 85.

potentially valid after they detect a positive emotion (either in a preacher or in themselves). Thus, emotions can serve as a stimulus for a reflection on the idea being communicated in the sermon. Furthermore, this study shows many pathos-oriented listeners appreciate the theological interpretation that helps them understand their feelings and provides guidance on how to respond to these feelings. Another intriguing finding is that although these listeners are not able to recollect the content of past sermons any better than congregants who listen on ethos or logos settings, they remember the felt emotions. The emotional outcomes of sermons thus "become a part of their reservoir of experience." Based on this, Allen seems to assume that longevity of sermons is best manifested among listeners on pathos setting, "Sermons continue to speak through the life of feeling, long after the voice and conscious memory have grown silent."[50]

These findings imply that by considering the specifics of each setting, preachers can reduce or even overcome the disinclination of their listeners and reinforce the likelihood of taking their sermon seriously. Yet there are some safeguards to be applied and limitations to be recognised by interested practitioners.[51]

5.3.3 Twelve Features of Inviting Preaching

The research team behind the *Listening to Listeners* study decided to present their findings from multiple perspectives. A book by Mary Mulligan and Ronald J. Allen puts forward twelve traits of preaching which the interviewees mentioned most frequently as the most inviting. However, given the vast diversity of responses, they strongly advocate that a preacher's elemental task should be discovering the specific dynamics within the culture of his congregation and treat the twelve traits as "*prototypes* that a pastor can investigate, test, adapt, or replace in view of local preferences."[52] What follows here is their succinct overview.

First, the interviews reveal there is a single general concern of listeners which propels the emergence of other qualities. People expect preachers (1)

---

50. Allen, 95.

51. For a more elaborate account of both opportunities and cautions that arise out of these findings, see Allen, 97–111.

52. Mulligan and Allen, *Make Word Come Alive*, 2.

to help them better understand who God is and what his expectations are concerning their lives. The awareness of the listeners' "ever-present desire for the Divine"[53] should always motivate a preacher's effort in engaging them with the sermon. The second lesson is summed up in the phrase (2) "Walk the walk!" The significance of a preacher's integrity is among the most frequent data in this study. It is the foundation of the trust listeners develop, either through personal knowledge of and relationship with the preacher or by making assumptions about the preacher's character based on their impressions gathered during the sermon. Both internal and especially external preacher's ethos can improve the experience of listening. On the other hand, Mulligan and Allen assert, "If the congregation is reluctant to believe the testimony of the sermon because the preacher is not walking the walk, the community's capacity to discern the divine purposes and to respond faithfully is significantly compromised."[54]

Another feature of engaging preaching is (3) a balanced reference to the preacher's own experience. The results indicate that many listeners find the personal experience to be emotionally appealing. Also, they may look upon a preacher's own struggle as a well-grounded impetus to take a sermon's claims seriously. On the practical side, there is a specific piece of advice to preachers: they would do well to " . . . share their own vulnerability with the congregation, seldom make themselves the heroes, or sheroes, of stories, and bring experience into dialogue with other sources of theological insight (such as the Bible)." This vulnerability is particularly substantial here; it paves the way for listeners' identification with preacher because they can ". . . feel their own vulnerability confirmed in that of the preacher, while also sensing that such vulnerability is "safe" in the grace of God."[55] Of course, the references to personal experience should not be too frequent and all personal material should always point beyond itself to the gospel.

Another useful lesson gathered from listeners' responses has to do with (4) "making the Bible alive." As a matter of fact, a request to "make the Bible alive" was among the top four priorities for 60 percent of participants who answered the question regarding what can help hearers to engage better with

---

53. Mulligan and Allen, 14.
54. Mulligan and Allen, 23.
55. Mulligan and Allen, 25, 30.

the sermon.⁵⁶ Listeners apparently often struggle with understanding the Scripture on its own. Preachers are thus advised to employ two effective methods of overcoming this problem; one is assuming the role of the biblical character, and the other is the expressive reading of the biblical passage before preaching. Also, an insight into historical context supplemented by the recognition of points of contact between the text and everyday life is warmly appreciated by a significant share of listeners. Almost a logical successor of the previous feature is the listeners' desire to (5) see how the gospel matters in a contemporary world. The reports prove that listeners can recall specific sermons precisely because they addressed "issues of current concern, former questions, and even future worship experiences."⁵⁷

Among the most articulated recommendations of this study is the message from congregants: (6). "Keep it short!" Regardless of their listening setting, the interviewees point out that short is better. But they regularly second that request with appreciation for the clarity and the usefulness of the sermon's content. Even if brevity is a relative notion, whenever a preacher ignores the natural stopping point or exceeds the established time frame, it can be interpreted as disregarding the listeners. Keeping the sermon short means decreasing the duration, but also holding to the focus, paying attention to the sense of the sermon's progression and conclusion, and avoiding unnecessary details. Still another trait, (7) the plainness of the sermon, is akin to brevity. Listeners openly communicate their need for preachers to speak plainly; their responses also reveal that they presume this requires proper study and preparation on the preacher's part. Of course, the diversity among listeners may tempt preachers to explicate too many points in order to please as many listening styles as possible. Yet, it appears that listeners prefer a clear focus and fewer points. Mulligan and Allen do not interpret this as a sign of listeners' superficiality; they read it as an expression of their desire "to have spiritual nourishment from the sermon that [is] small enough to ingest, yet significant enough to feed them during the week ahead."⁵⁸

The next three traits can be treated jointly, as they all deal with the content of sermons. The first of them says that contrary to the fears of most preachers,

---

56. Mulligan, Turner-Sharazz, and Wilhelm, *Believing in Preaching*, 21–22.
57. Mulligan and Allen, *Make Word Come Alive*, 52.
58. Mulligan and Allen, 71.

the majority of interviewed lay people agree with this statement: (8) "Not only *can* preachers "talk about everything," but they also *should* do so."[59] Many listeners candidly confess that they anticipate receiving theological guidance from sermons, including those on controversial issues. Some of them even point out a need to have preachers willing to think and preach on issues their congregations may not want to think about! The most common justification for this expectation is that the Bible itself handles a wide range of topics. They also admit that a preacher's attitude represents the crucial component in the creation of a safe and non-threatening atmosphere in which conversation will be stirred and different opinions listened to. Closely related is another suggestion, (9) "Do not oversimplify complex issues." Even if listeners wish for sermons to be plain and focused, their listening will still be impeded when they feel they are being treated as if they are not intelligent enough to grasp the complex nature of Christian faith. Allen and Mulligan aptly sum up this feature by saying, "Sermon information is appreciated when it helps people grow in their spirituality. And it is not appreciated when the sermon oversimplifies the faith life . . ." And finally, the third feature highlights (10) the listeners' inclination to expect sermons to help them to get their religious life right. Their listening becomes more attentive as they realise that an impetus for the change they feel is needed can be found in the sermon (more than in any other element of the liturgy). Listeners are time and again willing to go through a change, but they seek the preacher's assistance. Again, this quest is not a proof of listeners' helpless overreliance and it is "accompanied by a recognition that the sermon should not spoon-feed listeners but requires personal reflection and often results in pain from stretching and growing in the faith."[60]

The next quality is linked with the dimension of delivery; it consists of a number of factors which "work together with one another in a gestalt with the content of the message" and can be grouped under the title (11) "Talk loud enough so we can hear." Perspectives that explicitly affect this dimension are "being able to hear, variety in the use of the voice, energy and conviction, eye contact, gestures and body language, movement out of the pulpit, annoying mannerisms, and the preacher's pulpit presence being consistent

---

59. Mulligan and Allen, 73.
60. Mulligan and Allen, 85, 93.

with the preacher's personality."[61] For instance, in preachers who keep eye contact with them, the listeners are able to observe an energy, conviction, and enthusiasm and this creates an emotional connectedness that increases the appeal of the sermon. Body language and gestures can either add to or distract from sermons, while mannerisms should be avoided as they easily lead to the situation where, in the perception of listeners, they overshadow the content of the message.

Finally, a set of brief insights with potential positive influence on communication is presented under a somewhat humorous category called (12) "Don't forget to put in your teeth". Some of them are practical and simple bits of advice that can exercise a positive impact on preaching. For instance, a different approach to the preparation process is suggested: both feeding-forward and involving other believers in different pastoral duties can be beneficial. The former serves to turn preparation into a more communal enterprise while the latter redeems some precious quality time for the preacher. The listeners also observe that bringing variety into one's preaching style is a welcome change because sermons that differ from the ordinary pattern are more memorable. The use of humour can be helpful, but only insofar it is something discovered as a part of a real-life journey. Preachers would do well if they watched their tone of preaching; keeping it generally positive will actively engage their listeners. In the end, preachers should not be discouraged by the obvious fact that different listeners interpret the same sermons in different ways. Mulligan and Allen helpfully remind us that "[n]o amount of rhetorical finesse can give the preacher control over congregational receptivity," but also emphasize the responsibility and purposefulness of a proper preparation: "A well-prepared sermon gives the congregation an opportunity to welcome its contents when they are at a point in life to receive it."[62]

5.3.4 Concluding Observations

Being the most exhaustive of all studies in this chapter, *Listening to Listeners* stands out as an impressive exemplar of the pertinence of disciplines explored in the previous three chapters for the venture I am about to report on. I will conclude this chapter with a selection of observations made by members of

---

61. Mulligan and Allen, 103.
62. Mulligan and Allen, 120.

the research team behind that study. Some of those remarks undoubtedly show how advantageously homiletics, rhetoric, and congregational studies can be combined to understand how churchgoers hear sermons.

As an example, the analysis of numerous interviews leads researchers to declare that "... when identification is established, listeners tend to persuade themselves"[63] which is a perfect match with Meyer's concept of self-persuasion. When this assessment is placed next to the understanding of the importance of listening settings and the usefulness of congregational studies, the natural outcome can be phrased like this: "The emphasis on congregational culture ... reminds preachers that the preacher needs to pay careful attention to qualities in ethos, logos, pathos, and embodiment with which people *in the congregation* will identify."[64]

The research team had an initial expectation that the motif of a preacher's everyday behaviour being in harmony with his or her preaching will arise as a notable determinant, especially for those listeners who are ethos oriented. And yet, this theme appears in interviews both more frequently and more intensively: it is present in 90 percent of interviews.[65] Such an outcome clearly resonates with both Hogan and van der Geest's highlighting of preacher's ethos.

Aristotle's threefold notion of rhetorical appeal served as an elemental interpretive matrix, but the research findings entitle the team to offer three qualifications concerning these modes of appeal in the context of preaching:

> First, we believe that because preaching takes place over time in a particular situation, the role of local congregational culture needs to be expanded in rhetorical analysis. Second, we find that the interaction of ethos, logos, and pathos is more complex for particular listeners than Aristotle describes ... Third, whereas Aristotle reflected most fully on how these elements work together for individuals, we find that preaching affects a community as community.[66]

---

63. McClure et al., *Listening to Listeners*, 15.
64. McClure et al., 15–16.
65. McClure et al., 136.
66. McClure et al., 138.

As for the conjunction of these modes, even if one of them prevails, the other two are still effective and their interplay is more sophisticated than previously anticipated. What follows, though, is that preachers cannot at the same time communicate with all listeners with the highest possible efficacy. That corresponds closely to the notion of listening profiles and group preferences as explicated by Jeter and Allen.

In closing, these three research studies taken together present enough cumulative evidence for the tenability of deliberate exploration of the listeners' perception and experience of sermon listening. The potential benefits of such investigation are diverse and multiple – whether it is overcoming different communicational barriers between listeners and preachers, discovery of actual listeners' expectations and dynamics of their processing the sermon input, identification of mechanisms that set in motion their identification with the preacher or the sermon's message, or breaking the cycle of low expectations. Their common denominator is a compelling indication that such a move can initiate a noteworthy transformation of preaching into a more participatory practice that redefines the nature of the relationship between preachers and listeners and consequently alters the congregational understanding of what it means to be a church.

Before commencing the demonstration of the field study conducted among Croatian Baptists, one more step remains that demands a separate chapter.

CHAPTER 6

Croatian Baptists and Their Homiletical Practice

The purpose of this chapter is to delineate the immediate object of my interest and to provide some background information giving an explanation of Croatian Baptists as a particular denomination in a specific socio-cultural context. A short historical overview of Baptist presence among the Croatian people will be presented first, followed by a brief analysis of existing homiletical literature written or translated in Croatian. The next step will be a collection of observations concerning the nature of homiletical practice in Croatian Baptist churches. This will be followed by a justification of the study I conducted, including a brief description of my own insider's perspective and experience of both preaching and listening to sermons as a motivation for and starting point of this research.

6.1 History of Croatian Baptists

The emergence of Baptists among Croatian people is not easy to reconstruct as a historical phenomenon. For one, Croatians have a long tradition of having their national entity and sense of identity closely related to the Catholic Church. Since the period of Counter-Reformation, every occurrence of another form of Christianity has been received with distrust, if not open hostility. Thus, not much of a written record has been preserved. Besides, the very origins of the Baptist movement have been geographically isolated instances on a rather small scale, and some were probably unrelated or even chronologically distanced. However, there are several contemporary resources which helpfully consolidated the existing data in portraying the picture of this historical development in more detail.¹

During the latter part of the nineteenth century, Croatian lands were under the rule of the Austro-Hungarian Empire. This allowed the unobstructed movement and expansion of Baptists, especially from Hungary. On the other side, the religious freedom guaranteed to Protestant churches by the *Protestant Patent* (1859) of Francis Joseph I did not apply to the Baptist church, which meant that the beginnings of the Baptist movement faced strong Catholicism and a generally unfriendly climate. Knežević lists four major factors contributing to the emergence of Baptists in Croatian lands: (1) the mission and literary activities of colporteurs of the British and Foreign Bible Society; (2) the influence of German Baptists through Hungary, Romania, and Russia; (3) the influence of non-South Slavic Baptist congregations (mostly Slovakian and Hungarian); and (4) the activities of American Baptist missionaries and individuals.² Although the first visits and activities of colporteurs were not particularly successful, there is enough evidence for Knežević to conclude that 1863 could be considered the year of the indirect beginning of Baptist activities in Croatian lands.³ The first recorded house meeting was held in Zagreb, in 1872–1873, under the leadership of Heinrich Meyer. In 1893, Johann Lotz gathered the first group in Daruvar. The first Baptist church was founded in Zagreb in 1891 and, although not officially recognised, was tolerated by the legislative acts enacted in 1893 and 1895.

The outbreak of World War I at first had a detrimental effect on these rather isolated groups of Baptists. Their loose connections were broken, and the number of believers decreased for various reasons. For instance, it is known that the group in Zagreb had only five members after the war (as compared to twelve before the war), and their communication with the church in Budapest was discontinued.⁴ The turbulent events after the war led to the establishment of the Kingdom of Serbs, Croats, and Slovenes. However, its constitution included Baptists among the adopted confessions and paved the way for their future legal existence. A number of returning individuals

---

1. See Knežević, "Baptist History in Croatia," 130–131; Knežević, *Pregled povijesti*; Kolarić, *Ekumenska trilogija*, 477–97; Peterlin, "Počeci," 523–548.
2. Knežević, *Pregled povijesti*, 33; 37–62.
3. Knežević, 39–40.
4. Peterlin, "Počeci," 545.

(former soldiers coming from Russia or Hungary or immigrants from the USA) brought with them a Baptist faith and began to proclaim it among their neighbours. By the end of 1920, there are groups in various parts of Croatia – in regions like Međimurje, Zagorje, Banija, and the area around Daruvar. The Zagreb Baptist Church was officially founded in 1921, and the next year saw the founding of the Baptist Union of Yugoslavia (supported by the Foreign Mission Board of the Southern Baptist Convention). In 1922 Vinko Vacek came back to Zagreb; he was to become the Union's first leader and most prominent exponent of American influence, which, together with the German Baptist Church, proved to be the leading forces in shaping Croatian Baptists churches in both an organisational and theological sense.[5] At that point, there were probably eighteen "mission stations" and 114 believers. In the period of strong evangelism and structural development which lasted almost until the outbreak of World War II, the number of believers grew to 600, the first chapels were built, national youth conferences were organised, and Baptists were gaining some sense of denominational identity. The first periodical, *Glas Evanđelja [Voice of the Gospel]* was first published in 1923. On the eve of World War II, in one of its editorials (Volume 3–4 1940) editor Ivan Bistrović addressed the resistance to investment in theological education, particularly of the preachers:

> All shortcomings in the life of faith come from spiritual poverty. Therefore, it is our primary need to dig deeper into the Bible, and to hold firmly and to preach what we find there. Also to pay more attention to the education of our preachers, and to improve our spiritual condition . . . We should not be satisfied by knowing a little bit from the treasure of the Bible . . . we must be full of life, we must be attractive to the lost.[6]

Also, in the late 1930s, the growing tension between American and German factions reached its pinnacle. It could have ended up in a schism if it were not prevented by the terrible war.

During World War II, under the Independent State of Croatia – a German puppet state – the Baptist denomination was declared illegal, and church

---

5. Knežević, *Pregled povijesti*, 56.
6. Knežević, 86.

buildings were confiscated and converted to military depots. The Union terminated its activities, but believers often persisted with meetings in secret. However, by the end of the war, the entire German Baptist population had been evicted from the country. The number of full-time preachers was reduced to only six. Yet the renewal after the war began rather quickly; in 1945 the Union was reestablished, and in 1946 a new Constitution was enacted. This recovery included the emergence of the determination to establish a theological institution for the education of its leaders.[7] At the same time, the period between 1945 and 1953 was characterised by the government's rigid attitude toward Baptists; occasionally they were accused of collaboration with foreign intelligence services, of agitating for reactionary regimes, and of being sectarian. There were individual instances of imprisonment and repression, but generally, this pressure remained within the boundaries of disinclined tolerance.[8] The turning point came in 1953 when all denominations were given equal legal status and the same level of religious rights which clearly exceeded those in truly socialist countries.

During the period of 1954–1966 this coexistence with the communist regime allowed for several important developments: three new churches were planted in urban centres (Sisak, Karlovac, and Rijeka), the opening of the Baptist Theological Seminary, regular youth assemblies held on a national level, the continuous publishing of periodicals, and development of Home Mission.[9] The Seminary was founded in 1954 in Zagreb, only to be moved to Daruvar, and then to Novi Sad (Serbia). Until 1989, 56 students from Croatian Baptist churches were enrolled in its various programmes, while 34 of them graduated from the Seminary.[10] The institution's original intention was the training of preachers and church leaders, but this was later transformed

---

7. The strongest evidence of this dedication is the setting up of the committee whose task was to initiate a founding process. This decision was reached at the meeting of Serbo-Croatian regional Baptist conference, held as early as November 1945 ("Minutes from the Meeting of Serbo-Croatian Regional Baptist Conference").

8. Knežević, *Pregled povijesti*, 93–94.

9. Knežević, 98.

10. More detailed statistics were prepared by Rut Lehotsky, and for more extensive analysis of theological education among Croatian Baptists, including that on other institutions, see Peterlin, "Theological Education," 239–259. One of the key Baptist leaders in the later period, Dr. Josip Horak, is going to be a co-founder of another institution, Theological Faculty Matthias Flacius Illyricus.

into a more inclusive goal of providing a more general biblical-theological education.

In the years that followed (1967–1990) the dominant feature, according to Knežević, was the building of confessional distinctiveness: "In the 1970s and 80s Croatian Baptists became increasingly recognised by both Catholic and secular institutions, partly due to Billy Graham's visit to Zagreb in 1967 and the evangelistic project, EURO 70. Cooperation with other Protestant churches developed and in 1976 Baptists and Lutherans jointly founded the Theological Faculty Matthias Flacius Illyricus in Zagreb."[11] Also, starting from 1973, the publishing house in Zagreb, called Duhovna stvarnost [Spiritual Reality], developed into the most recognised source of Protestant religious literature in Yugoslavia. Its publications were very diverse and intended for various audiences, and over time they could be found not only in Catholic but also in all major secular bookstores.

However, toward the end of the 1980s, the tensions within the Baptist Union of Yugoslavia were more and more evident. The local churches never claimed the Union as something beneficial, but rather as something outwardly imposed. The structures of the Union were not developed with the idea of serving the purpose of coordination of local churches' activities and work while respecting their autonomy and ultimate authority. This notion was presented for the first time at the national conference in 1973, but it was never really put into practice.[12] Knežević lists other inner antagonisms[13] which gradually brought about the Union's dismissal that took place in 1991 at the session of its Executive Board. The conclusion was that new unions were to be founded within the borders of current republics. In this way, South Slavic Baptists managed to put an end to the common structural existence without hostilities that would almost immediately follow and lead to the bloody disintegration of the country of Yugoslavia.

The latest period, from 1991 to the present (and especially the last fifteen years), is apparently still not sufficiently documented and covered in the existing literature.[14] However, some observations can still be made. During the

---

11. Knežević, "Baptist History," 130.
12. Knežević, *Pregled povijesti*, 117.
13. Knežević, 117–119.
14. The most recent contribution to the investigation of that period is made by an American missionary, Eric Kane Maroney, who studied the conversion experience of Croatian

war years (1991–1995), the Union struggled to protect and preserve existing churches and even worked on founding new ones. Since many of the churches were in war zones, and many of their members were displaced, the Union also served many refugees and displaced persons, including those fleeing from Bosnia and Herzegovina. Receiving the strong support of organisations like the European Baptist Federation, Southern Baptist Convention, Canadian Baptists, and Baptist World Alliance, the Baptist Union managed to organise and coordinate the distribution of humanitarian relief without any discrimination, thus often winning the approval of the wider community and occasionally attracting new members.

In terms of structural changes, the Baptist Union of Croatia was founded in 1991, just before the outbreak of war. In 1993, it was admitted as a member of the European Baptist Federation and of the Baptist World Alliance. In 1996, the Union became a member of the *Conference of European Churches*. By the completion of these events, the Baptist Union of Croatia was a fully recognized entity within Croatian society. In 1998, the Union passed the *Constitution of the Local Baptist Church*. The proactive involvement in defining the relationship of Croatian Baptist churches toward society at large continued and brought about another crucial document: an agreement with the Government of the Republic of Croatia. Signed in 2003, this document specifies the rights of Croatian Baptists on a number of matters, such as religious education in schools; counselling in hospitals, army forces, and prisons; and church marriages. It also regulates the financial support from the national budget to be provided to the Union so that churches can continue "with a promotion of the general welfare."[15]

Today, there are over 2.000 adult Baptist believers gathered in about sixty local churches or mission stations. There are also around twenty full-time or part-time pastors. More than twenty-five years after the separation from the previous country and establishing a new Union, Baptists are still faced

---

Baptists between 1970 and 2010 in the contexts of war and major social changes. "Conflict, Change, and Conversion: Four Decades of Conversion among Baptists in Croatia 1970–2010" (unpublished doctoral dissertation, The Southern Baptist Theological Seminary, 2015). Accessed 28 May 2017, <https://search.proquest.com/docview/1757267797/abstract/792786A1B59E40A3PQ/1>.

15. *Ugovor s Vladom RH*, 2005, para. 23. Accessed 21 July 2015, <http://baptist.hr/ustrojstvo-saveza-baptistickih-crkava/dokumenti-sbc-a/597-ugovor-s-vladom-rh>.

with a number of vital issues which need to be resolved – both in the local and national context – if their presence is to be continually transformed into meaningful and faithful service both to the gospel and to society under the changed socio-political circumstances and a different moral climate. To properly respond to challenges that are (sometimes) significantly dissimilar to those which faced previous generations, Baptists in Croatia must become better equipped to understand and shape their identity in more positive terms.

The most recent articulation of an attempt to respond to these challenges can be found in a new Statute of the Baptist Union of Croatia and *2020 Strategy*.[16] These two documents contain five basic values of the Union, five principles on which the Union is founded, and five key activities by which the Union's mission and vision are to be accomplished by 2020. What pervades this strategy is the sense of more intentional openness toward society which is balanced with the awareness of the need for internal development. Two outward activities are the *new evangelism* (the mentality change required in order that every church member can become an agent in the mission field) and *integrative social projects* (the encouragement for believers to get involved in partnerships with civic groups and NGOs to help groups of people with specific needs). On the other hand, two inward activities are the *leadership development programme* (which includes lifelong education and development of pastors) and *"new giving"* (aimed at the financial independence of local churches despite prolonged economic instability, recession, and growing unemployment). The fifth activity to connect all those previously mentioned is *communication*, but it also needs to foster a dialogue with a wider community (and include various media such as bulletins, websites, internet, and radio stations). Although some of the elements of this strategy may find their implementation only in the future, the Union's mission is firmly committed to this immediate goal: "To make Christ present in our time, in ourselves, in the church, in the Union, in our Croatia."

---

16. "Statut Saveza baptističkih crkava u Republici Hrvatskoj," (Savez Baptističkih crkava u Republici Hrvatskoj, 2015). Accessed 20 October 2015. <http://baptist.hr/images/stories/pdf/Statut_SBC_u_RH.pdf>. According to Željko Mraz, the current Union's General Secretary, *2020 Strategy* is an internal document, but its core values have been incorporated in the new Statute. Željko Mraz, "Dokumenti Saveza," (email to the author, 15 July 2015).

6.2 The Existing Homiletical Literature

At this point, however, we must look back and review the available literature that can shed some light on Baptists' historical perception of preaching. Throughout their history, Baptist churches have placed exceptional emphasis on the centrality of preaching. Apart from the first few decades when there were no established congregations and the communication of faith was largely limited to the distribution of Bibles and Christian literature and to individual contacts, Baptists have used preaching to accomplish all their main purposes. Preaching has been essential in teaching and edifying believers, even from an early age (parents have usually been encouraged to bring their children to the church services even if there were no Sunday School classes). It was also seen as the focal point of almost all weekly church services. During the communist period, preaching also served as the main evangelism tool. Although public Christian activities were not allowed, the "internal" life of churches as conducted on their premises was tolerated. Thus, most churches tended to have "evangelistic meetings" or "conferences" to which they invited their non-Christian friends, colleagues, or family members. The central element of these meetings was always a sermon. Finally, leaders of local churches were interchangeably designated as "preachers" and "pastors," both in the official documents[17] and in everyday usage.

Although not all these observations have the weight of verifiable evidence, they at least signify the paramount role preaching has played in sustaining the Baptist identity. It would be worthwhile, then, to explore how much of its purpose is reflected in the existing written materials and other resources produced or used by Croatian Baptists. To begin with, there is an obvious disproportion between the number of published sermons and the number of homiletical works. Almost from the outset of Baptists' publishing work, their leaders believed that the dissemination of their sermons was among the most important and possibly most rewarding tasks. Practically every volume of all major periodicals issued by Baptist churches or publishing houses included at least one sermon.[18] More recently, the official bulletin of the Baptist Union of

---

17. For instance, see *Ugovor s Vladom RH*, para. 1.

18. For example, Franjo Klem regularly published his sermons in *Glasnik*, and occasionally in *Glas Evanđelja*. Vinko Vacek had his sermons issued in *Glas Evanđelja*. For many years, Josip Horak's sermons were broadcast over Trans World Radio from Monte Carlo and subsequently published in both *Glas Evanđelja* and *Glasnik*.

Croatia, *Glas Crkve* (launched in 1997) also has two columns where Croatian preachers regularly contribute their sermons. With the progress of technology, a tendency to produce a collection of sermons and publish them as books emerged. If the sheer number of published books is a relevant indicator, it can easily be concluded that Croatian Baptist preachers did not consider sermons a primarily or exclusively oral form of communication.[19] It is not always clear whether these sermons were originally preached in a worship context and only then revised for print. However, during more recent decades there have been more short Christian messages designed for radio broadcasting and then published verbatim as sermons in a book.

On the other hand, there is a striking absence of books on or about preaching. Interestingly, a Serbian translation of C. H. Spurgeon's *Lecture to my Students* appeared as early as 1909 and must have been known to Croatian Baptists in the following decades.[20] For many years, it seemed to be the only homiletical book available in any of South Slavic languages.[21] In 1961, a series of short instructions for preaching was published as a booklet, by Adolf Lehotsky.[22] He was a preacher and theologian whose origins can be traced back to the tradition of the German Baptist movement before World War II, and he served as a pastor in the Rijeka Baptist Church (1973–1975). These notes were compiled from different sources and based on his preaching experience and were intended for his lectures at Baptist Theological Seminary. Although this text can be called only a sketch for a textbook, the suggested sermon preparation process clearly includes the stages of invention, arrangement, style, and delivery, as well as some rudimentary examples for each

---

19. The following bibliography includes not only ethnic Croatians, but also those authors who have served in churches on Croatian territory and among Croatian believers, or whose sermons have been widely read and appreciated in those Baptist congregations: Josip Horak, "Zemljo, zemljo, zemljo! Čuj Riječ Gospodnju!" (Zagreb, 1967); *Jednostavni koraci na duhovnoj stazi* (Zagreb: Privately printed, 1979); *Propovijedaj Riječ* (Zagreb: Savez baptističkih crkava u RH, 2004); Martin Hlastan, *Mana sa Božjeg stola* (Daruvar: Privately printed, 1975); *Koraci vjere* (Novi Sad: Privately printed, 1976); *Upoznat ćete istinu* (Ljubljana: Beseda evangelija, 1989); Peter Donald MacKenzie, *Propovijedi o izgubljenom sinu* (Zagreb: Stepress, 2009); Đuro Samac, *Evanđelje na djelu* (Zagreb: Studio Moderna, 2012); *Samo vjera – Sola fide* (Zagreb: DADO, 2013).

20. Čarls Hedon Spurdžon, *Dobri saveti propovednicima Jevanđelja*, trans. by Mih. Popović (Beograd: Knjižara S. B. Cvijanovića, 1909).

21. It was translated into the Croatian language in 1971 (Charles H. Spurgeon, *Tako je govorio Spurgeon*, trans. by Gabrijel Jonke and Mirjana Lovrec (Zagreb: Branko Lovrec, 1971).)

22. Adolf Lehotsky, "Kratke upute za propovedanje."

stage. It also reflects a high respect for the linear movement of the sermon, with explicit divisions and subdivisions.

However, given the pronounced attention of this thesis to the role of listeners, I should not overlook two articles which demonstrate at least traces of evidence that preachers in Croatian Baptist churches felt that their hearers would (or should) be given a more active role. In one of the handbooks published by Baptist Theological Seminary, several articles dealt with homiletical issues. In his article on issues of authority and preaching, Stjepan Orcic asserts: "If there was equal authority given to everyone in the church, then everyone would preach and there would be no one to listen."[23] What can be discerned from this statement is his implicit presupposition that preaching is a one-way process in which the preacher is not expected to listen. Yet there are a few perceptive observations about changes in the listener's role. For instance, he says that "the old times," when "the pulpit authority" meant that listeners would obey the preacher's message without questioning it, are now gone.[24] From his perspective, listeners have become ready to make decisions on their own about which parts of the sermon are acceptable, and which are not. He is convinced that what the preacher says is now exposed to "scrutiny, evaluation and refusal."[25]

In another article, prominent Baptist leader, preacher, director of publishing house *Duhovna stvarnost*, and the future first president of the Croatian Baptist Union, Branko Lovrec, discusses language and communication in preaching. He advocates the use of language which avoids mere repetition of expressions that are meaningless for modern hearers. At one point he mentions the need for an "open system" in a church, where communication would be possible "from the congregation toward the pulpit so that this communication becomes a two-way communication."[26]

Lastly, the above-mentioned Stjepan Orčić (1930–2000), a prominent Baptist leader, and an ethnic Croatian, served as an editor of *Glasnik* and as

---

23. Stjepan Orčić, "Kriza autoriteta i propovedanje" [Crisis of Authority and Preaching], *Priručnici 1* (Novi Sad: Baptistička teološka škola, 1978), 21–27: 21 (translation mine).

24. Orčić, 23 (translation mine).

25. Orčić, 24 (translation mine).

26. Branko Lovrec, "Jezik kao značajan činilac djelotvornog propovjedanja" [Language as Significant Factor of Effective Preaching], *Priručnici 1* (Novi Sad: Baptistička teološka škola, 1978): 31 (translation mine).

a teacher and president of Baptist Theological Seminary in Novi Sad (Serbia). His lectures on preaching were gathered and posthumously published in Serbia.[27] Since this is virtually the only full-scale homiletical textbook written by a Croatian author, its key features deserve a closer look.

To begin with, it seems his lectures were partly motivated by his perception of the current state of preaching in Baptist churches: very often sermons are dull and boring, and preachers take their authority for granted and thus abuse the pulpit. Preaching fails to address both listeners and their contemporary issues. Sermons sometimes lack the proper content – the word of God – and thus miss their primary purpose – to change hearers.[28] In order to fulfil this ultimate purpose, preaching needs to bridge the gap between the Bible and listeners and create an encounter with Christ. He argues that preaching should have an almost sacramental value for Protestants. What he means is that preached words both perform and act, thus creating for listeners an experience of the real presence of Christ. This presence is possible only insofar as the sermon moves hearers' will, reason, and emotions. The preacher also needs to deliberately craft the goal of his sermon which includes its extension into the everyday life of listeners. Such preaching to church members "does not include saying things they do not know, but rather asking them to respond like they never responded before."[29]

He also insists that Protestant worship is necessarily subjective, that is, people- or listener-oriented with preaching as its pinnacle. This is precisely why the truth of the sermon's message must be incarnated in the preacher's life; otherwise, it remains only a passing on of information.[30] Expressed a bit differently, a sermon must affect both preacher and listeners. In that light, the Bible, Orčić warns, must not be a self-serving goal, but rather a tool which God uses to address people, to create tension, and to establish a relationship with them. His attitude is summed up in the following sentences:

> [A] sermon is not a mechanical transmission of insights about the biblical text, but the word of God directed to a particular

---

27. Stjepan Orčić, *Ludost propovedanja*. In the same year, Aleksandar Birviš authored an article that covers topics from the last three of Orčić's lectures which were not found in the book. 'Dopuna knjizi "Ludost propovedanja," *Teološki časopis*, 7 (2007): 21–24.

28. Orčić, *Ludost propovedanja*, 22–29.

29. Orčić, 51 (translation mine).

30. Orčić, 70–71.

environment through a particular person. And that "particular person" needs to experience this text and to communicate it in a convincing way.[31]

Of course, there is a question of how relevant his views were for Croatian Baptists. An answer would be that these lectures undoubtedly exercised some influence, but his book appeared far too late to receive a wider reception among them. Being published in Serbia, sixteen years after the separation of Yugoslavia, this work simply could not get a wider circulation among Croatian Baptists. By that time, Croatian Baptists' communication with believers from the country which was normally considered to be the aggressor became infrequent and occasional, and their newly discovered sense of denominational identity meant they were more concerned with the literature published within Croatia. Nevertheless, this book remains crucial evidence of an attempt to systematically teach homiletics and influence Baptist pastors and preachers by presenting a mindful and more comprehensive approach to the preaching practice.

This overview allows us to offer at least three tentative conclusions: (1) Croatian Baptist leaders put a premium on preaching, and the number of printed sermons supports this evaluation; (2) in their homiletical education Croatian Baptist leaders generally either used a few homiletical tools developed elsewhere in other contexts or learned how to preach simply by imitating other preachers without having an analytical approach to their homiletics; and (3) there is no evidence that Croatian Baptists ever produced a written record of the awareness of the need for a systematic, structured and empirical understanding of listeners' contribution to the preaching practice. In a similar fashion, there is no homiletical work written by a Croatian Baptist that seriously considers the contextual nature of preaching.

6.3 The Homiletical Practice of Croatian Baptists

This chapter would be incomplete without an attempt to offer some information on the nature of homiletical practice among Croatian Baptists. Unfortunately, apparently no studies with such an objective have been

---

31. Orčić, *Ludost propovedanja*, 151 (translation mine).

conducted. Therefore, I will limit myself to partial and fragmentary observations and comments, and inferences from the official documents.

There are some passing remarks in the studies that deal with the history of Croatian Baptists. Peterlin suggests it is highly probable that in the period before 1925 services in Zagreb Baptist churches typically included the reading of Scripture and its interpretation, i.e., preaching, collective prayer, singing, and celebration of the Lord's Supper (Eucharist).[32] Observing the situation ninety years later, Catholic author Juraj Kolarić writes that the central Sunday service in bigger Baptist churches is usually comprised of three main parts: worship, prayer, and a biblical sermon. The Bible reading functions as an introduction to the sermon on a specific topic delivered according to the previously established schedule. However, he remarks that although this may be a rough outline in larger congregations, every local Baptist church has the autonomy to shape its own church service model.[33]

The absence of a more detailed and mindful description of preaching practice in the past could lead us to make two conjectures: either the preaching practice has been largely taken for granted and as something self-explanatory, or Croatian Baptists simply lacked resources for such investigation and were concerned with more pressing issues. Indeed, it would be surprising if these two reasons were mutually exclusive. In any case, we can turn to more recent official documents for more insight.

In a document that defines the relationship of Baptist churches with the government of the Republic of Croatia, the practice of preaching is not explicitly mentioned, which is to be expected since the main purpose of the document is to regulate relationships in of education, culture, and counselling in certain public institutions. However, at the very beginning, the term "priest" is defined as synonymous with the terms "pastor" and "preacher"; all of them denote a "church minister who conducts a church service."[34] This inclusion underlines the Baptist tradition and contemporary praxis according to which the congregation's leader is expected to regularly preach as the pastor's central duty. At the same time, it is still acceptable that preaching is sometimes done by a person who is not a pastor. This is in line with a congregational

---

32. Peterlin, "Theological Education," 468.
33. Kolarić, *Ekumenska trilogija*, 496.
34. *Ugovor s Vladom RH*, para. 1.

ecclesiology of Baptist churches, yet in this document, there is no mention of any agreed-upon criterion for deciding on eligibility for preaching.

However, the Baptist Union of Croatia's original Statute was enacted in 1991,[35] while an annexe was issued in 1997. This annexe basically contains the statute of the local Baptist church. By this annexe, the Union affirms the autonomy of the local church in the creation and organisation of its ecclesial life and spiritual praxis, but in the preamble, the key purpose of this statute is expressed. It says that this statute "in principle regulates the organisation of the local Baptist church and serves as a framework for the process of drawing up the statutes of individual local Baptist churches."[36] I will look briefly at articles that address the role of the preacher and the purpose of preaching.

In Article 4, several central ministries are listed as requirements for any local church to be constituted, including preaching (together with the ability to manage the church and counselling). Apparently, a capacity to organise regular church services is dependent on the ability to repeatedly deliver sermons. Then, in Article 6, there is a distinction between reading and interpreting the Bible for individual growth and preaching as a service of the Word which builds the community of believers. Preaching can be done only by those individuals recognized by the congregation, by people who have charisma: demonstrated as a spiritual gift and ministry. This article remains slightly unclear, perhaps by intention, and does not specify whether the preaching ministry remains reserved for ordained pastors and other ministers. Article 8 mentions that the *Order of Worship* (see below) serves as a principle of the organisation of worship in Baptist churches, but confirms that individual churches have the freedom to create their own worship model. Yet in Articles 9 and 10 the holders of ministries in the local church are described. Any member can be recognized as a holder of a specific ministry, but the congregation identifies those who hold the leading ministries – pastor or preacher, elder, and deacon – in a special way. All three ministries require a process of ordination. There are also several qualifications for the pastor's office. This is

---

35. "Statut Saveza baptističkih crkava u Republici Hrvatskoj" (Savez Baptističkih crkava u Republici Hrvatskoj, 1991), accessed 29 July 2015, http://www.baptist.hr/slube-u-savezu7/159-sbc/dokumenti/81-statut-saveza-baptistiki-crkava-u-republici-hrvatskojj.

36. "Statut mjesne baptističke crkve" (Savez Baptističkih crkava u Republici Hrvatskoj, 1997), para. 23, accessed 26 September 2015, <http://www.baptist.hr/dokumenti-saveza/59-dokumenti/83-statut-mjesne-baptistike-crkve> (translation mine).

the most responsible ministry in the local church. It combines the ministry of preaching and counselling, and preaching has both a proclamatory and teaching dimension. The preacher is generally expected to hold a higher education degree in theology. The term of office is four years, and there is no limitation in terms of how many times a preacher can be reelected. And again, we have another clarification for the simultaneous use of terms "pastor" and "preacher," which both denote the same ministry in the local church in conformity with the previous praxis in local Baptist churches.

There is another document which requires more attention despite the fact it has never been officially enacted by the Union. It was offered to member churches in 1998 or 1999, but after discussion, it remained only as a suggestion and continued to be a helpful tool for conducting specific rites, such as baptism, funerals, and weddings.[37] The document is called *Order of Worship*, and its most relevant section for our purposes is *A Service of the Word*.[38] What can be found there deals predominantly with the use of the lectionary – the text explains the practical and theological benefits of lectionary preaching. It also suggests singing of Psalms and recommends that reading of Scriptures should be carefully prepared and entrusted to believers who can read clearly and intelligibly. It is fairly evident that this document aims at providing more orderliness in the practice of preaching since the free church tradition typically leaves a preacher with a lot of freedom to tailor his or her preaching strategy. Yet, such freedom can be abused, and this advocacy of the lectionary tries to help preachers prevent this deviation.[39]

As for the sermon itself, this document suggests expository preaching instead of topical sermons. The reason is that expository preaching "in some measure" prevents preachers' own ideas being read into the sermon and exposes the word of God as He intended it. The justification could be that previously much of the preaching in Baptist churches has been topical and had a predetermined agenda not always compatible with the function of the

---

37. Mraz, "Dokumenti Saveza."
38. Giorgio Grlj, "Bogoslužbeni red baptističkih crkava," 8–10.
39. My personal observation and conversations with pastors, however, suggest most of them still avoid the lectionary. If they do use it privately when selecting the biblical text for the sermon, they likely do not make it publicly known through the practice of reading three selected portions of the Bible. I also suspect many Baptist believers are distrustful of the use of lectionary, convinced this is a "Catholic tradition" and therefore an unbiblical practice.

biblical texts used to support it. A sermon should also, the text goes on, lead people toward a decision, which is a prerequisite for change. To meditate on the possible decision, the congregation should be given a short pause before the prayer which concludes the service of the Word.

Looking at these documents, we can get some understanding of what preaching in Croatian Baptist churches *should* look like. We can also infer that it belongs to the very centre of local Baptist church worship and identity. However, we do not have any comprehensive source or study that would tell us *how* it is done and *what* is going on during the preaching,[40] and we know practically nothing about the role of listeners and their participation in the practice of preaching. Therefore, the last section of this chapter will be devoted to presenting the justification of my research.

6.4 The Need for the Research

After setting out a brief history of Croatian Baptist churches and giving a glimpse at their homiletical practice in the present, the material of chapters 2–5 provides strong reasons for undertaking the research I present in the latter part of this thesis.

The first reason comes because of a serious appreciation that a multidisciplinary approach shows that any perspective on preaching practice which sees listeners as recipients with no active contribution to offer is an anachronism. Also, there is no reason to assume that listeners in Croatian Baptist churches are that different from listeners in other parts of the world. They are not so isolated from cultural changes, the influences of technology and (largely) secular media that their patterns of thinking, hearing, and learning do not require a better and stronger attention to their actual or at least potential participation in the preaching.

---

40. There are some local churches and some pastors who regularly publish video clips or audio recordings of their church services on their Web sites or publish the sermon transcripts on their blogs. These materials, however, usually do not disclose much (or enough) about delivery, style, worship context or listeners' reactions and feedback. For examples of such sermons, see "Prijenos Bogoštovlja – Baptistička Crkva Mačkovec," accessed 14 July 2015, <http://bcmackovec.com/prijenos-bogostovlja>l; *Nedjeljne propovijedi – Baptistička crkva Rijeka*, accessed 12 January 2016, https://drive.google.com/folderview?ddrp=1&id=0B0lz01Z7YoZgSFdYTjQ4RVpma2c#.

The second reason is that the available historical witness proves that preaching held a precious place in Baptist theology and praxis; the sermons (or their transcripts and radio broadcasts) have been a major proclamation tool while the practice of preaching *and listening* to sermons continues to be unrivalled in its determining impact on Baptist liturgy. And yet, up to this present moment, there has been no empirical research that probed this practice in a more systematic and comprehensive way. Thus any future empirical study which tries to understand what is *actually* believed about preaching, *how* sermons function for listeners, and *what* engages and promotes active listening will, at the same time, be both welcome and ground-breaking.

The third reason has to do with the Croatian Baptist churches' prospects. Given the Union's goals laid down in *2020 Strategy*, the intentional increase in attention given to preaching (especially to its contextual nature) may prove to be the leverage that determines their fulfilment. Empowered listeners, for instance, may help to evaluate the real effectiveness of preaching and acquire a renewed self-perception which could incite them to take a more active role in both new evangelism and integrative social projects. In addition, a leadership development programme could be refreshed and invigorated with some data provided through the well-defined channels of feedback from sermon listeners. Instead of working on the uncritical assumptions of what listeners supposedly think and believe, such input could help to shape a more realistic and relevant education of leaders and preachers. Finally, this could encourage lively conversation *within* congregations, without which the proposed dialogue with a wider community could easily turn into part of a burdening agenda which lacks its internal driving force and vitality.

CHAPTER 7

Presentation of Methodology

As indicated at the beginning of the previous chapter, this is where the presentation of an actual field study is called for. To make the process of conducting this study as transparent as possible, this chapter has a threefold structure. I will begin with locating my own position as a researcher and disclosing my motivation which urged me to undertake this research. This will be supplemented by highlighting the areas of personal involvement that could bear upon the process of data gathering and analysis. In my next step, I will seek to describe *how* the research was conducted and provide specific details about the method used, the time and location of research, and the actual number of participants. In the closing section, I will explain the procedures applied during the research, especially the choice of method and the overall strategy.

7.1 Personal Motivation and Involvement

Being raised in the local Baptist church, I have been immersed in a contextual expression of Baptist identity from my earliest years. I can trace my initial, conscious experiences of sermon listening back to 1980s, and somewhere in the 1990s I began preaching myself. All my life I have been a member of a Baptist church, and my interest in and attachment to preaching have grown stronger over the years. During the last seven years, I have been a member of a preaching team in my current local church, involved in Sunday preaching but also in the annual planning of the preaching schedule and occasional evaluation as well.

The single most notable concern that spurs my motivation for this research is a growing awareness that perpetuating the preaching practice without its critical evaluation – which includes the identification of listeners' expectations and opportunities for their feedback, as well as full recognition of the contextual nature of preaching – serves only to widen the gap between the preacher and listeners. The stimulus behind my efforts is a desire to check whether establishing a conversation with listeners can help to bridge that gap and whether the practice of preaching can be restored to its full potential, to which the congregational emphasis of Baptist ecclesiology should be more than conducive.

Consequently, my position is by no means neutral. I engage in this study with the rich dual experience of being both a regular listener to sermons and (less) regular preacher and this experience must be considered while assessing my analysis and interpretation of the data. I also approach this study as someone who is an insider because I belong to the same Baptist denomination as the people who took part in interviews. At the same time, I approach it as an outsider because (in most cases) I do not belong to their local congregations, may not share their views or values, and have no access to their particular subculture.

Let me be more specific. For instance, almost all the interviewees have heard me preach at least once. Those belonging to my church have listened to my preaching several times over the last few years, while most of the others heard me preach at the church service just before the interview. In other words, my role as an interviewer could not be perceived by the respondents as that of an objective and distanced questioner, and their responses must have interacted with their impressions about me as someone directly involved in the preaching practice. On the other hand, my own approach to the interviewing process was to some extent predisposed by my preexisting experiences and homiletic knowledge. Also, being a member of the Baptist denomination and having a history of interactions with other Baptist believers, I had some assumptions about their congregations and, consequently, certain expectations about the nature and content of their responses. Thus, I will try my best to draw attention to the instances when these touch upon my interpretation and arguments.

7.2 Description and Details of the Research

The research took place from 16 June to 11 September, 2016. It was conducted at several different locations since the participants were selected from five local Baptist congregations in four Croatian towns. Eighteen individual interviews were taken either after Sunday service (usually when interviewing required a visit to another city) or at the previously arranged time during the weekdays. All interviews took place within the church facilities, courtesy of the local pastors. In most cases, those rooms provided an environment with minimal or no interference from the outside. The duration of individual interviews varied from 50–150 minutes, but on average lasted around ninety minutes.

The question of accessing the data was resolved by a two-stage approach. During the first stage, the purpose and goals of the research were presented to a number of Baptist pastors at the Baptist Union Executive Board meeting in April 2016. As the local pastors have been identified as the "gatekeepers," this presentation placed a particular emphasis on explaining the potential benefits not only for the listeners, but also for themselves as preachers and for the quality of their preaching ministry. The intention was also to introduce my research and motivation in a transparent fashion and to eliminate any possible misunderstandings concerning the research purposes (one of them being that this research would tend to evaluate the individual preachers' performance and thus encourage the believers to make comparisons among them). By reminding pastors of the crucial role of preaching in Baptist ecclesiology, I drew their attention to the potential advantages of this research in enhancing their respective congregations' identity. The final step in this stage was to suggest they invite me to present my research to their congregations directly and invite the believers to participate in it. Several weeks after this presentation, two telephone conversations followed where I made the same proposal to two pastors who had not taken part in the meeting.

The next stage in obtaining access to the data took place during several visits to individual congregations following invitations from their pastors. In each of those churches, I was given an opportunity to personally present my research to the potential participants during the Sunday service. In those ten-minute addresses, an appeal was made to the adult members who were regular sermon listeners to approach me after the service and ask for more information on how they could participate in the research. On that same occasion, I communicated the key purpose, goals, and benefits of the research, together with a basic description of the interviewing process. I also provided some essential facts about confidentiality and anonymity, as well as the possibility of withdrawing from participation at any point without further explanation. After the service, I answered the questions asked by the potential participants. The only exception from this two-stage process was my home church, where I felt confident to omit the first stage because its church leadership was already acquainted with my research and I was able to approach the potential respondents more straightforwardly.

Candidates for my research were the churchgoers who regularly listened to sermons, adult members (18 years or older) of the local Baptist congregations in Croatia. Starting from this framework, I created a sample by means of purposive sampling. Three main selection criteria were employed in this study: age, gender, and personal history of belonging to the church. There is a twofold reason for applying these criteria. First, this ensured that the main groups would be adequately represented, and secondly, the diversity achieved in this way helped identify a greater number of characteristics that influenced the listeners' reception of sermons. Age was selected as one of the criteria because the Croatian Baptist churches generally include members of all age groups and yet it can be assumed that there may be notable differences in how they hear sermons. The gender criterion is equally important; although most sermons are preached by male preachers, this disproportion is not visible among the listeners since female listeners often outnumber male churchgoers. Finally, there is a personal history of belonging to the church, or faith history. As can be seen from the previous chapter, the Baptist movement in Croatia is still relatively young and many believers join Baptist churches either coming from a secular background or after being raised in Catholic families with very loose previous connections to the life of the local parish. Their previous engagement with faith practices is often only minimal. Such believers, whose numbers increased in the 1990s, can be designated as "first generation" Baptists. On the other hand, there are also believers who have been brought up in a Baptist home and who can be considered as "traditional Baptists." When all these criteria are applied, the resulting sample matrix is shown in table 1.

Table 1. Sample matrix

Age		Gender		Faith history	
18–34	4	Female	9	First generation	11
35–50	6	Male	9	Traditional	7
51–69	6				
70+	2				

A few additional remarks must be made here about the interview structure. Essentially, I have borrowed and adapted the questions used in the *Listening to Listeners* field study.[1] The reason is rather simple; they provide a clear and neat grid against which the respondents' feedback can be evaluated through the major rhetorical categories. By arranging the questions in three groups, which correspond to the three rhetorical modes of appeal (logos, ethos, and pathos), I also made a conscious decision to test one of the major findings of that study: the notion that "nearly every listener reveals that one setting is the mode through which they listen to the sermon." Although the study conclusions suggested that this particular setting or "initial mode of hearing the message" is not the only setting through which a hearer processes input from a sermon, nevertheless it "functions as a medium through which a listener synthesizes the other settings."[2] So, expecting a highly diverse feedback from interviewees in this study, I chose to follow the structure of *Listening to Listeners* interview questions in hopes that it would allow a greater visibility of listeners' distinct settings of hearing and help me as I navigate them through different perspectives of an encounter with a sermon. Naturally, I translated and modified the original wording to make it more comprehensible and engaging for respondents in their specific context(s). The full list of questions used in the study is given in the appendix.

However, the decision to use logos, ethos, and pathos also as the main analytic categories that shape the interpretation process requires additional explanation. For one thing, employing the categories that correspond to the three prearranged groups of questions helps to present the results in a more orderly fashion. More importantly, it pays due respect to the historical fact of

---

1. Allen, *Hearing the Sermon*, 135–136.
2. Allen, 8–9, 145.

Aristotelian rhetorical influence on preaching over the centuries. Finally, it acknowledges the reality that the most comprehensive empirical research on listeners' perception of preaching (*Listening to Listeners*) has confirmed the value of these three rubrics as a structure suitable for the assessment of raw data on preaching gathered through qualitative research. Yet, some inherent limitations of this decision need to be underscored as well.

To begin with, the use of these categories can easily become an imposition when the interpretative process is done without the awareness that this is only one of many possible models for addressing this subject and the collected data. There is intrinsic risk of selective appreciation of only those findings that fit well within this structure and of neglecting those that do not. Also, there is a temptation to force all the participants' feedback into this structure and to arrange them under one of these three categories to verify the decision to organise the data evaluation around them. It could easily result in a reductionist interpretive procedure that would not do justice to the wealth of experiences of listening to preaching as reported by the interviewees.

To mitigate these risks, I tried to make use of logos, ethos, and pathos as valid starting points for gathering and thinking through the hearers' responses to sermons while remaining prepared to depart from them whenever the research data indicated that their interpretation would benefit from surpassing this initial framework. As will be shown, articulating the answer to my research question required going beyond the rubric of ethos, pathos, and logos and comprehending themes that fall outside the frame of reference defined by these rhetorical modes of appeal.

7.3 Research Strategy and Procedures

A description of the overall research strategy is necessary to fully understand the intended purpose, including its being conditioned by two crucial notions: a phenomenological strategy and practical theology. The phenomenological approach to research has several advantages in this situation which can be applied in answering the research question. A phenomenology is a fitting approach for distinguishing different types of personal experience and for appreciating specific issues or situations through the eyes of "the other." Listening to sermons certainly is a highly personal, unique, and unrepeatable experience. Also, in the Croatian Baptists' context, preaching is a phenomenon that has virtually never been discussed or reflected upon from the perspective of the listeners; this is why the perspective of that "other" side is so crucial. Denscombe labels this as "raw data" and clarifies: "A phenomenological approach to research . . . concentrates its efforts on the kind of human experiences that are pure, basic and raw in the sense that they have not (yet) been subjected to processes of analysis and theorizing."[3] Further, a phenomenological approach is highly efficient in shedding light on various details and properties of everyday social life that are normally taken for granted. In this case, being exposed to sermons on a weekly basis is a pivotal point in the ecclesial life of Baptist congregations, yet at the same time it is so routinely assumed and neglected that it effectively represents a vast *terra incognita*. Likewise, this approach focuses on the individuals' perceptions, beliefs, and emotions because it presupposes that they make sense of this world through their experience. In other words, adopting this strategy builds on a presupposition that different listeners construct different and multiple meanings through their firsthand experience of sermon listening.

However, the strategy embraced in this research is not exhaustive in its phenomenological outlook but is enhanced through the addition of a reflective stance typical for practical theology. The phenomenon of preaching and sermon listening must be studied and observed, but an additional dimension is called for by its theological context. If we agree with Swinton and Mowatt when they describe the emergence of practical theology ". . . as a response to and recognition of the redemptive actions of God-in-the-world and the human experience which emerges in response to those actions,"[4] then we will affirm sermon listening as a distinctively Christian activity based on the listeners' effort to respond to God's action described, referred to, or experienced in preaching. In that case, we need to admit that doing practical theology implies a goal that goes beyond the parameters of human experience, although it takes that experience seriously as "a 'place' where the gospel is grounded, embodied, interpreted, and lived out."[5]

If we follow the lead of practical theology a bit further, we will soon reach the point where preaching (and sermon listening) can be recognised as a

---

3. Denscombe, *Good Research Guide*, 95.
4. Swinton and Mowatt, *Practical Theology*, 11.
5. Swinton and Mowatt, 5.

Christian "practice" in the sense of an activity developed within specific communities over time that functions as the carrier of tradition. These practices "... contain values, beliefs, theologies and other assumptions which, for the most part, go unnoticed until they are complexified and brought to our notice through the process of theological reflection."[6] If so, then a seemingly straightforward and ordinary practice such as sermon listening deserves not only a descriptive analysis, but also a critical reflection. My field study represents, first, a modest attempt at what Richard R. Osmer has termed the first task of practical theological interpretation: the descriptive-empirical task.[7] Secondly, its findings are also subjected to theological critical reflection in order to answer the following question: How does this practice square with the claims of Scripture and tradition? Finally, some pragmatic proposals are offered as a suggestion on how the practice of preaching might be revised and improved. Put simply, the phenomenological approach helps us understand how Croatian Baptists listen to sermons, while practical theology suggests how this could be transformed and aligned with the vital message of the gospel.

In my Introduction, I pointed out that a semi-structured interview was the chosen data collection method. This choice may need further validation. First, Denscombe affirms that this method is particularly advantageous when the data is based on opinions, feelings, and experiences. Such data needs to be investigated exhaustively and not just briefly mentioned.[8] Since the participants' feedback on preaching is likely to abound in these types of response, the interview seems like a natural choice. Secondly, the experiences of sermon listening can contain some personal and sensitive issues for the respondents, and honest answers can be best elicited through careful interviewing. Furthermore, if we are to grasp how Croatian Baptists listen to sermons and what they expect to receive from that experience, we need to employ a method that will allow us to plunge into their personal histories. Their life stories are often interwoven with some life-changing moments which occurred as a part of their listening histories. Individual interviews allow time and space for an indepth understanding of this highly personal perspective and it is implied that they will be conducted face-to-face in a

---

6. Swinton and Mowatt, 20.
7. Osmer, *Practical Theology*.
8. Denscombe, *Good Research Guide*, 174.

physical encounter between the researcher and the interviewee. In a similar way, the interviews are a suitable method because this study also seeks to explore the impacts of preaching on the listeners and only an interview can guarantee that a thorough personal focus will be given to every participant. At the same time, since sermon listening always takes place within a communal context, the choice of the individual interview is justified as it prevents personal connections among the participants from inhibiting their input.

There is another set of reasons why the interview is the most appropriate method here. Although the listeners represent the enormous majority in every preaching event, their perspective on preaching is rarely or never heard or made public. Functionally, they are a minority and preachers can easily monopolise preaching at the expense of those without whom the very practice of preaching would lose its original purpose. But the listening party does not need to be the "silent" party – and listeners have the full right to reflect on their perception of preaching and to vocalise their concerns. Through individual interviews, this silent voice of minority can blossom into a full spectrum of diverse perspectives and opinions that too often remain cloaked by the preacher's "Amen!" at the end of the sermon.

Besides, the interactive character of the interview had further benefits for my research purposes. It is "generative" in the sense that the participants have often been prompted to consider the ideas or thoughts they never scrutinised before, which may generate new knowledge or views.[9] That the participants themselves generate the data while being interviewed means, in effect, they are empowered through involvement in this research, which corresponds to my fundamental concern to create opportunities for listeners to offer their feedback – which in turn may help bridge the gap between them and their preachers. Crucially, only a semi-structured interview possesses both adequate structure to predefine the initial set of questions, and enough flexibility to accommodate participants' ideas and responses. It capably combines planned questions and open-ended answers which allows respondents to reply in their own language and elaborate on the subjects they find critical.

---

9. Ritchie and Lewis, eds., *Qualitative Research Practice*, 142.

CHAPTER 8

Data Presentation

Before proceeding with the data presentation, several initial clarifications are necessary. I will use the basic structure of my interview questions as a framework for putting forward the response from participants. My initial plan was to simply present their feedback to questions related to ethos, then continue with their responses related to logos and close with their input on questions pertaining to the dynamics of pathos. However, studying the transcripts persuaded me that this plan needed some revisions, as explained below.

The phenomenon of the primary listening setting, as described by researchers in the *Listening to Listeners* study,[1] appeared in this study as well. Answering the interview questions, some participants would indirectly reveal the setting on which they listen to sermons. Others would continuously go back to their basic setting, use a particular indicative language and expressions or pick up themes that imply their listening preferences. Many also answered questions from one category by introducing material that belongs to another category; for instance, asked to describe a particularly memorable sermon (logos category), a participant may answer by placing a great emphasis on relationships within the congregation (ethos category). Also, it seems that a dominant setting serves not only as an initial point of entry into the sermon but also determines how the hearer manages the input from other settings. So, even though proving the existence of a primary hearing setting was not among the objectives of this study, it is worth mentioning it here since it provides a supplementary perspective on understanding how people hear sermons.

---

1. See 5.3.1 and 5.3.2 above.

It is equally important to emphasize that my designation of particular interviewees as ethos, pathos, or logos-oriented listeners is not to be taken as a rigid classification of scientifically established categories. It is based on my subjective evaluation of their listening preferences that recognizes their proclivities as expressed in using particular phrases or in bringing up specific themes at various points of the interview. So, whenever a particular setting is associated with a specific participant in this analysis, it is best read as my personal and subjective assessment of their primary listening channel that by no means neglects the intricateness of their unique ways of listening, perceiving, and connecting to the sermons preached.

During the process of rereading transcripts several topics that cut across the three categories of ethos, logos, and pathos emerged repeatedly. The observation that these three modes are delicately interlaced and that certain other themes stem from interviews led me to this conclusion: the neat structure of presenting listeners' perceptions question by question would not do justice to the complexity of interview sessions and participants' perspectives. Thus, I present the gathered data by referring to findings that roughly belong to the categories of ethos, logos, and pathos and continue by presenting the data that points to the distinguishing preaching capacities with the potential of (dis)connecting with the listeners. The data exhibited here will not follow the strict order of interview questions but rather reflect the vividness of experience and involvement of interviewees and will be sorted in a way that helps us to recognise both emerging trends or common themes, and divergence from the dominant patterns.

The rest of this chapter will be based on excerpts from the transcripts.[2] I will either offer a textual description of participants' experience or provide verbatim examples of their comments. Whenever a quote represents other similar quotes, I will identify this by words such as "Many congregants claim." On the other hand, I will also signal if a quote can be found in only one or few interviews. Facts such as gender, age, or the size or geographical context of the congregation are supplied only when they are highly relevant to a specific comment. Care was taken to ensure participants' anonymity so any particulars that could reveal a congregation, town, or person's identity

---

2. All material from these interviews are documented in footnotes using a matching interview code.

has been excluded. However, some details of the context of the interviewee's answer are given when necessary.

At this point, several remarks about the language are also appropriate. All interviews were conducted and then transcribed in the Croatian language. Quotes that appear here are translated but I tried to render them in a way that preserves the properties of oral communication; thus they may contain fragmented sentences, grammatical errors, repetitions, and similar elements that depart from standard English usage. My goal was to make the translation as literal as possible to keep participants' input intact. Yet, minor editing was done in cases where it guaranteed a better understanding or where it was essential to protect the anonymity of the participants.

Lastly, apart from quotes and the descriptions, this presentation also includes my comments on how particular themes operate for particular respondents. These are the points where the descriptive approach blends into the interpretative task, although hopefully, they are only precursors of a more elaborate process of interpretation that will follow in the next chapter.

8.1 Ethos

Traditionally, the ethos as a mode of appeal incorporates concerns related to the character of the preacher. Here, however, the interview questions are also aimed at discovering how congregational culture bears upon individuals' predisposition for listening. Therefore, this section brings data gathered in interviews that relate to the dependability, character, and personality of the preacher but also material that discloses a communal perspective in which the practice of sermon listening goes beyond the mere individual experience and incorporates ways in which preaching affects the congregation as a community.

8.1.1 Communal Dimension

For many listeners in this study, growing intimacy with other members is one of the most important aspects of their community's life. At the same time, it is a marker of ethos as their primary setting. Consider how this is voiced by a respondent in a description of her engagement in the project of visiting older, lonely members initiated by two young people from the church:

> We hug each other, we love each other, but it is too short. I see some people only when they come on Sunday. This is too short for me. And now this project by Andreja and Boris . . . it makes us get to know each other better apart from Thursday and Sunday [meetings]. To get connected and that makes our faith stronger and makes us encourage our neighbours.[3]

The same notion is further enhanced by earnestly attending church meetings other than Sunday service and by their grateful involvement in additional church activities. The flip side of this concern can be seen in their tendency to verbalise their dissatisfaction with other people in the congregation who do not spend enough time together or to confess that they miss more open conversations or sermons about issues relevant for the congregation, including uncomfortable ones. For instance, a respondent claims that people may be threatened by "explosive" themes precisely because they tend to come and only "absorb like a sponge" or receive other people's time and money without ever giving anything from themselves. Her closing words reflect concern for the wellbeing of the community: "So, I think some themes might be more dangerous than others, but this should not prevent the pastor from preaching on them. Because if they are not preached on, they get swept under the carpet. And what gets under the carpet once it escalates only gets worse than it would be if it was talked about regularly."[4] This high regard for the fellowship is also evidenced by the relatively frequent use of terms such as "family," "organism" or "body." The same participant explains:

> This is why we are a living organism – because we are weak sometimes and we need someone to pull us, or to carry us, or to serve us. And sometimes we are stronger and we can carry others, but if we don't act, if we come and go without greeting or seeing anyone and if we do so Sunday after Sunday, then we are not part of the congregation.[5]

Another interviewee recalls that she moved around a lot in her life but never lost connection with her home church. She explains why: "I never lost

---

3. B1.
4. B3.
5. B3.

that, but I think this is because of relationships. I mean, this is where my friends go to . . . You may find God in other congregations as well but here is my family. That's how I see it. The other family. The spiritual one."[6] This congregational dimension can be perceived as crucial even when a particular respondent struggles with diversity within a community. Such is a case of a young doctor who uses bodily imagery:

> God teaches me that I need to change, that people are different, they are like an image of a body. Within the body, every cell is different . . . somebody is a heart and it beats, while others are static but they are needed as well. It wouldn't work without them . . . In my Bible, until recently I saw only "Love the Lord your God with all your heart," but I didn't see what comes next ["Love your neighbour as yourself"].[7]

These and other comments unveil a special relational aspect that these listeners regard as a safe environment necessary for listening to sermons. How safe they feel is directly affected by their perception of the quality of fellowship and intimacy between members of their congregation. For that reason, we may suspect that their listening inclinations are both framed and swayed by this communal dimension. To test that, let us examine their responses that describe their listening involvement in more detail.

First, a number of interviewees describe the experience of listening in terms of feeling connected with others, of belonging to the "Body of Christ." This bond is felt either through the perception that a particular message is addressed to the congregation to which the listener feels attached to or through the recognition after listening to the sermon that others may have also been touched or moved. The other person's reaction may additionally intensify the listener's experience. In any case, the reception of a sermon takes place simultaneously with the deepening of solidarity and it helps people to "open up" and begin to share their problems which they previously may have considered unique to them.

Also, these listeners tend to consider ethical living as a crucial test of their response to preaching. This is the "hardest part" and it may include forgiving

---

6. B2.
7. A2.

one's brother "seventy times seven" or "praying for your enemies." Trying to clarify how listening translates into everyday life, a respondent, who is a former member of the local human rights committee, says, "These examples from the Bible make us take a stand toward life, toward our neighbour, toward the stranger. It is important, morality is. If something is absent nowadays today, it is morality. And the need to bring joy to other people's lives."[8] At one point that person delivers a very strong statement: "One actually lives through the other people – through them one becomes aware of who he is."[9] Another respondent recalls a sermon during which he became aware of the need to approach another church member, a single mother with three children – she was a regular attendee, but this particular sermon urged him to make a decision to talk to her and check whether she needs help or to see how he can address her needs in an appropriate way. Interestingly, he does not remember anything specific about the sermon – what scriptural passage was read or what were the main points.

Particularly impressive is the case of a respondent who remembers the first sermon after the burial of her spouse following his premature death. She interpreted the message about this loss as an invitation to the entire congregation to resume his ministry and service to the community. She was able to hear because the preacher attributed meaning to her personal and collective emotion of pain by placing it within the congregational framework. She says, "At the end, we all cried, but I think nobody was really sorrowful ... He provided a purpose to it ... I think it was really felt. This fellowship of all of us who were present there."[10]

This picture of communal dimension changes, though, with several participants who enter the sermon through the logos setting. Although some of them also hold a high opinion of fellowship and believe it is the most notable part of their congregation's life, the scope of those relationships is usually much narrower. The intimacy found within a congregation is precious for these respondents because there they can find *a few* like-minded individuals or couples. In other words, for their fellowship, only a small company of people who share something essential is needed. Their relationships with

---

8. B1.
9. B1.
10. B3.

others outside of such groups do not possess the same quality or magnitude. One such respondent, in her fifties, puts it this way: "I have no time to think about others . . . If I can find three people in my life, three friends who think and reason in the same way, that's enough for me . . . And what the majority [thinks], I honestly don't know, and I am not even interested to find out."[11]

8.1.2 Authentic Life of a Preacher

Among listeners who take in sermons through ethos settings, there is another area where it seems they express almost unanimous agreement. To begin with, these participants consider a preacher's approachability as something crucial, especially when a preacher is also a pastor. He or she should be ready to discuss believers' questions and provide time for them when they express their pastoral needs. However, more than one respondent implies that timely provision of pastoral care has intrinsic consequences for their readiness to listen to sermons. In the words of one respondent, "But preacher who is present [in a pastor's role] . . . must know how to make both himself and the word of God reachable . . . that is, he must be approachable in a preached word and in his behaviour."[12] One of the participants openly admits that she does not feel particularly related to the pastor as she prefers a certain personal distance, yet, she also considers honesty and open communication as a basis of good relationships and a requirement of the pastor's job.

An even more dominant feature in these comments is the integrity of the preacher's life. For me, it was a striking discovery that this feature has also been singled out by some respondents for whom ethos is not a primary setting.[13] Regardless of other listening preferences, whenever a preacher lives an authentic life of correspondence between his sermons and his daily living, it enhances their listening disposition. When asked to describe a pastor who is also a good preacher, a respondent refers to her pastor and clarifies, "He does not live a life different from what he preaches." After being probed whether this is important in a sense that listeners will hear him better because of such

---

11. A1.
12. B3.
13. This reality is evidence that individual listening preferences cannot and should not be limited to a single setting but rather appreciated as an intricate composition within which the most outstanding note can be easily heard. Yet, this does not exclude the existence of other, subdued but equally contributing notes.

lifestyle, she replies, "Yes, it is. When you feel that he indeed believes in what he preaches."[14] The same respondent then supports her claims by contrasting his case with the discrepancies in the life of priests of another church.

Another participant illustrates this by retelling a story of her pastor who is widely known for his engagement during the war when he was ready to perform funeral services, even if the deceased were irreligious or members of a different religion or denomination. This was risky at a time when the town population was deeply divided across religious and ethnic lines and where everyone's life was endangered at any given moment. His funeral sermons often contained a direct invitation to extend forgiveness while other local religious figures usually used their public addresses for agitation against the "other" side.

An interviewee who decided to leave his secular job more than twenty years ago and join his pastor in a Christian charitable ministry did that largely because of the conviction that his pastor was fully authentic in his sacrificial lifestyle. Commenting on the connection between someone's preaching and way of living, he states, "For instance, if I feel that one's preaching is not backed up by his life, if his preaching is only intellectual, it causes a counter-reaction in me. If there is preaching on the need to be hospitable and, at the same time, you never open your home."[15] Thus, the authentic life of a preacher serves as a persuasive argument to listeners that she herself truly believes what she preaches. The related concept is a preacher's consistency; one of the respondents who has been raised in a Baptist family mentions that those most fitting to evaluate it are members of the pastor's family, especially children. If such consistency is missing, this interviewee imagines their reaction will result in problematic behaviour.

A respondent with an experience of interaction with three different pastors presents a perceptive suggestion which implies that a pastoral and preaching integrity includes a willingness to assume the role of receiver of pastoral care or to leave his vantage point. He states it succinctly, "But if the pastor is one to give advice, then he needs to learn how to take advice."[16] The same train of thought can be followed in comments of a younger participant who has been a

---

14. C2.
15. E3.
16. E2.

church member for the last four years. His life-changing decision came about after numerous, intensive conversations with a current pastor. In retrospect, he isolates some of the critical pastor's characteristics that impacted his life: "I know the Holy Spirit is within him when I see him humble and hear him say: 'I missed it, I made a mistake, I don't know enough.'"[17] Such an unexpected attitude obviously earned the respect of this participant and eventually made him more receptive to the pastor's sermons.

All of this shows that for a number of respondents a preacher's lifestyle outside of the pulpit has the potential to either create a ring of truth to her sermons or to repel her listeners. However, I will also mention a single comment that shows how listeners tend to make assumptions about preacher's character and presumed conduct even if she is a stranger to them, and how these assumptions bear upon the reception of the message. A young respondent mentions an instance of listening to the sermon of a visiting Christian director. Prior to the sermon, his wife observed that the preacher looked arrogant and he himself noticed a big ring on his finger. This created a prejudice which was not shattered until after the sermon when the visiting preacher in the local cafe secretly paid for a drink for the entire youth group.

8.1.3 Internal Ethos

Apart from the comments related to the preacher's character as perceived outside of the pulpit, the respondents also made several observations which deal with what Hogan and Reid call a preacher's persona.[18] They refer to elements that contribute to the preacher's projection of their character within the sermon, even if the preacher is not aware of her involvement in that process.

In the first place, there are factors that may weaken persuasiveness from the start. A respondent brought up in a Christian setting who personally knows several preachers says it is easier for her to hear a preacher she is not related to. For her, the *external* ethos of a preacher (i.e., the sum of all her judgements and perceptions of his character) she knows personally overrides the possibility of development of an *internal* ethos (i.e., making decisions about his trustworthiness as his sermon unfolds), and thus represents a hindrance to her listening.

---

17. A3.
18. See the discussion under Section 3.3.1.

In a similar fashion, the sloppy use of illustrations, deficient reporting on supposedly true stories, or insufficient knowledge of the subject, all create distrust in listeners. A consistent response from participants shows they naturally resist sermons in which they feel a preacher patronises them. Respondents named several manifestations of this attitude; one of them is the use of language that promotes exclusion. By continuously addressing listeners in terms of a *me-you* relationship, preachers create a gap that places them on a higher moral ground.

A related symptom of patronising is a straightforward judgemental stance – by refusing to take the listeners' side or appreciate their positions, a preacher distances himself from them in a way that makes their identification with his position inconceivable or at best highly unlikely. An interviewee provides a metaphorical description of being exposed to such sermons: "There was this barrier and a distance as if he [the preacher] is three light-years closer to the Lord than us."[19] Thus, patronising in preaching conveys a negative ethical message about a preacher that effectively abolishes anything else communicated through other modes of appeal.

Of course, the participants also talk about factors with a reinforcing effect. For instance, certain elements of delivery can easily function as a test of the preacher's truthfulness – his facial expressions, his entire behaviour during the preaching, or speaking "from the heart" – all of these may render a preacher's performance as persuasive because they suggest honesty and dependability. Also, some interviewees point out that preachers, especially those with a full-time ministry, should preach using their maximum potential. Standing next to the entrance after the church service is over and being ready to converse with listeners, to provide a word of clarification or simply to receive a comment or two is perceived by one of the respondents as meaningful in a sense that it proves that the preacher takes both her sermon and audience seriously and allows this relationship to develop even after the sermon is over. Still another respondent contrasts preaching when the words are read from the manuscript with a sermon where listeners get the impression of the preacher's full immersion in the moment. All these individual traits demonstrate that the exposure to such preaching is engaging and increases the believability of

---

19. A5.

the message. Still, these are mentioned only by occasional listeners in contrast to the next dimension of internal ethos: preaching from personal experience.

No matter what their orientation to listening is, preaching from personal experience receives wide recognition from listeners in this study. They repeatedly and extensively point out various advantages of the sermon which contains an element of personal experience. For one thing, a fair number of them prefer the real-life experiences to fabricated stories that were probably used in previous sermons. Also, some of them may come with an expectation to hear an actual experience of a real person that may reverberate somehow with an issue they are trying to deal with. Life is not easy and ready-made answers simply do not fit. Further, there is an assumption among some interviewed congregants that the preacher's claiming the sermon as his own (because something experiential happened during the preparation) makes the sermon better for the listeners as well.

For several listeners, the value of the personal experience of the preacher can be identified in their anticipation of a visible link between her experience and the passage she uses in the sermon. Their statements call attention to the notable consequence of that connection: the appropriate use of stories and illustrations from personal experience can indeed help listeners to remember and appropriate the message. The proof is the ability of some of them to trace back specific episodes or illustrations from a sermon and connect them to particular portions of the Scripture; several of them did just that while being interviewed.

Furthermore, preaching from personal experience (and from failures, in particular) can be much more convincing when the purpose is to urge listeners to examine themselves or to correct certain behaviour. By providing her own example, including the eventual experienced consequences, a preacher may help listeners to overcome excuses and make decisions. A logos-oriented respondent offers an emphatic argument for such use of personal experience in sermons: "Look, what is written in the Bible and those books, all of that is more or less only a theory, but when one tells you something from his own life, well, that is quite something. I always say that one can learn from others' mistakes."[20] Another respondent also alludes to the relationship between lived experience serving as a stimulus for the preacher, the listener's impression of

---

20. E4.

being spoken to by God, and their perception of the preacher being inspired. It does not come as a surprise, then, that when comparing such a sermon with a sermon that mainly provides historical background information, a participant clarifies why the former is superior: "I am always moved more by someone's life experience because I can identify with it and I see the comparison – a life experience, God, us – and this is somehow the most powerful for me . . . It is as if this [sermon] directs a spotlight on you, on your life, on things you do and contrasts it with God's [plan]."[21] The only warning concerning the use of personal experience comes from a participant who suggests that the preacher's experience should not stand in the way of listeners' acceptance of the word of God through their own personal experience. In other words, a preacher's personal apprehension should not overshadow the word of God.

Some respondents in this study reveal at least one more feature responsible for the development of the preacher's *persona*: vulnerability. According to them, there is no universal recipe for it. A preacher can render it by an honest recognition of having problems with certain biblical truths or Christian practices, or by publicly confessing some sin or weakness, or by some other act of sincerity. The bottom line is that exposure of his human nature, shared with his listeners, seems to prompt hearers to look upon the preacher as a trustworthy person. If this happens, they are more likely to perceive the sermon as something worked out by the Holy Spirit.

To sum up: The participants in this study express noticeable susceptibility to ethos-related concerns that to a variable extent affect their listening. For many of them, these concerns literally determine their primary setting through which they hear a sermon. For them, a strong sense of communal identity and fellowship are both the preconditions and the payoff of sermon listening. They listen located within the community and their response to preaching is tested by means of their ethical behaviour within that same community. Also, there are other ethos-related considerations held important by participants regardless of their primary setting, pertaining to the preacher's qualities. One is a credible way of living defined in terms of integrity (a life attuned to one's preaching), approachability, teachability and intensive pastoral commitment (in the case of a preacher with pastoral duties). Another is the preacher's internal ethos. A preacher's stance and use of language that

---

21. A2.

promotes exclusion of his listeners through a patronising or judgemental approach are features with a negative impact on listeners' inclination to hear. On the other hand, there are manifestations of character capacities that stimulate congregants' active reception. If the preacher's performance suggests the use of her maximum potential (usually perceived by listeners as "well-prepared"), she is more likely to earn listeners' attention and respect. Also, exposing her human nature during the sermon in some act of vulnerability increases the probability of hearers' acceptance of her character as dependable. Above everything else, the participants mention preaching from personal experience because of its high identification potential.

8.2 Logos

My next move is to depict the spectrum of themes that arose as I probed the appeal of reason in preaching. The key idea is to understand what sort of content and argumentation in preaching will facilitate or obstruct listening. The gathered data often focuses the researcher's attention on the sources of authority and the substance of sermon messages.

8.2.1 Role of the Bible

As I was beginning my research, my initial expectation was that the theme of the Bible would gain a lot of attention from the participants. Given its outstanding status in both the theology and practice of Croatian Baptists, it is not surprising that this expectation did not prove unfounded. However, I will investigate what they really think and believe about the Bible in relation to the preaching.

To begin with, among logos-oriented participants, I discovered a consistent presence of statements claiming that the Bible is simply essential for preaching. Consider, for instance, these two opinions: "I think there is no sermon without a Bible. I don't think it can be. If it were, I would leave that very moment,"[22] and "It [the Bible] is a required literature and every sermon begins from the Bible and must return to it."[23] In addition to this, it is possible to notice a hint of identifying the Bible with God's spoken word. For

---

22. C3.
23. D1.

instance, a theologically educated participant explains the role of the Bible in preaching by saying, "It is a source, a foundation, a basis. It's something a pastor studies and prepares from . . . So, the Bible is the most important. Without it, there is no . . ., I mean, Word is a Word."[24] Given such proximity between the written and preached Word, every pastor has a "responsibility" to use the Bible from the pulpit. However, another rather telling comment and suggestion come from an ethos-oriented participant who happens to be a traditional Baptist. He argues for using a hardcover Bible instead of small paperbacks, wall projections of the text on the screen or operating with electronic readers. When asked to explain the difference, he replies:

> Well, only this awe, awe for the Word, although Word has the same significance [regardless of media]. Maybe it is about small signs of holiness, some relics. Maybe we have too few relics in our church, maybe we should introduce icons, statues, maybe some symbols. Of course, the Bible is always the first and personal symbol.[25]

For him, the Bible in its most material form is so precious that he ascribes to it almost a sacramental value. The fact that he deliberates about the use of "symbols" in worship and believes the Bible should be highest among them, although the typical Baptist worship is devoid of almost any visual element, is probably the best indication of how central the Bible is for him, and not only in relation to preaching.

When urged to further account for the Bible's role in preaching, the participants offered various cues. One of them is that a sermon is supposed to be "biblical." This does not necessarily mean long scriptural portions being read at the beginning or numerous biblical quotations being recited during the sermon. For them, it primarily means an alignment with the truths of the gospel or having a foundation in Christian principles. Another listener directs our attention to the potential of the Bible to supply a diversity of preaching subjects. What happens, though, is that preachers sometimes have their "favourite" passages that get preached about often, while others remain unknown to the listeners. Somewhat contrary to that, a concern for biblically illiterate

---

24. E5.
25. E2.

listeners and newcomers obliges another participant to counsel preachers to use Old Testament texts only as a supporting evidence for the sermon based on the New Testament passage because they can be a source of confusion if preached about on their own. Another respondent, with some personal preaching experience, is far more aware how dependent the role of the Bible is on our interpretation. He holds that preaching should be aware of culturally determined elements in the Bible. Besides, the Bible is not capable of portraying the exhaustive picture of life, human existence, and God. Yet he claims that the Bible still remains normative and concludes, "That is, we must take into account cultural and every other factor, but if we dislodge the Bible I don't know what would be our foundation for preaching?"[26] And then there is the only dissonant voice that comes from a pathos-oriented interviewee:

> Well, in my opinion, it [the Bible] is only a skeleton. And the meat is experiences, testimonies and stories so that it can become familiar and realistic because in the Bible it is abstract and unreal. So, I think preacher can make those verses closer to me through narration and sermon because I wouldn't reach some of those conclusions, images, ideas or something by myself.[27]

This person evidently does not find the biblical text sufficient in a way a majority of participants do. In order to hear, this person needs preaching that will make a biblical text come alive and appeal to his emotions.

8.2.2 Authority

The next vital theme in hearers' experience of sermon listening is the issue of authority. The participants were asked straightforwardly: When is the sermon authoritative for you? The gathered responses essentially disclose two hubs of authority. But after they offered an initial answer, asking them to provide additional clarification caused a state of perplexity in a number of respondents. A nonverbal reaction of some of them almost led me to believe they are struggling with questions they never honestly asked themselves.

Now, the first hub does not come as a surprise, given the distinguished role of the Bible, as discussed above. More than a few respondents with various

---

26. E4.
27. A4.

primary settings agree that they consider a sermon as authoritative when they find that the sermon's message is in harmony with the Bible. When asked, "So, the sermon must be based on the word of God?" a respondent speaks for several others in her answer, "There is no other way. A preacher can't preach from the pulpit something contradictory to what God tells us in the Bible. If it's related to, if it's connected to, if it's in agreement with what God said, then what is preached is authoritative."[28] For those congregants, a sermon is authoritative whenever it is rooted in the Bible.

But when it comes to the criteria of making a judgement on this correspondence, they are not single-minded. There are interviewees who simply check the sermon against the wider biblical testimony. A comparison with a listener's own interpretation is also mentioned here. There is also the listener who thinks that a sermon has an authority *per se* because of its equivalence with the word of God: "Well, if we equate sermon with the word of God, then I wouldn't dare to say that it doesn't have authority over me."[29] Yet, a believer who relatively recently joined a Baptist church, refers to a sermon he heard in another congregation and claims that it felt "not right" although everything the preacher said was correct and in accordance with the Bible. It seems that, at least for some listeners, a mere conformity to biblical truths does not necessarily ensure a sermon's authoritative appeal.

This is probably why another hub can be identified, especially among ethos-oriented listeners. There are individuals who recognise the authority of a sermon not only in its Bible-based nature but also in the preacher's role and in his or her ethos. Holding a preacher's position in high esteem and, in the case of their pastor, maintaining a relationship characterised by trust and confidence makes these listeners prone to accept the sermon as authoritative for them. A long-time believer clarifies this, "A pastor has his own authority, and the emphasis is given on who the pastor is and why he is a pastor so that the sermon itself has an authority, too. I mean, a pastor has a conditional authority which means he can preach his sermon with an authority."[30] In other words, some hearers can grant *bona fide* authority to the preacher prior to the sermon, provided they respect his position or have

---

28. B3.
29. A5.
30. E2.

respect for his character and lifestyle. Yet, if a sermon fails to meet the biblical criterion, listeners will probably ignore it (partially or entirely) despite their positive relationship with the preacher. Listening to such a sermon, one of the respondents graphically uses an industrial image of rejected material being transported away from a production line.

Another intriguing detail is the fact that an additional requirement is mentioned among listeners whose entry point to the sermon is logos setting. One of them relies strongly on his rational capacities in processing the sermon but he evaluates its authority by measuring its outcomes: "It [the sermon] must have some subsequent effect. Usually, I experience something immediately or little after – I am lucky to experience it on the spot. It isn't anything sensational, but useful. And typically I will be reminded of that later and I will get back to it."[31] Still another congregant feels the authority of the sermon if it "challenges" or "motivates" her or provokes a "reaction." One additional response comes from a listener who longs for more demanding sermons that would draw him out of his "comfort zone." For him, it happens through solid interpretation and exposition of the biblical text (as opposed to the merely emotional appeal), "Whenever I can remember that he [the preacher] arrived at these conclusions through interpretation and elaboration and passed them on, I will be compelled to work on that and study them . . ."[32] In all these cases, the sermon's authority is reflected in the ability of its message to prompt listeners to act on it or to deal with it not only while hearing the preacher's words, but also at some point in the future.

8.2.3 Sermon Content

Many questions from the interview prompted answers discussing the matter of the content of the sermon.[33] This is a good reason to hear what they have shared about this specific theme. But before I proceed with the presentation of their comments, I start with a slightly astonishing finding: when directly asked to describe the content of any particularly interesting or relevant sermon,

---

31. A5.
32. E5.
33. This is true not only for logos-related questions 1–5 but also for the feedback on questions 2 and 7 from the ethos section and on questions 1–5 from the pathos portion, which occasionally also abound with insights and impressions about what is or should be the content of the sermon.

the respondents usually had a hard time pinpointing a specific sermon. Yet, as they continue to discuss other properties of their sermon listening experience, many of then gradually come up with the details of the content of individual sermons.

First, a few congregants who listen to sermons through the logos setting tend to define the sermon in terms of continuous learning. A respondent in her mid-fifties, brought up in a Baptist home, articulates this notion in the following way: "Hence I think this sort of learning is a lifelong learning. This realm of transcendent . . . is generally so unexplored that I think there is no end to it."[34] This learning process receives inputs during the sermon and then extends into the week, as demonstrated by another interviewee:

> There must be a trace of evidence that I learned something from the sermon, that I remembered something through those verses . . . That I have something to put into practice. I underlined important parts and I will revise them many times and they will come back to me during the week under some circumstances and it means that this sermon is a healthy seed which springs and works.[35]

Do they offer any insight on the subject matter of that educational development? The congregant who spoke of lifelong learning sheds some light upon this question: "Or to see through history, biblical history of people and how God acted in their time, how he approached them, and how this can be related with us today. How can this connection be established nowadays because we are separated by so many things."[36] She seems to be concerned with bridging the gap between the world of the Bible and the contemporary circumstances of listeners. That may demand that a preacher provide historical background data which makes it easier for listeners to grasp the original meaning and, to some extent, perceive its possible relevance.

Another question worth asking is: At what level does this learning take place? Apparently, listeners who enter the sermon through the logos setting are prone to think this content must reference substantial truths of the Bible

---

34. A1.
35. D1.
36. A1.

and offer reliable information that invites listeners to respond by rational thinking. A few of them affirm that this is the reliable part of a church service, since other elements, including worship, usually based on music and singing, may be too affected by emotional aspects. One of them puts it like this: "I consider worship as a sort of emotion and I view sermon as a rational part of the whole thing . . . If you depend only on worship, then I don't see how . . . Word and the truth are always the same. Whatever my emotions are, like it or not, it [the truth] is always the same."[37] In his view, preaching with this sort of rational content produces food for thought while everything else is too fickle and easily gets deflated. Some of them affirm that such preaching directly addresses their personal problems and situations. One of them expands on this by mentioning the cumulative effects of sermons: "For instance, I went through a period of switching a job . . . through that turbulent time I was exposed to a sermon every seven days which is four sermons a month for a half a year, that is, 24–25 sermons. This meant so much for my taking an attitude and deciding what happens next and what [to do] if something goes wrong."[38] So, considering all these comments, one can only state the obvious: these listeners are more disposed to hear the content of a sermon if they can perceive it as a part of the learning process that takes place on a rational level.

On the other hand, some listeners whose entry points to the sermon differ from logos are inclined to have a different attitude toward such sermons. One of them makes a comment on their helpfulness: "So, these are good sermons, useful and necessary. They make it easier for me to understand [the Bible] but nothing really happens then."[39] A similar impression is provided by a person involved in the worship of his local congregation who compares them with some theological lectures he attended in the past. They were "informative" but not "practical."[40] A pathos-oriented listener observes not being able to get answers she genuinely needs from sermons. She refers to the repetition of sermons that provide "basics," but fail to consider more complex questions or actual experiences of listeners. In support of her claims, she reports that sermons did not help her to understand the tensions in God's nature (i.e.,

---

37. A3.
38. D1.
39. A2.
40. D2.

kindness and the determination to punish sins) or to deal with her personal problem of not being able to see God as a father.[41] Responses like these propose there are congregants who consider such sermons as effective *only* on an intellectual level but without immediate bearing on their personal lives.

8.2.4 God in the Sermon

One interview question probes the hearers' hopes of finding more about God through listening to the sermon. Given that all interviewed participants are believers who, by definition, ground their faith in a personal transcendent reality, a careful approach to their feedback is called for. If we can postulate that their Christian identity is to a high degree determined by their notion of that ultimate divine being, then we will certainly profit from looking at how this notion is being shaped as they participate in the regular practice of listening to sermons.

Listening to participants whose primary setting is logos shows a recurring motive that can loosely be labelled as a need for logical and rational explanations. Concerns they express include the possibility of influencing God's decisions through prayer, the meaning and purpose of suffering, and the notion of free will. An example of such concerns, asked by a mature Christian:

> There is always that question: Why it must have happened that way? Why must it have been that way? When one sees all the evil, suffering and everything that takes place in this world for thousands of years, without any change apart from names and actors, I must admit that I sink into depression. God, why?[42]

A few sentences later, the same person expresses the same anguish even more vividly, "Preach the gospel of God's goodness if you can! I remember a person who was gang-raped during the war by her schoolmates. And you see this broken person, *[sighs]* and then, 'God is love, God is good.'"[43] Similar concerns are voiced in a response provided by another middle-aged interviewee, "That's right, [I want to find out] what is the purpose he has for humans and what does he expect from them. Also, why the suffering, why problems

---

41. A4.
42. E3.
43. E3.

in the world, why violence, why downfalls, why do we live in a controlled chaos, why is this happening and where the answers can be found."[44] These and some other respondents appear to have some established convictions about God but, as a matter of course, also have a collection of their personal experiences and immediate observations drawn from a daily life that does not automatically conform to their proclaimed faith. What they might hope to receive from sermons is something that will help them to reconcile these apparent contradictions and acquire some further knowledge that will help them to better understand the God they believe in.

At the same time, there is a need for logical disclosure of God's characteristics as a means of either advancement or consolidation of one's faith and spiritual well-being. Depending on their preferences and previous experience, respondents may expect a preacher either to reveal something new about God or to reiterate what was already adopted at an earlier stage. Consider this listener, an experienced Christian with a theological education, who reflects on a substantial finding related to the particular portion of Scripture: "I need discoveries like these to show me another feature of God, of Jesus. And this kind of interpretation of Sermon on the Mount, which is a major doctrine of the New Testament, really got me inspired!"[45] Likewise, another listener, a first-generation Baptist without advanced education, responding to the question of his expectation about a sermon helping his knowledge of God, says, "Most of all, I want to understand as much about him as I can . . . I want to improve [in that knowledge] and to affirm again, if necessary."[46] In both cases, these motivating impulses to find out more about God require a form of preaching that brings some logical facts, sound interpretation, or well-reasoned twists of existing knowledge.

A bit more surprising, though, is the curiosity about God's relational traits among logos-oriented respondents. Several of them clearly express a desire to hear about the reality of God as a person with whom it is possible to establish and maintain a relationship of love. This is a consideration shared with some interviewees who hear sermons on pathos and ethos settings. To be more specific, these listeners tend to listen to sermons with a special attentiveness

---

44. D1.
45. E5.
46. C3.

to anything that may teach them how to achieve intimacy with God or how to nurture that closeness in a daily life. An ethos-oriented listener, an educated musician and worship leader elsewhere laments about the domination of spoken word over the music and singing. But responding to the question of what he wants to find out about God, he says, "What plan God has for mankind, how can His mission become ours, how can I obey His will, how can I worship him properly, how can I be pleasing to him, how can I touch other people's life by God's love and what do I need to change?"[47] A similar emphasis on the importance of the appropriate response to God's love is echoed in the reply of a female believer who began attending church meetings twelve years ago. She declares, "Personally, I really want to know what sort of person I need to be in order to be a believer in God's eyes, someone who truly follows the rules. When I first started going to the church, I knew that psalm: 'I thirst for you, my whole being longs for you!'"[48] A more mature believer underlines a hunger for sermons that revive in listeners an awareness of God's caring relationship, "I like to hear that God is gracious, that God helps, that God is a friend during difficult times, that he is with us during good times, too . . . I like to hear that he cares even when I'm no longer able to care."[49] So, these congregants, irrespective of their primary setting, are ready to learn and take in new insights or be reminded of those already known insofar as they will enable them to better comprehend and, consequently, to nurture their relationship with God.

In summary, the respondents' opinions about matters pertaining to the preacher's appeal through different lines of argument can be grouped under four main ideas. First, many of them agree that the Bible is, in some sense, essential and indispensable for preaching. This belief is supported by various convictions about the nature of preaching, including the one that equates the *written* word of God with the sermon as the *preached* word of God. But there is also a broad awareness that its value for preaching is highly reliant on the preacher's competency to interpret the written Word and bring out its content in a way that will spur and enlighten his listeners' private reading of the Bible.

---

47. D2.
48. C2.
49. E2.

Secondly, the issue of what represents authority upon which persuasive arguments are to be built in preaching gives rise to two different, perhaps complementary, answers. One says that rootedness in the Bible is the ultimate test of a sermon's authority. There is not much clarity or agreement, though, among participants on what criteria are to be applied in determining this rootedness. The other answer focuses on the preacher's role, as some ethos-oriented listeners assign a conditional authority to the preacher's position and function, while there are also logos-oriented hearers who are more inclined to locate authority in the preacher's efficiency in crafting a sermon that evokes a response and brings about an outcome in and among listeners.

Thirdly, when it comes to the sermon content, there is a noteworthy dissimilarity between logos-oriented listeners and the rest of the participants. The former tends to be highly receptive to a sermon providing reliable information that stimulates rational thinking. They are also inclined to appreciate the practice of regular sermon listening as a process of "continuous learning." By comparison, other interviewees are far less captivated by lecture-type sermons that fail to address their real-life experiences.

Fourthly, the listeners' feedback on the question about what they would like to find out about God in a sermon demonstrates among logos-oriented participants a proclivity for preaching that enhances their cerebral knowledge of God or offers solutions for the contradictions between their convictions and observed realities. Yet some listeners with various primary settings also manifest attentiveness to those elements of a sermon that portray God's person and thus stimulate the growth of their relationship with God.

8.3 Pathos

The final set of questions is designed to elicit participants' view of the emotional dimension of their experience of listening to sermons. Asking these questions required congregants to identify when their emotions were aroused and what caused this to happen, to think about what they are more likely to decide or do when under the sway of feelings stirred by the sermon, and to identify the gamut of emotional responses a sermon can set in motion within them. Furthermore, apart from the level on which the emotional dimension of preaching appeals to individuals, some of these questions intentionally explore the level of congregational pathos; I will begin from there.

8.3.1 Congregational Emotions

There is a response that consistently appears across interviews with participants with various listening preferences. A number of them, when asked to describe a sermon that stirred their personal or collective emotions, recalled sermons preached during the time of crisis – usually a situation when a pastor or respected church member was very seriously ill or passed away recently. So, a female respondent describes the period after a sudden death of a committed church member: "During last two or three years, there was a sense of loss. And the pastor would burst into tears in the midst of his sermon. There was this grievance and then everyone would cry. And the reason why is . . . well, this bond and fellowship among people. Maybe the cause was not the sermon itself but this whole situation."[50] Another interviewee remembers the occasion when a respected member was ill and asked elders to anoint him with oil and pray for him. He recognises this particular service to be a moment when the congregation felt emotionally moved as they practised their compassion and love for their member: "It was such an atmosphere in which all of us felt as one and we felt God. He [the ill member] also testified the same, but only later on. That he felt it too. Not the healing, but some sort of presence."[51]

Interestingly, although instructed to evoke a *sermon*, the interviewees are usually not able to reconstruct the content of the sermon's message. What they are able to remember, though, is a sermon's occasion, its *Sitz im Leben* and the immediate or delayed effects of the sermon. This observation is valid not only in the case of crisis sermons mentioned above but also true for other occasions. For instance, a logos-oriented listener recognises a strong connection between sermons preached on Sundays when the congregation celebrates the Lord's Supper[52] and believers' reaction afterwards. She says that these sermons are "different" and people are "more positive." Her comments seem to suggest that following the ritual helps her fellow believers to emotionally "open up" and this becomes manifest during the informal time after the service. She describes it in this way: "We eat food, people bring cakes

---

50. B2.
51. E5.
52. Croatian Baptists, as a rule, celebrate the Lord's Supper on the first Sunday of each month.

they made at home, we have some tea and we stay at this facility here. And it's obvious that people mingle, talk, express more positive attitude and share with each other and so on." She goes on telling what happened once during that time, "When I asked somebody: 'Hey, how are you?' and she begins to talk: 'I feel terrible, awful . . .,' and she is on the verge of depression, literally. But I think that this is also necessary, right? It is important to know if there is someone with problems in the church and not to think that everyone is OK, right?"[53] Still another member of a different congregation takes note of effects of the emotionally inspiring sermon being present and visible even the next Sunday. He specifies, "At the beginning, people greet each other more often, they wish each other a nice day or God's blessing . . . they are more open for conversations, for anything really – for worship, prayer, singing – they are more open and willing."[54]

An intriguing coincidence occurred when two participants from the same congregation touched upon a specific example of preaching with a persuasive emotional appeal. They singled out two different sermons preached by two different pastors with a similar agenda: to motivate their listeners to make a financial contribution toward purchase or construction of a new church building. In the first case, these funds were used to help a congregation in another town. In a more recent instance, a pastor presented the project of moving to another location and constructing a new and bigger building. Neither of the respondents makes a reference to the actual content or key ideas of the sermons but both describe the outcome in terms of congregational emotional response. One of them explains the preacher's strategy: ". . . it is up to that preacher and his skill how much money will people give. I mention this only as an example because it works. And if he can *stir them up*, you know, or *set them on fire*, they will give more"[55] (emphasis mine). The other one uses the following words to depict believers' attitude during the church service when this offering was collected: "It was emotional as well – when something like this happens, the people are single-minded."[56]

---

53. B2.
54. E2.
55. E4.
56. E2. In Croatian the word *jednodušni* is used. It means that people are united in their thoughts and feelings. Literally, the adjective can be translated as "of the same soul." Obviously, a more emotional connotation is being communicated here.

Finally, a pathos-oriented listener articulates a congregational reaction to an emotionally loaded invitation from a pastor who demonstrated his vulnerability. Instead of only issuing an invitation or asking from believers to raise their hands in a response, the preacher plainly said, "I need you to pray for me!" This listener reports, "I believe that I, and possibly others as well, got moved by this act and emotions. Maybe we did not experience anything special on a cognitive level, but moments like this still help people who really want to do it [respond by committing their life] or to make some decision."[57] From her perspective, preaching can chiefly aspire to the listeners' emotions and still give rise to changes or facilitate their decision-making within the congregational setting.

The gathered feedback appears to suggest that both emotional appeal and emotional response can be triggered by the immediate situation shared by the whole congregation. The experience of pain and loss possesses a potential for making the congregation more connected, because it adds to members' sense of belonging and mutual responsibility. Under such circumstances, people appear to be more taken with the sermon's emotional stimulus.

8.3.2 Listener's Emotions

Certainly, the theme of congregational emotions cannot fully cover the variety of responses expressing the listeners' reactions to the affective elements of preaching. Quite often, interviewees describe their own, individual feedback and feelings without immediate reference to the congregational context; for example, different views of the value of emotions, insights on what triggers their emotional response, or the ways of its manifestation.

The congregants' answers show that their emotions involved in sermon listening may be activated by several different components. Sometimes listeners recognise the preacher's emotions as genuine and real and this recognition can rouse their feelings even if they do not share the experience that evoked preacher's emotions in a sermon. A congregant who is usually not given to expressing her emotions in public confesses it is hard to remain indifferent to the tears of a particular preacher: "Because I feel sorry for him when I see him struggling and then, he also says something. I guess there is something in his life situation – you see, I can't determine whether I cry with him because

---

57. A4.

he cries or I cry because I recognised something that moves me."⁵⁸ In other words, a preacher's emotional involvement with the sermon can create an empathy in listeners and elicit their emotional reaction even if listeners are not able to comprehend where this response comes from.

A personal or congregational crisis can increase the possibility of stirring emotions in listeners. A respondent who claims he is not often emotionally struck with sermons, in his response to the question "What does it look like when a sermon spurs his emotions?" admits nevertheless, "I rarely see that [being struck], but when I do it is usually related to the fact I have already been shaken up. Then it seems as if you want to hear something in every single word. And then perhaps you really hear it. And when I have the same problems, but I am not emotionally down and I feel disinterested, then I will not hear it."⁵⁹ Another listener remembers the sermon she heard at the time she quit her job. Being worried about her future and emotionally troubled made her more receptive to the sermon and she felt directly and emotionally addressed by it. Her anxiety has been relieved by a sermon she understood as a call not to be worried.

Another factor that respondents acknowledge as conducive to their emotional affective involvement is previous participation in worship, especially in singing. Although not a part of the preaching, worship is viewed by some participants as a preparatory stage of the church service that leads to greater openness for the sermon. One of them describes a typical Sunday service and when he comes to the worship, he states, "In this worship, you experience God as he moves you in an emotional way. By doing that, I believe he strikes you so that you can open up your heart, you can open up at an intellectual level."⁶⁰ Another interviewee concisely confirms that worship is a channel through which emotions can flow in, "Worship is about the emotions – to lift me up!"⁶¹

The other element is a novelty of approach. A respondent who genuinely honours her pastor openly admits that it is a sermon preached by a visiting preacher that emotionally lifts everybody. And she readily provides an explanation: "I listen to my pastor every Sunday, I know his gestures, his voice, I

---

58. A1.
59. E5.
60. A3.
61. B3.

know when he will make a pause, what he will say and when he will laugh."[62] Another interviewee, who has listened to sermons since her childhood, recounts a particular sermon preached at the youth camp by someone she never heard before. She claims the sermon struck her emotionally and goes on, "She [a preacher] literally used her hands and legs. I mean, she illustrated the cross with her body and expounded on that verse in many different ways . . . Everything revolved around John 3:16, but she managed to make me understand *for the very first time in my mind and in my heart*, I guess, that he loved me so much that he gave his own son"[63] (emphasis mine). These observations imply that a pastor or regular preacher can become predictable and some listeners grow more and more accustomed to her style and performance. The consequence may be their unintentional resistance to her preaching. For these listeners, there is a connection between listening to a preacher for the first time and the probability they will be moved on an emotional level.

Some listeners who tend to enter the sermon through ethos settings are touched during their listening experience because of the relational dimension. One of them mulls over her connectedness with others during the church service: "For me, the atmosphere is extremely important. Yes. Not even the personal experience but the atmosphere in which . . . you feel this warmth, this intimacy with people. It can be felt after the sermon. At the time we part, we are all stirred. We can hardly wait to see each other again on Sunday, on Thursday."[64] So, it is a sermon that elicits her emotional response and amplifies this sense of bonding with her fellow believers.

This link between pathos and ethos can also be detected in the words of a participant who feels strong emotions of inadequacy and gratitude as she was reminded, through the sermon, of the nature of God's relationship with a sinful human being. When reflecting on the reality of her relationship with God, she says:

> Well, say when we are not even aware that our sins have been redeemed and this gratitude. We don't, we don't experience enough of these big things, for instance, that we are forgiven, that God accepts us as we are. This really moves me . . .

---

62. B3.
63. A4.
64. B1.

What sort of feeling is it?

Well . . . What sort of feeling? Feeling of being worthy, of being something to God, of knowing that he loves you endlessly regardless of how sinful we are and sometimes I think, "Oh, God, we are unworthy of it."[65]

This last reply can serve as a transition toward the next question – Is it possible to pinpoint some explicit emotions or can we name some clear feelings identified by the participants? And how are those usually demonstrated? There are respondents who mention a feeling of being loved or accepted by God as their main affection experienced during the sermon. Similar is an emotion of gratitude and a sense of closeness to God. However, the recurrent response includes pairing some of these emotions with feelings that are not so easily identified. One of the respondents has a hard time labelling the exact nature of that feeling: "Because I don't know how to describe it, it's not . . . it's something between the sorrow and joy. And again, it's neither of these two but something perfect which hits you like nothing else can hit you."[66] This pair of feelings can entail both pleasant and uncomfortable sensations and seems to be commonly related to the listeners' self-perceptions as (forgiven) sinners.

Yet other answers disclose an even more nuanced scope of emotional effects. A middle-aged logos-oriented listener provides details of the development of his emotions: "Yes, well, one thinks through very hard and feels under a strain and then through the sermon a peace can be experienced. It already starts with hymns and you can experience peace and calmness. This is an emotion – you are tense and stressed out, you can't understand but then you reach an insight because of the sermon."[67] For another respondent who perceives sermons through the logos setting, the critical emotion is relief which results in his assurance about making a right decision at a crucial point of his life. On the other hand, a pathos-oriented congregant refers to her emotional experience in listening to a particular sermon as a "catharsis"[68] which helped her to feel cleansed and intimate with God. These remarks show that the emotional engagement in listening can involve a shift that leads a

---

65. C2.
66. A3.
67. D1.
68. A4.

listener from the inducement of one feeling to the shaping of another that will replace that first one. Also, all these emotions are reported as commonly accompanied by some physiological responses, the most frequent being tears. Other reactions mentioned are palm sweating, "floating on a cloud," a rapid heartbeat, and stomach cramps.

Though in these participants a whole spectrum of emotions is born out of intensive sermon listening, there are discernible differences related to their primary settings.

For one, respondents who approach sermons through ethos or pathos settings are more likely to consider emotions as a dependable and credible ground for the decision-making process. A vivid example is found in an instance already mentioned above. During a sermon, an interviewee was made aware of a single mother within a congregation and what compelled him to offer her practical help were feelings of compassion and admiration for her perseverance. Another respondent points out that a sermon can build on already existing emotions in listeners and boost them in a way that stimulates the listeners' actions. He specifically speaks of emotions experienced during his ministry to the Roma children and how those were later refreshed and sustained after listening to a specific sermon.[69] Yet another congregant assigns a supreme function to emotions – at first, she claims that emotions are what differentiate her congregation from other churches and when encouraged to clarify how important emotions are, she answers, "The most important! As a matter of fact, [emotions are] the most important part. To feel in your heart. A heart is God's temple . . . One can feel whether something is right or wrong in one's heart."[70] These listeners' propensity for listening is proportionate to the sermon's appeal to their emotions. Subsequently, the sermon is unlikely to kindle a change in them or propel them to action unless it arouses their emotions.

By comparison, many logos-oriented listeners have a different take on emotions. Some of them have reservations about a public manifestation of emotions, although they will not deny the reality of sermon's appeal to the listeners' pathos. Yet in their view, the stirring of emotions is only a second-rate effect. One of those respondents puts it this way: "It can be seen on

---

69. D2.
70. B1.

people present there, but what will happen when everything sinks down, this is what really interests me – will there be some reaction, will something happen then?" In her view, these emotions are real but it would be superficial to rely on them; a preacher's pathos may appeal to listeners' emotions and call forth their affective response, but that in itself will not cause a change. This same listener sums it up: "But what will really happen on Monday is that everything will settle down. And I am interested in to see whether something of it will remain there. I would like something more than just a handkerchief to remain."[71] This secondary value of emotions is additionally attested in the remark of the participant who believes the role of the worship is to pave the way for the sermon. According to him, the emotional response is profitable insofar as it creates a predisposition for the rational hearing.

Even so, logos-oriented listeners may also receive some benefit from an emotional appeal. A respondent's reaction to a sermon about the prophet Jonah serves as a case in point. In his lengthy explanation of that experience,[72] he reveals how he identified with Jonah's situation and the challenge placed before him; by doing that, the sermon's logos helped him to interpret his previous experience and provided him with some guidelines concerning his next big decision. At the same time, it also enabled him to recognise and name the feelings he struggled with until then and led him to experience relief and joy which set him free to make some decisions and to move on. This shift from anxiety to peace of mind is the point at which his predilection for the sermon's content as the key channel of his reception begins to acquire an emotional outline. Although emotions are not what he expects to attract him to the listening, as the sermon helps him to make sense of his present life and circumstances, they come as well. And they bring along some liberating power with them, too.

Some interviewees confirm that the experience of sermon listening can include negative emotions, too. When directly prompted, they unveil what triggers upsetting emotional reactions. There are those who acknowledge that being addressed by the Bible's teaching in a sermon occasionally elicits negative emotions, such as guilt, shame, or moral incompetence. But they also confess that those emotions helped them mend their ways. This sort

---

71. A1.
72. E3.

of response is sometimes accomplished by preachers asking listeners to reconsider the nature of their relationship with God. This is an experience the listeners naturally want to avoid, but these emotions can still have beneficial consequences. One of the interviewees speaks of a sermon in which the preacher issued a warning against "hiding behind people we know" and urged against the sin of omission when it comes to personal evangelism. She does not see herself as a person who enjoys speaking in public or talking about her faith with strangers. During the sermon, she struggled with sorrow, anger, and guilt and felt rebuked as if the pastor preached only at her. Still, in her reflection on how she perceived this sermon after she had some time to process it, she concludes, "So, at the end of the day, I believe this was a good sermon. Although, at that time I could have lived without it."[73]

On the other hand, the respondents also testify about occasions where their discomfort does not yield any positive thoughts or results. One of them observes that vulnerability of the preacher during the sermon may be interpreted by some listeners as an unwelcome intrusion:

> My explanation of the fact that people will later express their specific opposition toward that exposure is that they are simply not ready or that it is too much for them because at that moment there may be an expectation from the congregation to do the same [to expose themselves] and people either don't want to or aren't ready or are not aware that they could or should do precisely that and this is why they resist.[74]

In this case, it is possible to attribute the cause of his irritation to preachers' crossing the line in his attempt to challenge the hearers. However, the opposite behaviour of the preacher can also be perceived as imposing. When referring to a preacher making an altar call and inviting listeners to publicly confess their sins, a congregant objects to this evading the confession of the preacher's own deficiencies by saying, "And you are not going to say anything about your own life. And there is something to say. If you would say, 'Here, I have a problem with this and I present it to God and you. This is my handicap,

---

73. B3.
74. A4.

my problem. If you have it too, let's pray together.'"⁷⁵ This example in which this congregant apparently feels a resentment indicates that in similar situations listeners can be somewhat subtly pressurized and develop an aversion to the preacher and shut themselves off from the message.

The sincere feedback of a young, pathos-oriented congregant signals a potential danger in preachers' employment of the emotional appeal if they fail to provide guidance or follow-up which will help listeners to act upon their reactions. She provides a striking comparison: "It is as if I come to the psychotherapy session and someone opens me up and makes me aware of some processes but doesn't provide anything for me. I am left there with a question mark and what am I supposed to do with it?"⁷⁶ She reminds us that taking a step of emotional disclosure can result in negative effects for listeners unless they are offered specific suggestions how to work through their emotions and inner process.

Another potential source of distress is the occasion when listeners hear sermons saying something from the Bible which contradicts their beliefs, convictions, or intuition. Their discomfort is enhanced by the recognition it is not the preacher they disagree with, but the Bible itself. A male respondent in his late twenties recalls his reaction to a sermon on Paul's view of marriage. At that point, he has been engaged and he was not able to accept the superiority of celibacy as presented by apostle Paul. He sums up his immediate disposition, "There were some emotions, for sure. After we left the meeting, I didn't feel really pure . . . I felt bad. Am I allowed to? Am I allowed to feel this way? Am I allowed to say that out loud? That I disagree with something from the Bible?"⁷⁷

Finally, respondents also mention manipulation as a cause for their resistance. It can be either a deliberate and shrewd arousal and exploitation of listeners' emotions or the misuse of the Bible. A former Catholic remembers a sermon when the latter took place: "It was experienced once while I was still a member of a Catholic church. During a war, a priest had a sermon that ended

---

75. E3.
76. A4.
77. A3.

up in calling people to hate others. Then, well, I even had no connection with this church [a Baptist church] but I got really angry about it."[78]

The domain of emotional appeal is by no means easy to apprehend. These interviews perhaps offer a peek through a window of insight into listeners' pathos-related predilections. For the sake of clarity, I will only briefly mark out the key sections under which these results fall. On the congregational level, many respondents are receptive to emotional appeals during critical situations. Their feedback also shows that in retrospect, the immediate context and actual effects of the sermon on congregational life are more easily recollected whenever that sermon had an explicit emotional dimension. On the individual level, there are participants who confirm that a preacher's genuine emotions are likely to draw out the listeners' emotional reaction. Some also point out other factors that, for them, add to the likeliness of the emotional appeal, such as previous participation in worship or novelty in the preacher's approach and performance. An observation many congregants agree with is that sermons can incite a wide range of both positive and negative feelings. Accordingly, not all of them react in the same way to the emotional stimulus, neither do they experience the same feelings. For most logos-oriented listeners, the emotions created during sermon listening are only secondary and are too elusive and untrustworthy to be something on which believers should base their decisions or actions. Yet, some of them report experiencing true relief and peace of mind as they responded to an emotionally engaging sermon. In contrast to them, pathos-oriented listeners usually encounter more intensive and more relational emotions. As expected, both they and ethos-oriented interviewees hold that emotions aroused by sermons are a valid and reliable basis and guide for a decision-making process.

8.4 (Dis)connected

After several rereadings of interview transcripts, it became evident that I needed to step out of the threefold scheme of logos, ethos, and pathos if an honest and integral presentation of participants' responses was to be submitted. When my research questions are considered, the data appeared to suggest that listeners not only repeatedly refer to those major features of preaching

---

78. C2.

that help them to connect to sermons but also to the factors that interfere with their inclination to properly hear sermons. Indeed, my interviewees disclose a varied range of both "connections" and "disconnections" that I will try to present now. As I do, two questions may linger in the background and serve as a bridge toward the next chapter when the notion of listeners' expectations will be directly addressed. These questions can be articulated as follows: Are there any distinguishable qualities of a sermon that help preachers to establish rapport with their listeners? And what sort of approach by preachers will inevitably erect stumbling blocks for their listeners and prevent them from engaging with the intended outcome?

8.4.1 Connections

Sermons that manage to set up effective links between the biblical text and the life of listeners instil in them a sense of being connected and caught up. Respondents allude to such ties in many ways and at different stages of the interviews. For instance, when a female in her fifties tries to isolate the highlights of her listening experience, she is not able to retell the contents but she remembers a crucial element and effect: "Now, I can't remember anymore, but there was a very good connection between our lives and lives in the Bible which inspired people to live better, to mend their ways."[79] Another respondent, a traditional Baptist, explains her desire to hear and learn about God and specifies, "Maybe [to find out] from some history, a biblical history of characters from the Bible how he acted, how he approached them and how it can be associated with us today because there is such a huge gap between us and them . . ."[80] If preacher succeeds in establishing this connection, it will increase the probability of these listeners applying the sermon's ideas into their lives.

However, there is no single method of bridging this gap and fostering their receptiveness although some trends can be observed. Some congregants point out examples when sermons addressed specific real-life situations and report on integrated illustrations or word images drawn from their own actual life settings. When they can recognise these situations as realistic and close to their everyday experience, they are also prone to identify with the

---

79. C2.
80. A1.

wider message or impulse of the sermon and to claim it. Probably the most expressive account of this type of response is evident in the words of the oldest listener in this study. Being close to her eighties, she recalls a relatively recent sermon that focused on the importance of decisions. This sermon empowered her to reinterpret her entire life, full of hardships and difficulties, as a series of crucial decisions she was able to make with God's help. She says, "[The sermon] was about how decisions are important and it stayed with me – and I remember even now how decisions are hard to make . . . And then I applied it to my life – how many hard decisions I had to make – to decide to go to the school, to decide to endure life, to finish what I started in my marriage, at my job, and to earn the pension . . . There were many decisions to make."[81] At the same time, the youngest participant discloses a similar sense of being directly spoken to when a sermon addresses him in his immediate context: "When a sermon strikes an issue about which I had the dilemma whether I should have acted in the way I did, maybe at my workplace. And that dilemma got resolved in the spoken message."[82] Yet another listener had a similar experience with a sermon helping him in his work setting: "The message was that God is with us and that we have to pray in these moments. So there were occasions when I sat at a meeting but I would rather not be there. And then I remember the sermon: 'I am sending you out like sheep among wolves, but don't you worry!'"[83]

Apart from being moulded in a way that prompts listeners to relate them to their concrete life experience, sermons can also establish a meaningful connection if listeners perceive them as preached from authentic, personal experience. A first-generation believer vividly recounts her identification with the preacher's life experience and her words deserve to be quoted again:

> I am always moved more by someone's life experiences because I can identify with them and see the comparison – a life experience, God, us – and this is somehow the most powerful for me . . . It is as if this [sermon] directs a spotlight on you, on your life, on things you do and contrasts it with God's [plan].[84]

---

81. E1.
82. A5.
83. D1.
84. A1.

This identification brings not only recognition but gives rise to the sense of being spoken to, of being enlightened. That youngest respondent explains how such a sermon affects him: "I am most easily impressed when the preacher speaks from his own experience, when he starts with himself and without the intention to rebuke us . . ."[85] Another believer still has fresh memories of his youth pastor who often preached by referring to examples from his personal life. This certainly produced a good effect, since "I was able to identify with him because that man not only learned the theory and wanted to be a moralist of some sort to us, but he was also someone who himself went through all of it." Later on, he ponders upon his current pastor's preaching routine and observes that his sermons turn into a spiritual food for the listeners only when the pastor himself "goes through some phase and this reflects in his sermon instantly because it becomes more intimate, more human."[86] A respondent from the same congregation shares a comparable thought, "But there are some sermons where I believe that he learned something, that something clicked during his studies. Something he discovered during the preparation he then puts forward with more passion."[87] These responses reveal that for some hearers preaching that comes out of a genuine encounter of the preacher with her sermonic material adds up to authenticity of a sermon and increases its identification potential.

Several other hints for connecting with a sermon can be discerned from respondents' feedback. For instance, a few congregants realise that the reason for their remembering sermons is the fact that the preacher used some taglines or slogans. Simplicity of language is another characteristic that may advance sermon reception. One of the younger respondents points out that nonverbal communication can be critical for the listeners' reaction. She feels this on an emotional level and explains: "There is a difference if you appear to read from the paper placed next to your Bible with an indifferent look in your eyes or if you are so identified with what you talk about as if you went through it by yourself. And if you did, people really believe that person because she believes in what she preaches." And making a comment on a particularly stirring sermon, she states: "I can observe that I am usually won over by

---

85. A5.
86. E5.
87. E2.

any preacher who succeeds in arousing my curiosity at the beginning."[88] A similar notion is expressed by another respondent who declares that in order to connect, a sermon needs to produce a certain discomfort that "prevents you from lulling oneself to sleep, that invites you to action, or at least, pricks your conscience."[89]

In line with these two comments are the remarks about the usefulness of imagery and multimedia in the delivery of the sermon. Referring to a sermon where a film clip was used, a middle-aged congregant says, "Here [in the church] we [usually] never use the technology we have at home. This is why it was great for me."[90] For another respondent, there is a strong correlation between the use of images and applicability of the sermon. He remembers a preacher who employed word images: ". . . he derived practical images and placed them not only into the introduction, but also into the body of the sermon . . . not in an unrelated way, but so that everything fits. And then you will remember it as a good sermon."[91]

The final contributing factor to be mentioned here is humour. A certain amount of laughter and amusement seems to be more than acceptable to some listeners. One of them simply says, "I am the kind of person who is attracted to humour and then it [the sermon] becomes interesting in itself and I can listen without any effort. It's like watching a TV."[92] Another congregant, also in his twenties, agrees with him: "I like it when there is some humour or something like that. It also sticks in my mind quite a lot."[93]

8.4.2 Disconnections

Before proceeding to discuss the participants' specific observations on the causes of the disconnections, I must stress the more general reality of the state of (occasional or customary) disconnectedness between listeners and their preachers. Explicitly or implicitly, many respondents in this study report on their recurrent exposure to sermons they have trouble following; they cause them to switch off, keep them utterly aloof, or even openly irritate them. An

---

88. A4.
89. E3.
90. A1.
91. D2.
92. A3.
93. A5.

otherwise positive respondent, involved in a number of church activities, speaks bluntly of the regular Sunday sermon: "Personally, I don't receive much on Sundays."[94] She admits that she often struggles with listening and staying awake. Another listener from the same congregation says, "There are sermons when I leave the place and I don't know what it was I listened to. I didn't hear them, they didn't draw any interest, they didn't touch me, and my thoughts were elsewhere – who knows where."[95] An older interviewee, a worship leader, openly confesses that listening to a sermon while standing is his only way of preventing himself from dozing off.[96] So, if this is a verified occurrence, can the interviewed congregants help us to identify some (un)usual suspects as the roots of this detachment?

In the first place, listening to these listeners reveals that they can be turned off when the preacher gets excessively repetitive. This reaction is mentioned several times. Sometimes a preacher basically preaches on the same set of themes, Sunday after Sunday. Describing her pastor from a previous congregation, a young interviewee makes this point: ". . . you get an impression that you listen to the same sermon every Sunday. We always go back to the same topic whatever his starting point was."[97] The problem of repetition can also be detected in undue explanations within the same sermon. Too much description of a single point and the intensity of listeners' attention may peter out. A traditional Baptist in his late forties puts it this way: "For instance, a pastor may begin with a theme or title and he tries to communicate around that topic, with or without the success. Often, he gets lost in descriptions and then the unifying idea is lost, too."[98]

In the second place, the use of ready-made or generic illustrations and stories that neutralise listeners' disposition also can have detrimental effects. Those are easily recognised as fake and bogus. A believer with a long church experience sums this up when referring to some missionaries: "Americans, for instance, heap up illustrations as if I am a moron. They explain it by hundreds of images in order to reach the essence which is almost nonexistent.

---

94. B2.
95. B3.
96. D2.
97. A4.
98. E2.

But too many stories, this is killing me. Without a strong message, but with banal examples not worthy of being told."[99] A traditional female believer also mentions the stereotypical observations or "illustrations" usually told by male preachers and based on their family members' behaviour or habits. Some participants respond negatively to stock phrases or the use of Christian jargon used to cover the absence of any real substance in the sermon. When asked to list some stock phrases she often hears, a seasoned congregant makes this remark, "'God forgives us everything,' 'We are all good,' 'God knows our weaknesses' . . . some topics which are so general that they can't inspire or move us. We heard them so many times that we remain indifferent after hearing them once again."[100] These are seen to be at the opposite pole of personal and authentic experience as testified in the opinion of the relatively young believer: "He had no specific [experience] of his own, but he only went on and on with it, it may sound ugly, with some Christian slogans . . . But it was all too general and superficial."[101] Another problem is spotted by a logos-oriented participant; she is repulsed by tall stories, affected accounts sometimes used in sermons. She states, "It puts me off. This is something supposed to stir some emotions. But it only . . . [puts me off] (*laughs*)."[102]

In a similar fashion, there are some respondents who detect a problem with sermons loaded with too much content. Whenever a preacher attempts to incorporate a large number of different emphases, he runs a risk of messing up the listeners' capacity to follow the course of a sermon and benefit from its message. A frustration with sermons with too many "points" is expressed in a comment about a preacher announcing his "fourth point": "Now what? How come this will be the fourth point when you talked [without mentioning points] for the last twenty minutes? I can remember his emphases so far and I know that preacher needs some guidelines, otherwise, they may lose track. But this can be a trigger that shuts me off."[103] Apart from it being an overwhelming exposure, such preaching makes this listener feel he cannot get a grasp of a wider picture or a full perspective.

---

99. E3.
100. A1.
101. A3.
102. B2.
103. A5.

The next factor is also loosely related to the repetitive nature of a sermon. Broadly speaking, it has to do with a lack of focus. When asked to describe an unappealing sermon, a respondent replies, "Well, it [the sermon] is not interesting when there is no theme. It happens often, there is no specific theme. Everything is a theme, like, a sermon jumps from one theme to another."[104] Reflecting on a particularly confusing sermon, another participant comments, "After 30–45 minutes one sees that you can't make head nor tail of it. You simply see that person talks in a way she will never stop. And again, things she said were OK, but there was no clear direction, no beginning, no storyline, nothing that will lead to some conclusion."[105] What this comment underlines is that whenever a preacher does not appear to have a firm goal and some clear strategy how to lead the listeners toward that goal, it is likely they will conclude his train of thought is practically impossible to follow. And even listeners who primarily hear through the logos setting and typically appreciate receiving a considerable amount of information also get discouraged by listening to preaching about many different topics at once. One of them puts it like this: "I get lost, you know. When I see that the preacher will begin to talk about hundred different issues, I lose my motivation to listen further on."[106] Interestingly enough, in this study, this lack of focus is something listeners spot not only with inexperienced preachers but also with pastors who have a long-standing history of regular preaching.

A further recurring disconnecting element can be identified from responses that reveal a judgemental attitude of the preacher. This same respondent knew a homosexual person whose withdrawal from the congregation served as a trigger for a set of sermons about homosexuality and she felt that these were preached in an antagonistic mode. She also feels disconnected to preaching that manifests contempt for other denominations or different church practices. Upon hearing that, she raises a question about the legitimacy of such preaching: "But I've been listening to sermons that were very negative about others, about everyone else. They [the preachers] are the only ones who are right. And in my opinion, that can't be a sermon."[107] A similar

---

104. B2.
105. A3.
106. B2.
107. B2.

reaction can be expected when a preacher-outsider comes to admonish and storm against believers' alleged sins. An intruding message of judgement, in this respondent's opinion, will certainly impede listening and provoke some resistance. A participant from another congregation agrees because of his comparable experience with a preacher who addressed his audience in an extremely judgemental manner. Although he agreed with most of what this preacher said, he was offended by his attitude: "It was like he isn't aware that what he preaches applies to him as well . . . But this barrier and distance [suggested] that he is three light years closer to the Lord. There was a great distance between us who listened and this preacher."[108] Thus, preaching that creates or deepens the gap between preacher and listeners probably obstructs the listening process while the hearers are in danger of being alienated by this aggressive "preaching against."

Sometimes listeners may have preexistent doubts about a preacher's suitability. In that case, their disposition for hearing can be compromised. A female listener, a first-generation believer, acknowledges her inability to pay full attention to a sermon preached by another woman. She explains her initial reaction, "My first response was: 'Oh, my God, I will never come to this church again! What is this? This is not a biblical thing!' . . . It was hard for me to follow the sermon. Everything she said was fine and I agreed with it, but I was bothered by the fact she is female, and I thought 'This must be wrong!'"[109] In another instance, a participant recounts a joint church service when believers from different denominations celebrated Christmas together. However, a sermon was delivered by a church leader who was notorious for his negative view of Christmas. In the end, this preacher was almost interrupted by his listeners and the entire atmosphere was rather tormenting.

Another objection is pointed out by a couple of listeners who consider enforced uniformity to be contrary to their understanding of faith. These listeners are experienced believers, raised in Christian families, and they resent being treated simply as a part of the crowd and told what to do, even if it is done by a preacher. When specific types of response or visible expressions are prescribed and expected by a preacher, these hearers feel threatened and they retreat. One of them explains, "As soon as you start to manipulate – Come!

---

108. A5.
109. A2.

Stand! Kneel down! Lift up your hands! this is too much for me . . . This is something that irritates me in sermons . . . I simply don't like that."[110] Yet another participant describes how she feels about it: "When someone who preaches says, 'Now, all of you do this!' I don't feel as a part of a majority and my gut response is to retreat to myself and to walk out."[111] In other words, some hearers are not susceptible to being ordered when and what to do during the worship. If they are exposed to such procedures, especially by a preacher, their listening capacities will inevitably suffer.

The list of disengaging aspects of a sermon does not end here. In the opinion of some congregants, the sermon (and entire church service) can be (and sometimes is) just too long. They usually do not specify how long a sermon must be to become too long, but they squarely indicate they are distracted to the point of being unable to follow the sermon. It looks as if this does not necessarily have to do with the actual length of the sermon, but rather with meaningless repetitiveness or with the incompetence of the preacher to capture her listeners' attention for the duration of the sermon. Also, there is a participant who remembers the distractions caused by the process of consecutive interpreting of sermons in his previous, multilingual congregation. Presumably, the best explanation why "too long" sermons have such a disengaging effect can be found in a response from a traditional Baptist:

> All I wanted to say is that even if the Word [of God] has a great message, it will lose its significance if it's too long. There are very few instances when one is able to pay attention after a full hour and still remember things preached about. In most cases, at least for me, a too long sermon destroys everything good that has been said. It cancels out those positive effects.[112]

Interestingly, the next element that makes listeners withdraw from hearing the sermon is reported by traditional congregants only. They recognise that some preachers are either incompetent or inadequately prepared for the specific sermon. For them, this fact has an immediate consequence for sermon reception. One of them recalls sermons preached only to fill the time and says,

---

110. E3.
111. A1.
112. E2.

> I mean, one can actually feel whether someone gets prepared or not, and how much he prepares and whether he prays about it or not. I don't think we all need to get prepared for weeks, but [we can] see how much of it is committed to God and how much time is invested. We also feel when the preacher comes with some reservations or when she only reuses some old sermon. Such sermons are no good for me.[113]

Another participant establishes a connection between lack of practicality in a sermon and insufficient preparation. Yet another directly points out the fact of the preacher's deficiency as a key to her dissatisfaction: "This is a situation when you realise it's not that person's fault. He reached the certain level and can't go beyond that. And among his audience there is 50 percent of people or less, it doesn't matter, and they are way above that . . . This disparity between what he can offer and my need is an awful thing."[114] These participants have no doubts that the preacher may have very limited capacities or may fall flat in terms of putting his sermons together. In either case, these listeners will most likely feel disconnected.

Let me summarise what has just been said about connections and disconnections. The subjective impression of being engaged by the sermon mostly depends on the listeners' judgement whether a connection between the biblical text and message and their own life has been set up by the preacher. This engagement happens either when they realise the resemblance with their actual, lived experiences or when they are convinced that the preacher speaks out of a heartfelt encounter with the biblical reality or out of her own personal life experience. There are also other suggestions, largely related to the style and delivery. For instance, a simple language, catchy introductions and haunting slogans, humour, and use of multimedia and suggestive imagery – all of them increase the probability that listeners will feel engaged by the sermon.

The participants in this study are slightly less forthright when articulating their objections, but their overall feedback makes it perfectly clear that the sense of disconnectedness is more than just an incidental or transient problem. They specify that repetition in preaching, endorsed by sterile speech components, such as generic illustrations, stock phrases or Christian jargon,

---

113. A4.
114. A1.

can seriously disengage those who want to hear. The same applies to sermons that lack a focus or are overburdened with too much content. Moreover, there are recipients of sermons who feel forced to withdraw from a sermon preached with a judgemental attitude, although they may agree with the content on a cognitive level. Some traditional Baptists sense disconnection as soon as the preacher tries to impose uniformity through her sermon. Those with a family Baptist background are more likely to notice a preacher's incompetence as a barrier to a more enthusiastic reception. Lastly, the inappropriate duration of sermons easily nullifies all previously accomplished positive impact of the preaching.

At the close of this chapter, it is possible to pause at the raw data gathered in interviews and express an appreciation for the variety of impressions and experiences shared by the participants. Taking even a casual look at their responses, loosely sorted out by the categories of ethos, logos, and pathos, connections and disconnections, reveals intricate nuances of evidence that require further processing if the research question is to find its pertinent answers. Therefore, I dedicate the next chapter to this task.

CHAPTER 9

Data Interpretation: Listeners' Expectations and Receptiveness

Before I proceed, let me make a simple clarification: the articulation of initial and provisional answers requires the interpretation not only of findings presented in the previous chapter but also of additional data contained in participants' feedback that speaks of their expectations and the factors that shape those expectations more directly. I suggest how this study can offer an informed reply to the first part of my research question – that is, what are the real expectations and receptiveness of the Croatian Baptists as sermon listeners? The response to the latter part of the question (How can these findings be utilized to improve the quality of preaching?) will be addressed in chapter 11.

9.1 General Expectations

As I interviewed the eighteen people, I gradually grew more aware of how their assumptions about preaching are largely conditioned by their previous experiences of sermon listening. Overall impressions and anticipations they bring with them as they enter the church building Sunday after Sunday accrue over time and without understanding them it is nearly impossible to grasp listeners' concrete hopes and expectations of preaching. Here are my observations on their deep-rooted opinions.

9.1.1 High Hopes of Preaching

Given its historical role in the development of the Baptist movement, it is not surprising that for the majority of participants the central role of preaching is incontestable. When asked what would be missing if there were no sermon, some of them had difficulties even imagining this scenario, and many of them claimed that the sermon is an indispensable part of the church service. Since the sermon is most often perceived as the proclaimed word of God, if there is no preaching, listeners feel they would not be able to gather around the word of God anymore. Such a service would be crippled since it is the sermon that infuses all other elements of the service with meaning. When asked what would happen if a church would meet without preaching for a longer time, a participant replies that it would stop being a church and would become some sort of a "club."[1] Another participant has a ready answer to the question what would be missing if there were no sermon – he said openly that it is *he* who would be missing from then on. Still another participant mentions the habit of some believers in his church who regularly come late for the beginning of the Sunday service, but are anxious not to miss the sermon. Put differently, there is a strong inclination among participants to hold a high view of preaching.

This inference is additionally supported by the recurrent use of terms such as "spiritual food" or "spiritual growth," mostly by logos-oriented listeners. In their description of the sermon's function, they tend to use organic terminology – a sermon is sometimes likened to food and its absence during the service can leave congregants "hungry." Its provision, on the other hand, brings these listeners to the desired outcome of their sermon listening. At other places, the respondents use the images of "core," "meat," or "substance."

Furthermore, the listeners' observations on the preacher's role are also evidence of their high expectations. A preacher is here to provide answers to questions that would remain unanswered otherwise. He is someone who "knows more" and is able to "explain what God meant"[2] – that is, someone who is more experienced and capable of interpreting the Bible in a way that supplements listeners' own understanding of Scriptures. An ethos-oriented listener makes a slightly unusual statement – after saying the preacher is here to "deepen" the word of God for his listeners, she summarizes this relationship by pointing to a hierarchy: "word of God, then pastor, then us."[3] By some listeners, a preacher is thus effectively seen as a mediator between the Bible

---

1. B2.
2. C2.
3. B1.

and the listeners, even though not many of them would be willing to phrase it in this particular way. In any case, a certain level of competence, knowledge and commitment on the preacher's part is mandatory if such expectation is to be successfully met.

All in all, this study demonstrates that most participants share a high view of preaching, agree that the sermon is a pinnacle of the church service and life, and cannot see how their congregations would go without it. However, at the same time, there is more than enough evidence in their feedback that sermons they listen to do not always come up to their standards. If their actual, everyday experiences in their congregations as testified in these interviews are not consistent with their expectations, then it would be profitable to explore their take on what really happens with their expectations as they gather before the pulpit Sunday after Sunday.

9.1.2 (Somewhat) Rough Reality

A middle-aged respondent, also a regular member of a worship team, openly admits that sometimes his only way of avoiding falling asleep during the sermon is listening while standing. Another participant in his early twenties confesses that since early childhood he often experiences mind-wandering during sermons. A first-generation believer says that her attention rapidly decreases after half an hour because her mental capacity cannot receive more than "two or three new things."[4] An implication of her remark is that this probably occurs often enough for her to identify it as a problem. Although these hearers are aware of this attention issue, this is only a part of the problem.

A number of interviewees make remarks disclosing a sense of disappointment with preaching. Although some of them do that only implicitly, others openly speak about their irritation. For instance, when asked about her expectation from preaching, a mother in her thirties replies "I expect to get some food. Some spiritual food and to go back home and have something to think about for at least a few days (*laughs*), but it does not always happen that way . . . But I don't get that. Only rarely."[5] Her wording indicates that such letdown is a regular occurrence while her laugh discloses a certain uneasiness about this honest declaration of dissatisfaction. The middle-aged person

---

4. C1.
5. B2.

mentioned at the beginning of this section points to the modification of his expectation over the course of time:

> I would expect to hear something that sticks in my mind, not only during the sermon but also after that. To understand and see how God can work within me. This is, of course, something I wish, but in reality, I don't have many expectations anymore. I just leave it to go by.[6]

In his case, the prolonged period of frustration leads to a gradual lowering of his original expectations. Two respondents, coming from the same congregation, express similar opinions. One of them describes a typical Sunday morning: "Very often we just go home after we did our duty, I've seen my friends, we talked a bit more or a bit less with other people . . . Well, maybe sometimes I have expectations and sometimes, unfortunately, I have no expectations."[7] He feels as if the sermon fits into a routine and typically he does not expect the preaching to break through that routine. Another member believes that the pastor should captivate his listeners in his sermon's introduction: "And if he does that, then he'll get our attention and it will go well. But if at the beginning I see that it goes as it often does, then I won't have high expectations."[8] This last testimony suggests that once a lowered the bar becomes *modus operandi*, it may be extremely hard to reverse the trend. All these statements have a quite recognisable common denominator: being exposed to uninspiring sermons that fail to meet anticipated preaching standards over an extended period of time will gradually create a disappointment.

The example of two other respondents further illustrates how serious this issue really is. One of them remembers how she used to analyse every single word of the sermon when she was young. Today, in her fifties, she is far more easy-going, "And here [in the church] I am ready to turn a blind eye, to tolerate, and to find for myself at least a single sentence or single positive thought."[9] Her peer, from another congregation, in another town, recalls a conviction of his youth that being a Christian involves a truly radical change of personality. However, after seeing and experiencing so many different things in a

---

6. C1.
7. E2.
8. E5.
9. A1.

church, he reflects on the nature and likelihood of a real, profound change: "Then there is a question: How does a sermon change me? All that is said can be correct, but what about later, what about my life? Has it changed me?"[10]

Such musings describe the reality of adjusted expectations. Of course, one might ascribe these to the sense of realism that builds over the years and comes with maturity. But it still seems safe to observe that many listeners go through the period of life when they discover the gap between their high view of preaching and their regular experience of sermon listening. It seems the common outcome is that they decide to keep their high hopes and appreciation for preaching, but, paradoxically, they also choose to lower their immediate expectations by which they receive the next Sunday sermon. Possibly, this is a defence mechanism – it can ward off potential further disappointments and still allow them to occasionally benefit from a sermon if it surpasses the ordinary level of quality.

A striking observation must be made at this point. Among those who are more prepared to voice their discontent with preaching, the majority belongs to the traditional Baptists. This is true regarding their expectations of preaching, but also in that they are more likely to articulate their criticisms and disapproval of established patterns of behaviour or communication within their respective congregations. Although it is not possible to conclusively prove by the scope of this study, I assume that the lowering of the expectations in those areas seems to them as the best way of easing out of the frustration. On the other hand, the first-generation believers seldom raise objections or reveal their dissatisfaction with preaching. Even when they do, it is done implicitly or mentioned as a side issue. Is there a particular reason for this differentiation? Why are their perceptions of similar involvement sometimes so different?

I believe it is reasonable to conclude there are two complementary factors to consider here. As I indicated earlier, a high proportion of Croatian Baptists come from a Catholic background. Among first-generation Baptists included in this study, most of them have been at least loosely affiliated with a Catholic church before they joined Baptist congregations. After receiving the sacrament of confirmation, many Catholics continue to attend church service only on special occasions, such as Easter, Christmas, funerals, and weddings. There are also Baptists whose traditional church background is Orthodox,

---

10. E3.

but the crucial point here is that in both cases preaching was incidental to their participation in the life of the church and to their Christian identity. In retrospect, they often describe those sermons as lifeless and hollow, only loosely related to the Bible. One of them evokes the experience of attending mass in a Catholic church: "It was totally futile for me. There was nothing there to touch me." She then tells of attending the Orthodox church since her husband had an Orthodox background. She admired the architecture of the church building, but otherwise ". . . also nothing. Simply nothing. Nothing touched me."[11] Another first-generation Baptist remembers a sermon in a Catholic church when a priest openly roused hatred against a different ethnic group. In contrast, the sermon in a Baptist church for many of them was usually one of the key agents of change that led them to their experience of conversion. In all likelihood, from their perspective, the preaching in the Baptist churches is immeasurably better than sermons they used to listen to in earlier stages of their life. Therefore, they feel they cannot afford a luxury of "nit-picking" about those less than perfect features of the sermons they listen to in the present. As a matter of fact, a lady who was brought up in a Catholic home and joined the Baptist church twelve years ago, expresses this sentiment when she tries to explain why she has no objections to the preaching, "As I said, probably because I came here from a church that didn't have such a practice, I am more than satisfied here . . . Maybe it's because I came from another church where that [the preaching] was completely different, so this here is just great for me."[12]

Another factor responsible for the differentiation mentioned above is "the years of service" that traditional Baptists spent in the congregation. Brought up in Christian homes, usually intensely involved in church life during their childhood and adolescent years, they have a long-standing exposure to preaching that led them through initial decisions and various crises and helped them to reach a certain level of maturity. It should come as no surprise that the attitude of some toward preaching has become more critical and demanding. This should not be seen as bearing a grudge against preachers or a form of internal rebellion against authorities. After all, the traditional Baptists in this study generally have a high view of preaching and consider it

---

11. B1.
12. C2.

as a focal point of worship. It would be better, and more accurate, I believe, to attribute their objections to their natural need to continue their spiritual growth as Christians and humans. Their questions, doubts, and demands are simply not easily answered by preaching that successfully caters to their sisters and brothers who have only recently discovered their faith or who have not lived their entire life within Christian community. Indeed, their discontent and critical remarks are probably authentic expressions (although not always conscious ones) of their inner desire to see preaching tuned in to their real needs and high standards that they have been dampening to reduce their dissatisfaction.

Now, despite the observed reality in which some Croatian Baptists struggle with a mismatch between their hopes for preaching and their concrete involvement in the practice of sermon listening, they nevertheless keep investing their faith and sometimes venture to believe that preaching still has a noble mission in their lives. The proof of that is found not only in their commitment to attending church services and sermons but in their voluntary (and in some cases even enthusiastic) participation in this study. This alone is reason to move from a general examination and plunge into the specifics of participants' expectations, trying to discern what corresponding features of preaching have a positive impact on the enhancement of their receptiveness.

9.2 Specific Expectations: When Sermons Are Actually Heard

Naturally, it is impossible to organise particular expectations into neat categories, and it would be methodologically wrong to assume that those I mention here are representative of *all* Croatian Baptists. At the same time, though, I hope these findings are sufficiently illustrative and indicative of existing trends among Croatian Baptists and detailed enough to stimulate efforts to establish their applicability and transferability to other comparable situations.

At the start, let me briefly acknowledge those expectations that show up only sporadically. There is a respondent who believes that a sermon should be, among other things, "honest." This expectation corresponds with the appeal of a preacher's credibility and vulnerability made manifest in the sermon. Two participants claim that preaching is supposed to serve as a safeguard against false doctrines. Without preaching, one of them suggests, people can forget "basic stuff" and wander off "in the wrong direction."[13] The fact that only a couple of congregants expect sermons to function as a yardstick in doctrinal matters and as a means of highlighting unacceptable beliefs might be indicative: even though sermons may contain a prescriptive, doctrinal character, this might not be of the utmost importance for listeners.

There are expectations that occur more often and create a thick fabric of listeners' receptiveness, thus calling for more detailed exploration. Thus I will seek to unpack the findings presented in the previous chapter and interpret them in light of my research question.

9.2.1 Understanding the Bible – Finding Guidance for Everyday Life

The responses from several congregants reveal they anticipate sermons will provide a more thorough understanding of the Bible. They not only see the Bible as the sermon's starting point but also seek to acquire some actual knowledge from it. They assume that preaching is the occasion when substantial input on the biblical material is fitting. The term which appears several times is the word "deeper" – "getting deeper into the word of God is missing"[14] or "people want a bit deeper exploration of the Bible"[15] are just two examples of this attitude. In their view, a proper sermon must possess this informative dimension and their frustrations are, to a degree, caused by its absence. In other words, a sermon with thoughtfully prepared expositional and exegetical elements will probably be highly appreciated by these listeners.

However, this tendency toward deepening of knowledge is perhaps not ultimately motivated by the expectation of accumulating more information as such. Some listeners clearly want to have the world of the Bible drawn closer to their life to fulfil a heuristic purpose. This is vividly illustrated by one of the respondents when she argues for preaching on a shorter portion of biblical text (as opposed to skimming over large paragraphs): ". . . if it is a smaller part of the text . . . then it seems to me that we've reached a depth of something that changes my perspective of the text or of something that can

---

13. D2.
14. A5.
15. E5.

help me to apply it in life."[16] Put very simply, they expect to receive something that will come in useful. The knowledge imparted *during* the sermon should be something applicable *later on*. This notion can be discerned in the threefold expectation of this listener: ". . . first of all, I should listen, secondly, it [the message] should remain in my heart, and thirdly, I should be able to apply it in my life. In any case, I don't expect from every sermon to instantly rescue me from all the problems I am in, but if I listen to it carefully, sooner or later it will be drawn from a deep memory and something will become clearer."[17] Moreover, in the experience of several hearers, sermon listening can (and often does) bring about delayed effects. Therefore, it is relatively safe to claim there are suggestive indications of their awareness of the formative influence of sermon listening practised over an extended period of time.

This leads me to ask further questions: If they listen with the intention of picking up some solid biblical knowledge to be implemented later in their communal and individual context, what is the intended purpose of gathering and applying this information? What do they hope to achieve at the end? What do they think preaching should develop in and for them? Listening to those participants who begin their hearing from a logos setting will reveal that they are prone to expect a sermon to help them to resolve various issues. They may feel they need more guidance in life or more assurance about the next steps to make and they are ready to hear or extract some specific directions from a sermon. Or they may expect a preacher to suggest explicit actions for addressing a particular problem in the life of the individual believer or the entire congregation. In any case, they assume that (re)solution will bring some relief and, ultimately, make more sense in their life. In other words, they are more likely to hear a sermon that supports them in their striving to move from an uncomfortable or insecure situation toward a more pleasant setting where they feel God's direction. Preaching that opens up the Bible and provides a valid understanding of its material, in fact, secures their steps on that path. From their Christian perspective, this is what makes their everyday existence more meaningful.

---

16. A4.
17. A5.

9.2.2 Getting to Know God and Maintaining a Private Devotion

Of course, the conclusions from the previous section are by no means exhaustive. Among both traditional and first-generation believers, there are individuals whose response introduces opportunities to uncover another set of expectations. There is an implicit, yet strong, assumption that a church service, and the sermon in particular, is *the* moment when a meeting with the transcendent is anticipated. Listeners invest their hopes for such an encounter into sermon listening, imagining that the pivotal place of their church life is a locus where such a meeting is the most plausible. The evidence they submit for the reality of that encounter may come in different forms; for some, it is the sense of God's presence as a real, actual person, and for others, a sermon is both an event at which they met God for the first time in their life and a dedicated point in time and space where that same God reveals himself again and again and sustains their faith. Some believe that their moral development is a proof of the authenticity of such encounter. A first-generation congregant puts it straightforwardly as ". . . a person improves through sermons if he or she listens to them honestly."[18] All this is to say that there is a distinct expectation of a sermon's immediate outcome which is not necessarily contradictory to the delayed effect of implementing the knowledge learned from a past sermon. Given the high hopes for preaching many listeners cherish and the prominent status of sermon within the context of Croatian Baptist worship, this specific expectation is not surprising. Nevertheless, I am convinced it should be interpreted as a poignant reminder (and perhaps as an encouragement) to preachers how tenacious the trust in preaching can be, despite manifold factors that seem to communicate the opposite. At the same time, it should be read as a caution not to underestimate the potential of a sermon to become a transforming, on-the-spot experience for listeners, even in those congregations where the sermon is traditionally perceived as something to be heard first, and then remembered and applied later.

Yet this immediate impact of a sermon is related to another expectation, of a long-term process that happens through a series of incremental steps. A few interviewees establish a direct link between listening to sermons and fostering their private discipline of devotion. As both Baptist theology and

---

18. C2.

devotional praxis lay strong emphasis on reading the Bible, it is easy to see why listeners may be engaged by a sermon that inspires them to read the Scriptures, to understand them better and to find a devotional fountainhead in the biblical text. The sermon that connects well with those listeners stimulates their individual devotion, largely consisting of the devotional reading of the Bible, and reaffirms their conviction that the interpretation offered in sermons complements and upgrades their private reading. This is closely connected to the previously mentioned assumption that the preacher should be someone who possesses specialised capacities and skills for unpacking and communicating the message of the Bible, something not easily accessed by "regular" church members. A participant who devotionally reads the Bible daily supports this notion by her brief answer to the question what can be accomplished only by preaching: "Our better understanding of the word of God. It is one thing when I read it at my home, but quite another [when it is read] here. That Word is then deepened, contemplated, enhanced. And this is the significance of the sermon."[19] Another respondent reasons in a similar way when he tries to imagine what would happen if he would not be attending a church for a year. He thinks he would not lose his faith because he would continue to read, interpret, and meditate on the Bible on his own. But he still believes God is more active in the church service during the sermon, and he calls it "the upgrade, in fact, the reinforcement of my faith."[20] Thus, it is rather safe to suggest that these listeners will be more eager to hear whenever they feel the sermon corresponds to, builds on, and nourishes their private time of devotion.

I believe it is not difficult to see how these two expectations can be mutually supportive. Whenever the hope of meeting God in a sermon gets fulfilled, it incites the listeners' desire to keep this experience alive, and to do that they invigorate their devotional practice of Bible reading. The same connection can be identified the other way around: a listener who devotionally reads the Bible on a regular basis is more likely to see a buildup of his or her hopes of encountering God during the Sunday sermon. Even though individual listeners may express these expectations with varying intensity, nevertheless they are closely linked.

---

19. B1.
20. C3.

9.2.3 Spiritual Battery Charging and Identity Affirmation

To properly introduce the next expectation, I need to refer to my initial observations concerning the high hopes of preaching. Besides the frequent use of expressions such as "spiritual food" or "spiritual growth," the respondents quite often refer to their conviction that the sermon is a source of nourishment that enables them to make it through the next week. When describing what would be missing if there were no sermon on Sunday, one of them specifies, "Well, the message would be missing. I mean, there must be a message, something *to help you to keep up through the week*. I'm not saying this is the only thing that holds you up, but basically, this is food, right? The food for you and your life" (emphasis mine).[21] The implicit assumption here is that the everyday life wears down believers' stamina and spirit and that they, to a certain extent, depend on the sermons for the replenishment that enable them to resume their spiritual journey. Another interviewee uses a different image to express the same idea: "The sermon must have a power and force to keep me nourished for the future period so that the Word can change me for the better, and this is related to the spiritual growth. One could say, *to charge my batteries*" (emphasis mine).[22] Responses like this paint a picture where a church service, and more specifically a sermon, can be imagined as a dedicated "pitstop," a place where congregants come to assemble their thoughts and regain their inner balance between the two stages of the race of life. Preachers will probably do well if they keep this expectation in mind during their sermon preparation, especially when the Sunday service is the only place and time of contact between preacher and listeners during the week. Their preaching should, therefore, seriously take into consideration Craddock's advice that it should not "put down, insult, violate, or ignore those whose investment in the message is no less than that of the speaker."[23] These listeners have made a conscious decision to refuel their energy there and gathered around the pulpit to quench their existential thirst there and not somewhere else (even though, more often than not, their expectations may not have been fulfilled in the past). In my opinion, preachers would do

---

21. B2.
22. E4.
23. Craddock, *Preaching*, 25.

well to make themselves aware of that decision Sunday after Sunday and seek to find appropriate ways of expressing a due respect for it.

At this point, a noteworthy undertone of this expectation must be mentioned, too. It resembles van der Geest's dimension of security because it reveals the listeners' craving for reassurance, for the affirmation of their deeply held beliefs, for the consolidation of their identity. They congregate from a world of insecurity to hear a sermon and as they desire to have their strengths renewed, they also want to be reassured they are at the right place heading in the right direction. This explains why they do not want to listen to repetitive sermons, and yet they still expect the preacher to remind them of well-known, heartening truths. A mature believer in his early fifties exemplifies this expectation's undertone by saying, ". . . it is good to be reminded, especially when the sermon is well constructed because it provides an encouragement and this will keep you up for some time, for a month, two months, or a year."[24] Even more striking is a statement from a first-generation believer in his late sixties who meditates on the nature of the sermon and makes a mental picture of God addressing him: "You came here not for me to tell you something new, but for me to reveal myself to you again. To reveal the same me as I was last Sunday, as I am since Genesis, to convince you so that you may believe, to strengthen your faith."[25]

From my view, there is more than one interpretation of this expectation. One could, for instance, understand these listeners' assumptions as a reflection of their apprehension that the Christian life is a process to be endured, during which a believer is heavily dependent on the spiritual support and provision administered by ministers and preachers. However, the relief they receive is only short-lived and forces the listeners to come back week after week to get more of it in order to survive until the next Sunday. Such an interpretation would tend to view these hearers as castaways who passively wait for a preacher to lend them a hand. They are content with the status quo, with having their identity reaffirmed, and they feed on sermons because they do not want so much to thrive as to subsist. Yet, another interpretation is at least equally feasible. These people are aware of their own frailty, have no illusions about the harshness of everyday life, and realise they often resist

---

24. E2.
25. C3.

forces much stronger than themselves. If this is a correct evaluation, then these expectations are nothing less than realistic and sensible goals set by believers who choose to seek their refuge, courage, and sense of belonging within a congregation substantially shaped by preached words.

In any case, it is time to reflect on the next expectation which seemingly goes against the striving for assurance and stability described in the three previous paragraphs.

9.2.4 Challenge to Change

In the previous chapter, it is possible to locate several clues to the weight of a sermon's applicability. Answering the questions, some respondents express their hope that preaching can offer them a sense of direction for their life. Faced with these correlated fractions of their feedback, I began to follow this line of reasoning: If a listener thinks she should apply something in her life and feels that guidance is needed, then some aspects of her life possibly truly need a modification or improvement. A mandatory in-between step is a change on her part. Such a reading opened for me a new way of looking at their perceptions of the purpose of preaching. For several hearers, behind their wish for a sermon to produce some discernible outcomes, or the longing for a sense of direction, or the desire to leave the church with something worthwhile of being applied, there is a common but resolute conviction. And this conviction translates itself into the last expectation: a sermon's function is to cause a change in listeners.

This conviction conceals a delicate, yet vital distinction – preaching cannot and should not be simply equated with the transformation process itself. Sermons are, after all, verbal and made of preacher's words that may call upon or put forward a potential change; but the change itself must take place within listeners and be shaped in their concrete actions. But if this change is to happen, listeners must recognise the need to modify their current condition, agree *that* particular adjustment or reversal is required, and summon their inner capacities to carry it out.

Yet, as some of the participants' responses tell us, believers sometimes swing between sheer inertia and the dynamic longing for change. The listener who talked about the necessity of leaving his "comfort zone" explains, "I think I am not able to do it on my own, I am lazy. I don't want it because sometimes it is easier that way. But, you know, I get used to it and I let it go, and then, at the end of the day when I think about it, I'm not satisfied."[26] A respondent from the same congregation describes this duality even better: "Sometimes I am content with the way things are, and sometimes I'm not. Sometimes I would like to change, but I don't feel like doing anything about it and this is when I think to myself: 'I wish for this sermon to touch me somehow!'"[27]

9.3 Are Expectations Sufficient?

What are the potential implications of these findings? First, it can be suggested that listeners' expectations to hear reassuring reminders of already known facts and insights that will provide reinforcement needed to "keep up through the week" or to "charge their batteries" is counterbalanced with their latent craving for sermons that will, at least occasionally, present them with a challenge. The coexistence of these two expectations is not contradictory. It is better to think about it as a true to life demonstration of the complexities of human nature, and it should not be a surprise if many listeners spend most of their time sliding between these two polarities.

Secondly, even if listeners appear to be tranquilised recipients, this does not mean they will reject a challenge if the preacher succeeds in presenting it. Their previous exposure to sermons that mostly protect the listeners' status quo does not necessarily entail their indifference toward a positive transformation – but the impulse for change must come from the outside! Thus, hearers seem to cede the responsibility for their mobilisation to preachers. In a real-life setting, there are listeners who are willing to settle with very little, but they still guard their dormant expectancy of a sermon's potential for stimulating a change and can respond favourably to such preaching. Obviously, this accentuates the preacher's liability to craft his sermon so that it may resound as a wake-up call at the ear of the listener.

Thirdly, there are listeners in this group who believe that concrete actions are the ultimate test of sermon reception. In their view, if a sermon does not extend its life in tangible acts of the listeners that were induced through the direct impact of preaching, it is basically preached to no purpose. Put differently, a sermon will engage them and prompt their attention only insofar

---

26. E5.
27. E2.

as the preacher shapes and delivers her message having in mind at least some practical and actual actions to be taken by them in a response. These listeners will not resent preachers making suggestions about possible ways of responding because they are likely to perceive them as a valid way to receive a sermon and transpose it into an everyday life. In other words, these listeners not only expect from a preacher a challenge to change; they also have a pragmatic hope that the sermon will urge them on to take certain steps and set about performing some clearly defined deeds.

The last question here remains: What is then to be gathered about the expectations of the interviewed Croatian Baptists? An overarching generalisation is not possible. Their individual experiences differ but also change over the course of time. There are also diverse hearing settings that to some extent affect their expectations. Yet, some leanings can still be discerned.

A good number of participants oscillate between their high view of preaching, deeply rooted in them through both Baptist tradition and theology, and their lowered expectations that gradually came about from continuous exposure to preaching that is below par. They seem to be torn between their strong and unfaltering faith in the enormous potential of a sermon and the central position of preaching within the worship and life of the congregation and their experienced, sometimes bitter, reality in which listening to sermons often fails their expectations. This dichotomy is also inherent in a responsibility they feel and express as they participate in listening to sermons. That is, they feel that preaching, being so closely related to the word of God, must produce some outcomes but they also know that these outcomes are conditional on their attitude and response. That means they come ready to listen and hear and they also come with strong, even if subdued, anticipation. Having adopted such a stance, they are generally able to detect in a sermon anything, however slight, that meets their expectations. But if preaching does not get through to them, it is likely they will assume the cause is their own shortcomings. The resulting frustration and sense of disappointing inadequacy can easily accelerate the process of adjusting and lowering their expectations to protect themselves.

It is against this background of beliefs and disappointments that their expectations are best understood. Their weight can be even better appreciated if for a moment attention is paid to the question "What is *not* an expectation of Croatian Baptists?" For instance, they do not expect to acquire a systematic knowledge of Christian doctrines or of historical developments.

In a similar way, they do not anticipate sermons will teach them how to win in an apologetic discussion or how to demonstrate the superiority of Baptist belief over Catholic doctrines. Quite fascinating is the fact they barely mention evangelism in relation to their expectations. They are also unaware of various preaching methods and techniques, so they have no specific expectation in that field, either.

Their expectations, however, look far more pragmatic and existential. Yes, they are concerned with a better understanding of the Bible, but its undercurrent is their emphatic yearning to find a reliable, well-founded and accessible source of guidance in everyday life. Naturally, most of them will expect sermons to be securely tied to the Scriptures, but that can also be regarded as their search for making sense out of their lives with all their problems and ambiguities. They expect sermons to address *their* problems and look for applications to use in *their* mundane circumstances. Yes, some of them anxiously expect sermons to enrich their private devotion and prayer life but the key thrust behind this desire is to keep their existing experience with God alive and prolong it into the future. How this encounter with God will be solicited, what means or devices will the preacher use, and whether her message will be doctrinally orthodox, may be of no or only secondary concern to them. Yes, their expectation to recharge their batteries and have their sense of identity reaffirmed on a weekly basis may appear to prove their over-reliance on their pastors; but the fact they come again and again to receive in spite of the ruthless circumstances of their everyday life should never be downplayed. Yes, they occasionally may seem content with status quo-biased preaching and yet, they are appreciative of the need to have their lives confronted and questioned to the point where they need to make, and act upon, far-reaching decisions.

Previously, my interpretative efforts were focused on tracking down listeners' *expectations*. I believe there are good reasons to allow listeners to voice their expectations for themselves and to open space for this silent majority to articulate their own needs. Besides, I am convinced that churches, particularly their leaders, need to recognise the reality of preaching being contingent on the listeners. Only such acknowledgement and willingness to revise their role can help congregations to keep preaching vibrant and formative amid ever-changing social contexts, local and global. However, to explore the listeners' expectations would sanction the concept of preaching according to which listeners are only at the receiving end. Over the course of this study, listening to my participants made me aware that their active, contributive capacity must be both surveyed and strengthened. Put differently, I concluded that my original outline of this chapter needed to be expanded to include a discussion on listeners' *responsibilities*.

9.4 Responsibility: Backing Up Expectations

Conversations with my participants leave no doubt about the general sense of responsibility for their participation in the practice of preaching. The awareness of their own liability for the success of the sermon seems to be deeply implanted in them if its widespread occurrence and variety of is expressions is a sound indicator. Most of them have a high view of preaching and the preacher's role, and yet almost all of them appear to assume that one has to back up his or her expectations from a sermon. They also share the understanding that ultimately it is not a preacher's responsibility to create a positive listening experience for them. If they expect to receive from a sermon, they need to invest in it. If a sermon is to leave any significant mark on them, they need to make sure to adjust their attitudes and approach in a fitting way. However, it is possible to discern two different levels of responsibility: the passive and the active.

9.4.1 Passive Responsibility

A typical response that aptly represents a number of similar comments comes from an experienced believer: "In my opinion, if I am half-hearted, if I don't have a need for spiritual growth, if I don't work with God on my problems and deficiencies, it is not very likely that a single Sunday sermon will change me."[28] This basic attitude of willingness to get involved with God, to grow in a spiritual dimension is simply an indispensable prerequisite. It has to be followed by a more specific stance to be taken by a listener every time he or she comes to listen to a sermon. It is up to the listener to enter the church building and to lend an ear to the sermon with an expectation of an encounter with the Divine. A respondent describes the elementary qualities of this stance: "One has to come to the service with a clear head and be ready to hear the Word.

---

28. E3.

And before listening to the sermon one should maybe pray to God to give him a peace or concentration . . ."[29] Different participants mention different consequences of such an approach, but some go so far as to say that God's presence during the sermon is directly dependent on the active approach of the listener. When comparing various attitudes with which people come to the Sunday service, one of them comments, "And yet you can come because you want to be there and you know this could be a holy place, a special place because God is present . . . But this may not depend on whether God will come or won't come but on how did I come."[30]

When such an attitude is adopted, it enables the listener to become particularly attentive to the positive aspects of the sermon, even when a pastor did not do particularly well in terms of meeting the hearers' expectations. An experienced traditional believer, whose comments are relatively critical, admits that she often feels as if preachers she listens to do not possess the capacity to deliver a satisfactory sermon. Yet, she takes these sermons as a basis on which she will build on and refrains from any criticism. Instead, she looks for a sentence or a verse she can "take with her."[31] A first-generation believer expresses a similar point of view: if the sermon happens to be meagre, she still tries hard to draw something from it. If nothing else, she can remember a Bible verse that was read and take it as spiritual food for the week to come. At this point, a thought-provoking question can be asked: what makes those listeners, otherwise quite capable of spotting disengaging elements of preaching and of recognising the inadequacies in matters of content, style, or delivery, so benevolent and willing to search for and accept even the slightest grain of a helpful nutriment in such sermons? There are at least two probable explanations. One has to do with hearing through the ethos setting: enjoying a good relationship with a preacher and finding her character and lifestyle to be authentic can lead a listener to excuse her weaknesses and imperfections in preaching and still benefit from a sermon.[32] The

---

29. E4.
30. A1.
31. A1.
32. For instance, a participant who is clearly a highly relational person and holds his pastor in high esteem provides a list of justifications for occasions when his sermons are not especially inspiring: "Pastor could be tired. He is very, very busy. He gets so many calls. He has two ceremonies in a day and then the TV show, too" (B1).

other reason is related to perceiving the preaching as speaking out the word of God. If, by default and definition, every sermon *is* a message from God, perceiving any *particular* sermon as irrelevant, boring, or wrong creates a paradox for its listeners. The resolution of this paradox is reached by (some) hearers when they take on the responsibility to make sense out of the sermon; if this is a word from God (and it must be), then something useful must be in it, and they feel obliged to find it.

Yet, there is more to it than just focusing on every beneficial input available from a sermon. The reason I am inclined to classify this attitude as a "passive responsibility" may be found in the surprisingly frequent occurrence where listeners tend to blame themselves for any failure to resolve the paradox I have just described. Several participants imagine that in the case of a sermon they did not find engaging or responding to their needs and expectations, they are the ones at fault. Let me give several examples. A first-generation believer explains his initial negative response to one of the preachers in his congregation: "At first, I was judgemental about him . . . but then wait, God placed him here for a reason and this is why he is here. He didn't come out of nowhere and I need to look at myself. And then you look inside yourself and not outside." He recognises that God wanted this preacher to preach something and this could have been done in a more or less skilful way. He concludes, "And if I don't like it, I mean, if it's boring or I don't feel like listening, that's a problem with [me as] a listener, and not with a speaker."[33] Another participant ponders the possible cause of a "hollow" sermon: "The problem is usually with me. I don't see how the preacher could be a cause of the problem unless he lost his focus. But this is a communication problem."[34] Yet another participant admits that there are sermons she was not particularly connected to and yet she explains, "I think I need to change my attitude – I see that the problem is with me, it is about my relationship with God, how much will I receive."[35] There are even more striking examples. Take for instance the response of a participant who grew up in a Christian home. She struggles to explain why sometimes she is not moved by a sermon when everyone else in the congregation seems fully absorbed by the preacher's words. She concludes:

---

33. A3.
34. D1.
35. A2.

> And then I wonder what is wrong with me. Because obviously there is something wrong with me. It comes to my mind that I am not well prepared, that I didn't pray, that I arrived with some antagonism, that I am simply not ready. Something must be wrong with me at that moment because it [the sermon] is clearly aimed at the people and God surely speaks to everyone but not to me. And it's not God's fault but probably mine. I guess so.[36]

If I interpret this phenomenon correctly, then what we have here is a case of internalising a problem that could very well be a shared problem or even a preacher's problem. But these listeners seem to have no mechanism for exploring other possible causes of the disconnection from the sermon. Instead of trying to solve the problem in a conversation with other participants in the process, including the preacher, they shrink back and attribute this breakdown to their deficiencies (although they usually cannot be sure what exactly these are). A result of their taking up a responsibility is not particularly rewarding; the gap between preacher and hearers widens and they are left to their own devices to analyse their seeming shortcomings. In the long run, this trend certainly can contribute to the lowering of expectations but can also prove to be auto-destructive for some listeners. These listeners are usually predisposed to take on a certain level of responsibility in the practice of sermon listening, but are also likely to blame themselves whenever the sermon does not fulfil its purpose. Whenever that happens, an opportunity for dialogue and reciprocal communication is missed.

A word of clarification of my understanding of this passivity is necessary here. These listeners approach the sermon in an active manner, wishing to hear and understand, with engaged mind and heart. They are eager to direct their attention to the productive elements of the sermon and neglect the disengaging ones. But in all of that, their role remains prevalently passive: they are still only recipients of a message shaped by someone else, left with no access to the process of sermon construction. The preaching they listen to is so often a hit-and-miss affair in relation to their actual expectations, questions, and doubts. Their only choice is to sift out the sermons, hoping they will find gems of meaning that will address their needs, meet their anticipation, and stimulate their further participation in the life of the congregation.

---

36. A4.

9.4.2 Active Responsibility

However, a few participants express opinions pertinent to a more active type of responsibility. Extracts from their comments help me to elucidate this concept. A listener, who typically begins to process a sermon at the intersection of logos and ethos settings explains that she likes her pastor a lot and hates conflict but she does not "think that all of us have to think the same way about everything . . . I think we can have some of our own opinion on biblical topics we study."[37] Likely other participants also have their own points of disagreement with their preachers and the sermons they preach. But this input is perhaps unique; it implies that within the congregation such differences in understanding or interpretation of the Bible are plausible and conceivable. Though personally not prone to conflict, she can discuss and question the pastor's claims in a direct and open conversation with him.

This implication seems justified by a comment made by another member of the same congregation. When recalling a particularly moving sermon, she also established a connection with something this pastor said almost twenty years ago at the time she was preparing for her baptism. According to her, he said, "Everything I preach from the pulpit, everything somebody else preaches, you write down and reexamine. The fact I stand up there does not mean I am always right. You are required to read, think through, ask questions and seek for answers, no matter what you think my opinion is."[38] This instruction made a lasting impression and over the years shaped her attitude of active responsibility.

Another aspect of this attitude is demonstrated by a middle-aged respondent, a traditional Baptist who often feels preachers possess inadequate capacities for their role. Nevertheless, she indicates that not only do both preacher and the listeners share responsibility for preaching and listening matters but also these two are interlocked. In her view, listeners, and especially more experienced believers, should provide support and uphold a preacher as he presents their expectation of an encounter with the Divine during the service and the sermon. As a matter of fact, she uses a powerful biblical image here: "It's like when you hold up Moses' arms so that he can keep lifting them up."[39]

---

37. B2.
38. B3.
39. A1.

Admittedly, only a few respondents show a potential to take passive responsibility to the next level. Yet, in their perception, preaching is more of a joint, collaborative service with shared responsibilities. At least implicitly, they sense that preaching should surpass the typical role distribution where preachers preach and listeners listen, or preachers give and listeners only take. One of them mentions a captivating image in her description of preaching and listening to a sermon: "... we who sit and we who preach ... all of us are an audience and the only one who preaches is God himself."[40]

What makes an *active* responsibility substantially different from a *passive* responsibility? As I see it, active responsibility includes the recognition of mutual accountability: both parties are to be held accountable for the "success" of a sermon. This has at least two crucial repercussions. For one, if a sermon does not connect, if a preacher does not manage to engage his listeners, and if the message comes across as unpersuasive, the source of miscommunication might be found on both sides. Listeners understand that preachers are imperfect just as they are, and both preaching and listening can be impaired. That leads to another consequence: the hearers intuit that they are entitled to discuss the sermon, to question and evaluate what is being delivered through preaching, and possibly to contribute to future sermons. Although the data of this study shows that among Croatian Baptist churches there are no established procedures for obtaining listeners' feedback or input into the preaching process (comparable to the McClure's roundtable pulpit or feed-forward groups), the listeners who are conscious of their active responsibility seem to be keen, when opportunity arises, to partake in the creation of a sermon's meaning.

---

40. A1.

CHAPTER 10

Theological and Theoretical Reflection

An encompassing purpose of chapters 7–9 was to articulate some intelligible and solid data-based answers to this query: *What are the real expectations and receptiveness of Croatian Baptists as sermon listeners?* Using Osmer's terminology of practical theology's tasks,[1] it could be said that these chapters cover the descriptive-empirical and interpretive dimensions of my research. The qualitative study conducted among Croatian Baptists served me as a tool to (begin to) spell out *what is actually going on* from their perspective as sermon listeners. The accumulated findings that emerged from the accounts of their experience supplied me with material conducive to interpretation and this analysis enabled me to suggest some reasons *why* it is going on in the way it is. At this point, I turn to the second part of my research question: *How can these findings be used to improve the quality of preaching?* This signals the need for moving to the next two tasks: the normative and the pragmatic. In other words, concerns shaped by the questions "What should listening to sermons in these congregations look like?" and "How can we respond to make it happen?" will govern both this and the next chapter.

This shift of focus, though, requires a change of interpretive lens. What was gathered through a phenomenological approach to the qualitative study needs to be considered from a theological perspective. The meaning of the participants' input must be reflected on theologically, a repositioning which is not an unnatural step. The participants' answers graphically demonstrate they themselves think *theologically* as they attempt to understand and make sense of their experiences of listening to sermons. Their explanations reflect

---

1. Osmer, *Practical Theology*, 4.

particular and genuine theological stances, no matter how underdeveloped or fragmentary these may appear. What follows, then, is that theological reflection is already going on, so my intention is to add a critical edge. In other words, I seek "to put together the depth and complexity of the experience . . . so as to discover God's presence and action in the midst of the contingencies of this situation."[2]

This is not to say this reflection will remain a theological soliloquy, since I will also try to expand on the relevant insights from other disciplines already mentioned in chapters 2–6. The goal, however, is to construct a normative theological prescription for the practice of preaching. I will seek to take a critical attitude toward myself as being affected by my comprehension of the events, the course, and the outcomes of this research, and report on any significant self-observation.

Let me begin with some retrospective thoughts. As I prepared this research and immersed myself in its beginning stages, I was fascinated by the prospect of a deeper understanding of a relationship so intensely conditioned by the silence of one of the involved parties. I felt that the majority's compliance with allowing the minority to monopolise the speaking role is too easily taken for granted, especially when the listeners may disagree with the preacher's sermon. I wondered: Why is preaching so resistant to any questioning or evaluation, even if this *silent majority* functionally becomes a *silenced majority*? The question is even more alarming given how much is at stake when preaching in a typical Croatian Baptist congregation. A sermon, as I have learned from my lifelong involvement with various local Baptist churches, is the heart of congregational life, the hub of communal identity, and the hearth of spiritual growth for individual believers. In this context, my deep intuition kept suggesting there is more to this silence. I even suspected it could become a tacit accomplice in the preservation of the status quo, although there may be some valid reasons to upset this condition. At some point, as I was arranging the interviews, I came across the concept of "eloquent silence" as presented by a Nobel laureate, novelist José Saramago. In a single sentence, describing the moment when his main character leaves his daughter and her husband alone to settle their disagreement, he seemed to voice all my fears regarding what silence in listening to sermons may hide:

---

2. Ballard and Pritchard, *Practical Theology in Action*, 128.

... and say, Here he is, and then close the door and leave them inside until words came to their rescue, because silences, poor things, are just that, silences, everyone knows how often even apparently eloquent silences have given rise to mistaken interpretations, with serious and sometimes fatal consequences.[3]

On the other hand, I also imagined that this mute posture concealed something far more productive, something that might transform both preaching and listening. My personal experiences, mainly from a listener's perspective, steered me to the point where I began to assume that the listeners' side must be reinforced, and their role upheld in order for an equilibrium to be reestablished. Could this "eloquent silence," provided it truly existed among the participants, be converted into something contributive, active, and more faithful to the nature of relationships within the Christian community as envisioned by God's revelation? Can the existing preaching practice benefit from the processes of including the hearers? Are the findings from my study adequate in terms of presenting a case for preaching that is more inviting to the listeners?

10.1 Theological Framing

Preaching is essentially a Christian practice and, by definition, an exercise of Christian faith enacted (although not exclusively) within and by a Christian congregation. If, on the other hand, theology is a conceptual discourse with a threefold task that Elaine Graham and others have termed as helping the *"formation of character,"* "building and maintaining the *community of faith,"* and "relating of the faith-community's own communal identity to the surrounding culture,"[4] then this reflection surely can derive advantages from some theological framing. This is why the three doctrines mentioned at the end of chapter 2 will now come to my aid.

10.1.1 *Imago Dei* and Formation of Character

If we accept that every sermon is essentially an effort to establish and maintain a communication between God and human beings, then the pressing issue

---

3. Saramago, *Cave*, 215.
4. Graham, Walton, and Ward, *Theological Reflection*, 10.

is: What does it take to turn this effort into a meaningful contact between the Divine and those made in the divine image? This is even more intriguing if the listeners are perceived as embodied, visible images that also refer to something beyond them that is invisible. Even more importantly: What are the consequences of the fact that those who are addressed by God through sermons are already created in the image of that same God and are the bearers of His likeness?

The biblical motif of the human as created in the image and after the likeness of God is mentioned only at three places in the Old Testament: Genesis 1:26–27; 5:1–3; 9:6. Yet, it has been the subject of numerous treatises and works of many distinguished theologians and biblical scholars since the earliest days of Christian theology. The scope of my work here does not allow for a more detailed investigation of the various contributions to the understanding of the doctrine of being created in the image of God.[5]

I will instead sketch a more contemporary approach to this Christian teaching. The recognition that in Gen 1:26–27 God's decision to create humans is accompanied by an abrupt change to the grammatical plural ("Let *us* make man in *our* image, in *our* likeness") and that the first biblical reference to this image is the fact that humanity is created "male and female" grants a licence for an interpretation that focuses on the social and relational dimension. Plantinga, Thompson and Lundberg signal that twentieth-century "theologians such as Barth, Brunner, and Bonhoeffer took this gendered qualification of humankind as a key interpretive principle in order to emphasize

---

5. There are a number of disputed questions: Is the "image of God" to be understood as a reference to the primary human condition and "likeness" as a description of the ultimate state at the end of history? Was this image destroyed by the fall? What else, apart from baptism, can help its restoration? Concerning the question of what this image consists of the theologians of the past usually pointed to some of the human faculties – be it reason, conscience, or freedom – or particular endowments, such as dominion over other creatures. They also tried to locate the single point of likeness between God and humanity that defines this image. More recent contributions in the field, however, critically reassess these views. Daniel Migliore, for instance, argues that in this respect the longstanding emphasis on human reason "fostered an intellectualization of Christian anthropology," resulting in a "depreciation of the emotional and physical dimension of human existence." On the other hand, the concept of dominion over the creation corresponds to the worldview of hierarchical relationships whose consequence can be exploitation, especially of nature. And the stress on human freedom as the content of that image in this contemporary culture too often coincides with mere independence from others or even with sheer self-gratification. Migliore, *Faith Seeking Understanding*, 144–45.

a more social and relational theological anthropology."⁶ In this view, human existence inevitably "reflects the life of God who eternally lives not in solitary existence but in communion."⁷ Furthermore, this male-female duality should be read as a paradigm for the diversity of relationships defined by our race, gender, gifts, or ethnic identities. The *imago Dei* thus implies certain mirroring of ways in which the divine Persons relate to each other and holds a capacity for living a life with the "other" being the chief interest of our actions and behaviour. Pannenberg reasons in a similar way when discussing the notion of human personhood as related to the *imago Dei*: "We can attain to the totality of our own lives, notwithstanding its fragmentary form, only in the relation to our Creator. But we achieve our particularity in our encounter with others. Both types of relations are in their own ways constitutive for our individual personhood."⁸ The divine immanence is thus profoundly involved in and tied to our relationships with our fellow humans. This relational concept then invites humanity to a life of mutuality and dialogue that is initiated and propelled by God's act of creation, but also results in an active responsibility of the bearers of *imago Dei*: "humanity is called to reflect God's likeness and character in the range of its relationships – not only to be the visible image of God (noun) in creation, but also to image God (verb) concretely in all of its tasks and activities."⁹ By creating human beings in his image, God addressed them and entangled them in this God-relationship.

However, this relational model can be complemented with another model, the one that brings the representational dimension to the forefront. Plantinga and others understand the image of God in Gen 1:26–27 as referring to the custom of Near-Eastern rulers who would erect statues with their image in the territories under their rule. Thus, human beings are to be viewed as God's living statues with a representational function. Their reading of the passage suggests that the image can only be understood as including the entire human being (and not some of its capacities) and implying that "the general human vocation has a sacramental quality about it, pointing beyond itself to the reality of God." Equally important, the bodily aspect of human existence

---

6. Plantinga, Thompson, and Lundberg, *Introduction to Christian Theology*, 186.
7. Migliore, *Faith Seeking Understanding*, 145.
8. Pannenberg, *Systematic Theology*, II, 200.
9. Plantinga, Thompson, and Lundberg, *Introduction to Christian Theology*, 190.

is not to be ejected from the image of God "since the function of an 'image' resides in its visibility."[10] This interpretation goes along almost perfectly with Moltmann's idea of humanity's double identity.[11] In Moltmann's reading of the Genesis creation account, human beings are certainly given a transcendent identity by virtue of being created in the image of God. But humans also have an immanent identity as creatures made in the image of the earth. These identities make humanity distinct from the rest of creation and yet humans still share enough creatureliness with nonhuman creatures so as not to have a basis for dominating or exploiting nature. In addition, this intersection of immanence and transcendence turns human beings into priestly mediators between God and creation. We represent God to the creation through the *imago Dei*, but we also represent the earth to God through the *imago mundi*.

This actualizes the necessity to introduce the New Testament perspective on the Genesis material. The epistles, especially those from the Pauline corpus, repeatedly depict Jesus Christ as the image of God (2 Cor 4:4; Col 1:15; also Heb 1:3). He is presented as the true and exact image to which human beings, although bearers of the *imago Dei* by creation, must conform (Rom 8:29; Col 3:9–10; 2 Cor 3:18; Eph 4:22–24; 1 Cor 15:49). The New Testament clearly underscores that the restoration of the image of God is necessary and possible only through Jesus Christ. The question is: What is the nature of the relation between Christ's perfect likeness to God and our likeness imprinted on us by creation? In other words, what is the interrelationship between our creation and our redemption? Of course, the necessity of redemption derives from the reality of human sin and its effects on the *imago Dei*.

Throughout history, theologians have offered various answers – usually by describing the different degrees of damage caused by the fall. For instance, Calvin agrees with Augustine in his assessment that man's natural gifts (such as the soundness of mind and the integrity of heart) were corrupted by sin, while his supernatural gifts (such as "the light of faith and righteousness") were withdrawn. Drawing both on the history of human thought and the biblical witness, he affirms that human mind continues to seek the truth "to which it never would aspire unless some relish for truth antecedently

---

10. Plantinga, Thompson, and Lundberg, 184–85. See also Pannenberg, *Systematic Theology II*, 207.

11. Moltmann, *God in Creation*, 185–90.

existed." He also acknowledges the existence of diverse gifts, as expressed in the manual and liberal arts, which are distributed to all human beings by their Creator. Although these "have ceased to be pure to polluted man," they cannot be "polluted in themselves in so far as they proceed from God" and in their diversity "we can trace some remains of the divine image distinguishing the whole human race from other creatures." On the other hand, in matters of spiritual discernment – the knowledge of God, the way of salvation, and the righteous conduct of life – human beings are left blinded as a result of the fall and are in need of enlightenment by the Spirit. So, even though the proper knowledge of God requires supernatural intervention ("when the Spirit . . . forms the ear to hear and the mind to understand"),[12] Calvin still seems to imply that this act of God includes the renewal of human capacities that are already present in every person, albeit corrupted and inadequate in their present state.

Of course, there are also other, more radical interpretations. Perhaps Karl Barth's reasoning is a suitable example. When discussing the knowability of God and man's readiness for God,[13] he maintains that man has lost the "conformity to God," that is, there is no point of contact between God and man, and hence no possibility of receiving God's word. The reason for that is, according to Barth, the fact that "the image of God is not just . . . destroyed apart from a few relics; it is totally annihilated." Therefore, a person may be open to God, but that does not mean he or she is ready for God. Given that, because of the fall, a human being always keeps "an indivisible remainder of enmity against the grace," the only possibility for knowing God opens up in Jesus Christ, a real man and Son of God – in Him, God is knowable to himself and also to human beings. In his campaign against the natural theology of his time,[14] Barth is anxious to demonstrate the superiority of the theology of revelation. Hence, the word of God comes to us only when "the knowability of God which is bestowed upon us in His grace is received and accepted as

---

12. Calvin, *Institutes*, 165, 168, 169, 170.
13. Barth, *Church Dogmatics*, I.1, 239–241.
14. Natural theology, in his words, begins and ends with „the affirmation that even apart from God's grace, already preceding God's grace, already anticipating it, he [the human being] is ready for God, so that God is knowable to him otherwise than from and through Himself." Barth, *Church Dogmatics*, II.1, 135.

such by us."[15] By faith, people can then participate in Christ's person and work. In that sense, it could be maintained that, for Barth, the *imago Dei* is defined almost exclusively in christological terms:

> The image of God in man of which we must speak here and which forms the real point of contact for God's word is the *rectitudo* which through Christ is raised up from real death and thus restored or created anew, and which is real as man's possibility for the word of God.[16]

Also, theologians have tended to explain the fall by employing the doctrine of original sin, as maintained by Augustine. Thus, all sins have their shared source in the fall and all humans receive that sin "by virtue of the common stock into which they are born (i.e., human nature)."[17] However, some contemporary scholars have tried to revise this doctrine, differentiating between "propensity" toward sin as a part of the general human condition and guilt for the sin that comes from committing particular sins. In that way, the *imago Dei* is affected both by that propensity, shaped by our being born into a sinful world corrupted by structural and societal sins, and by our actual sins.[18]

At the same time, other scholars show that the Bible never implied that the fall distorted this perfect first estate or that the *imago Dei* ever included immortality. Some of them indicate on exegetical grounds that Paul "ascribes immortality only to the second eschatological man."[19] According to their understanding, the fullness of the image of God historically occurs only with Christ as the end of an ongoing process. Believers can then participate through character formation and transformation into the likeness of Christ that not only restores the *imago Dei*, but also places them into a new, unprecedented relationship of intimacy with God. This agrees with the relational model according to which the *imago Dei* describes human life as the totality of its relationships. Consequently, the distortion of the *imago Dei* through sin corrupts three basic human relationships: with God, with one another, and with nature. These corruptions can then be seen as consequences of sinful attitudes: "our acts of sin express attitudes of either excessive self-love

---

15. Barth, II.1, 161.
16. Barth, I.1, 239.
17. Migliore, *Faith Seeking Understanding*, 198.
18. Plantinga, Thompson, and Lundberg, *Introduction to Christian Theology*, 194–203.
19. Pannenberg, *Systematic Theology II*, 213.

or stultifying self-loathing. That is to say, we sin both 'above ourselves' and 'beneath ourselves.'"[20]

Perhaps there is no need to follow Barth's distinct division between creation and redemption. Perhaps we were created for communion *and* communication with God in the first place, so the restoration of the human ability to hear and respond to the word of God through Christ's redemption is not an entirely different act of the same God. Also, if we decide that the *imago Dei* can be seen as a work of "preliminary" grace bestowed upon humans in the act of creation, then human experience as the point of contact does not need to be located outside God's grace. Similarly, the reality of creation can be conceived as the initial act of God's revelation to be followed by revelation in Jesus Christ, made possible by His embodiment in human form. I am inclined to agree with Pannenberg as he comments on the New Testament perspective by saying that, in Paul's statements about Christ as the image of God,

> . . . the Christian doctrine of the divine likeness must see an elucidation of our general destiny of divine likeness. But in so doing it may not expunge the differences between the fulfilling of our divine likeness in and by Jesus Christ on the one hand, and the OT statements about Adam's divine likeness on the other. To do this is to miss the point that our destiny as creatures is brought to fulfilment by Jesus Christ.[21]

What can be made of these theological considerations when juxtaposed with the data from my study and the insights of other disciplines? Several answers are relevant.

First, unless understood in terms of total depravity, the doctrine of *imago Dei* always reveals something in humans that effectively points to God. As a result, the act of preaching has the potential for meaningful communication because there is an inherent possibility of contact between God and human beings. Given that the *imago Dei* encompasses the entire human being, the listener's experience is a fully-fledged candidate as the location where this contact will be established. Feedback from the participants proves that when identification or recognition takes place, it is because the preacher managed to strike a chord with something in their personal experience. Thus, the

---

20. Plantinga, Thompson, and Lundberg, *Introduction to Christian Theology*, 201.
21. Plantinga, Thompson, and Lundberg, 210.

listener's experience should never be considered as something subjective, volatile, or nugatory. Instead, it should be viewed as a realm in which momentary glimpses of the *imago Dei* can be seen as they fall on the soil of the *imago mundi* and from which numerous sermons could find their beginnings, points of contact, or cruxes.

Secondly, the relational character of *imago Dei* affects both preaching and listening in manifold ways. The social constitution of the image of God helps explain why for some participants sermon listening is a fundamentally communal experience, during which a sense of connectedness (or its absence) with fellow believers and the preacher decisively shapes their involvement. Also, if the diverse nature of humanity is carved into an *imago Dei* at the point of creation, then human beings can hope for the restoration of that image only when they live in dialogue and exchange with other humans. Evidence of their advancement on the road toward the destiny of divine likeness often takes the form of the growing importance of mutuality and a self-sacrificial attitude. With that in view, it is easy to realize where the basic human need to be heard and understood comes from. Taking their seats on Sunday morning, the listeners come in order to hear that they have been taken seriously and to have their questions, fears, and hopes recognised by their preachers, but also by God. None of that can happen unless preachers infuse their preaching with a dialogical attitude. Browning is right when he qualifies listening as the most evident expression of love and terms it "an act of descriptive theology – an act that in itself witnesses to God's grace in creation and redemption,"[22] which is such an endorsement of the *imago Dei* doctrine as presented above. This is also why preachers should take to heart Carrell's assessment that studying the "text" of the listeners is equally important as studying the biblical text[23] and intensify their intentional efforts in the former activity. This is also why Tubbs Tisdale's invitation to preachers to exegete their congregations by employing congregational analysis in their daily involvement with congregants aims at developing a listening stance that will allow them to get to know their listeners better and incorporate the world of their listeners into their sermons. At the heart of all preaching should be an awareness that every hearer has been created after God's likeness, and the appreciation of this reality should

---

22. Browning, *Fundamental Practical Theology*, 286.
23. Carrell, *Great American Sermon Survey*, 209–10.

be manifested in the practice of preaching. Sharing the image of God with her hearers, a preacher will show her dependability and conjunction with them by preaching in a way that discloses her honest work of hearing and understanding them.

Thirdly, an earnest acknowledgement of the *imago Dei* adds to the eschatological aspect of preaching. The history of God's dealings with humanity, which reached their climax in Jesus Christ as the perfect image of God, represents a continuous movement of God's promises and salvific actions whose ultimate purpose was to reestablish God's blessing of the creation, originally intended to take place through the "general human vocation" derived from the *imago Dei*. Correspondingly, preaching should acknowledge the image of God in listeners and encourage them to continue their journey toward their eschatological destiny which is the full actualization of the *imago Dei*. To reach that destiny, however, sermon listeners must experience change and have their character reformed in order to conform to the character of Christ. Thus, the very practice of preaching and listening at once testifies that the preacher's speaking and the listeners' hearing are cognitively impaired by sin and reveals the redemptive grace of God at work in preaching that uplifts and intensifies the present transformation as a precursor of the eschatological full conformation to the *imago Christi*. This spiritual and moral betterment of all participants in the preaching practice correlates to the homiletical give and take between hearers and their preachers, no matter how flawed it may be in our present circumstances.

The particularly valuable discovery of this study discloses that a number of the listeners' true expectations reflect precisely this longing for their continuous improvement, even if it is often contrasted with their sluggishness caused by uninspiring preaching. Preachers should help this process of character formation by their vigorous integration of listeners' perspectives, by treating their listeners' experiences seriously, and by allowing their various voices and concerns to be heard and evaluated, believing that this is their joint participation in the reestablishment of God's original blessing of all peoples.

10.1.2 Incarnation and Building the Community of Faith

Although there are several scriptural portions traditionally employed to support the concept of incarnation, narrowing down my attention to the Johannine prologue (John 1:1–14) and the Pauline hymn (Phil 2:5–11) is,

I believe, a tenable decision. The Gospel of John is a signal that the early Church, after trying to interpret Jesus through the eschatological framework of the future renewal, began to understand him as a specific person in whom divinity and humanity were brought together. By attributing to him the title "Word," the Evangelist highlights that Jesus is not to be taken as a prophet provided with the word of God to be proclaimed, but as a human embodiment of that self-revealing Word presented to the entire human race. His bold statement, "the Word became flesh and lived among us" (v. 14) refers to the process by which God took on a human life in Jesus, and the Greek word commonly translated as "lived" could be more expressively rendered as "pitched a tent." As such, it alludes to Israel's journey to the Promised Land. The Pauline hymn, on the other hand, celebrates Christ's voluntary decision to humble himself in becoming human, and seems to imply his preexistence.[24] It affirms his sameness with God, which did not prevent him from appearing and living in this world as a mortal creature.

Historically speaking, however, the question "How has the Divine 'become' human?" did not come to the forefront of theological considerations until the great controversies of the fourth and fifth centuries, when the Church tried to define its orthodox attitudes against a variety of beliefs about the relationship between the human and the Divine. Today, scholars seem to agree that the formula reached at the Council of Chalcedon (AD 451) did not decidedly resolve the problem, but defined the borders of the orthodox. Stanley Grenz puts it this way: "Chalcedon claimed foundational importance for orthodox Christology. As a result, the incarnation became the focus of theologizing after the fifth century."[25] Let me point out several examples of modern-day contributions whose developments are well-suited for my purposes.

In Tillich's understanding of this doctrine, we are dealing with the effort of expressing "the paradox that he who transcends the universe appears in it and under its conditions." This appearance "is not a metamorphosis but his total manifestation in a personal life."[26] In order to fully perceive its meaning, he suggests we focus on the claim that "the Word became flesh":

---

24. Other references that hint at Christ's preexistence include Matthew 1; Luke 1–2; Galatians 4:4; 1 Corinthians 1:24; Colossians 1:15; Hebrews 1:1–3; John 6:62 and 8:58.

25. Grenz, *Theology for Community of God*, 399.

26. Tillich, *Systematic Theology*, 149.

> "Logos" is the principle of the divine self-manifestation in God as well as in the universe, in nature as well as in history. "Flesh" does not mean a material substance but stands for historical existence. And "became" points to the paradox of God participating in that which did not receive him and in that which is estranged from him.[27]

Thus, this situation can be read from a communicational perspective: the human partner refuses to accept and chooses not to understand the divine partner. To abolish this alienation and lack of communication, God makes an astonishing manoeuvre and crosses to the other side. If humans are to understand God, he must understand them first, which is to be effected only by His coming closer to them. The only efficient way of coming near is His identification with the human condition. Looking back at the feedback from this study, I can confirm the participants are usually capable of recollecting the sermons that were experienced as engaging precisely because of their high identification potential. If preaching from personal experience promotes listeners' identification with the preacher or triggers their recognition of the similarity in their circumstances, and if, as a consequence, the probability of their awareness of being addressed by the sermon increases, then the reality of incarnation has compelling implications for preaching!

Secondly, the incarnation also entails God's solidarity with human beings. The process and significance of identification are not exhausted by merely taking up human existence and living as an individual human being. The very fact of incarnation is evidence of God's determination to take part in human suffering and the cross is its ultimate verification. It confirms that God entered, as Michael Welker frames it, "into the full depth of creaturely distress, including unfathomable suffering and the entanglement of human culpability . . ."[28] This is exactly why the author of Hebrews confidently describes the Son of God as a high priest capable of feeling sympathy for our weaknesses (Heb 4:15). Identification meant solidarity and solidarity meant "God's *com-passion* or 'suffering with' the world."[29]

---

27. Tillich, 95.
28. Welker, *God Revealed*, 257.
29. Plantinga, Thompson, and Lundberg, *Introduction to Christian Theology*, 219.

It is impossible to overlook some further implications of Christ's identification for the practice of preaching. Craddock recognised that identification in preaching requires a two-step movement: (1) The preacher needs to live in a way that will allow her identification with her listeners; (2) She must find common ground as she prepares and begins to deliver the sermon which will pave a way for listeners' identification with her message.[30] Solidarity may be expressed in having not only sympathy for, but also readiness to grapple with the temptations of faith that the listeners may discern in the sermon and identify with. Van der Geest advises preachers to become "the questioning listeners" who demonstrate this type of solidarity.[31] A very similar notion reverberates in Carrell's suggestion to the preachers to "decentre" their sermons in order to lodge the listeners' perspectives at the heart of their communication.[32] Identification and solidarity, modelled after the incarnation, surely require that the preachers should modify their preaching by respecting them more and by demonstrating readiness to see through their eyes.

Thirdly, the dynamic concept of incarnation presented by the image of "pitching a tent" provides a welcome supplement to the ideas of reestablishing communication, identification, and solidarity. It depicts God as someone who joins us in our quest, who will walk in our paths, who will explore the crossroads with us and share our everyday hardships. God is not some distant glory in the cloud on top of a mountain anymore; God is now a fellow traveller and a dependable, caring companion. In this image we can, together with McGrath, comprehend that incarnation means God "achieving a double entry into our situation, coming *among us* as *one of us*."[33] In other words, coming among us was not and is not enough; becoming one of us was the best possible way of making God known.

Again, the analogy with preaching is rather self-evident. If this double entry demanded humbleness and sacrifice on the part of God who desired to reveal himself, then undoubtedly a similar driving force should inspire preachers in their undertakings to communicate the word of God. There is no reason they should forget they are the same as their listeners, that they

---

30. Craddock, *As One*, 57–59.
31. Van der Geest, *Presence in Pulpit*, 126.
32. Carrell, *Great American Sermon Survey*, 219–20.
33. McGrath, *Landscape of Faith*, 127.

share far too much with their hearers not to be able to imagine themselves sitting in those same pews or chairs or to allow their lives to be touched and moved by the lives of their congregants.

When understood in the categories of solidarity, identification, and compassion, the reality of incarnation emerges as a narrative in which it is impossible to separate the message from the messenger. The most straightforward way of expressing it is that Jesus of Nazareth does not show a *way* to God – he *shows God*. There is no greater normative implication for preaching than this. The results of this study suggest there are listeners who intuitively embrace this incarnational dimension of preaching whenever they implicitly or explicitly allow the preacher's ethos to function as a gateway to their involvement with the sermon. At the same time, the preachers cannot incarnate the Divine in the same manner as Jesus did. Yet, their role as messenger should be defined not only by how convinced they are of the message they wish to convey, but even more by how authentically they embody that message in their preaching and personify it through their lives and relationships. In a way, their entire life is preaching, and the words of a sermon are only the tip of an iceberg.

Finally, there is a long tradition of interpreting the incarnation by means of a kenotic model. Broadly speaking, the preexistent Son of God abandoned some of his divine attributes and "emptied" himself of the divine powers that could prevent him from becoming fully human. Over the centuries, this model was often at the brink of Docetism or had difficulties defending its deity claim – that is, how can we still consider Christ as divine? Therefore, various modifications have been proposed. One of those, for instance, posits that,

> in the incarnation the *Logos* did not lay aside the divine attributes themselves, nor those powers inherent to deity. Rather, the Son gave up the independent exercise of these powers . . . the earthly Jesus refused to draw on his divine abilities merely at his own whim.[34]

---

34. Grenz, *Theology for Community of God*, 400.

Christ's *kenosis*, then, can be regarded as a continuous exertion of "free self-limitation and self-expenditure"[35] as he employed his divine facilities in total obedience to the Father's will and under the guidance of the Spirit.

However, there are also some risks in referring to the kenotic understanding of incarnation as the ethical model to be followed. For instance, various feminist scholars have rightfully pointed out that the concept of *kenosis* has too often been imposed as a vehicle of oppression and as a means to prevent different oppressed groups and individuals from questioning or resisting abusive or oppressive relationships. Thus, the ideal of self-emptying and self-giving has been used to convince women that suffering is a recipe for imitating the life of Christ. Defined and applied in this way, *kenosis* amounts to powerlessness as the legacy of a patriarchal system nested within ecclesial structures.[36] Yet there are an increasing number of feminist theologians who argue that such understanding is inadequate on several grounds.[37] Considered in the light of these contributions, the doctrine of *kenosis* remains a substantial theological catalyst that precipitates the embodiment of love of God by and for all participants in the preaching practice, encouraging them to empty themselves of everything that hinders them from openly communicating with others, or promotes the relationships of inequality that are alien to the reality enacted by Christ's kenotic act.

So, without further delving into this rich doctrine, here it should be sufficient to point out the voluntary nature of the kenotic movement. All participants involved in the preaching practice (not only preachers) could benefit from mirroring this attitude. For listeners, this can involve a decision

---

35. Migliore, *Faith Seeking Understanding*, 186.

36. See, for example, Hampson, "On Power and Gender," 234–50; and *Swallowing a Fishbone?*.

37. Sarah Coakley, for instance, shows how kenotic movement implies vulnerability that signifies the interdependence of both men and women, which has potential both for the rejection of oppressive systems and for the empowerment of women ("Kenosis: Theological Meanings and Gender Connotations," and *Powers and Submissions*). Anna Mercedes presents *kenosis* as a framework for feminist theology and relates it to the body of Christ. This emptying act must be followed by an outward action by which an individual believer reaches out to the Christian community and offers Christ to the wider world. In the process, *kenosis* becomes a way of imitating Christ through self-giving that enables his followers with a "power for" living for the specific other (*Power For: Feminism and Christ's Self-Giving*). Annie Selak reminds that the human analogue of Jesus's *kenosis* has a "different starting point," meaning that self-emptying must be preceded by filling with God. This process is "fundamentally an act of empowerment and liberation" ("Orthodoxy, Orthopraxis, and Orthopathy," 529–48).

to invest themselves more actively in providing feedback and responding to every preacher's cue or invitation that can lead to a more collaborative enterprise. Instead of quietly putting up with the status quo, they can refuse to accept the role of disappointed listeners who may have ceased to consider their preacher capable of offering engaging sermons. Their role can become more proactive if they locate and begin to do away with anything on their side that hinders them from accepting more responsibility for the preaching process. For the preacher, this can require a prayerful assessment of his inner convictions, outward manners, and pulpit performance with the purpose of surrendering anything that elevates him above his listeners and thus making him unapproachable and distant. It may also include a sincere revision of his a priori presumptions of what his listeners expect (or *should* expect) from a sermon. The ultimate purpose is to recognize that anything thwarting the communication between preacher and hearers needs to be abandoned.

10.1.3 Priesthood of All Believers and the Relation of Community Identity to the Culture

The last doctrine to be addressed in this reflective process is the New Testament concept of royal priesthood or the priesthood of all believers. Of the three notions, this one is presumably the closest to the theology of Croatian Baptist communities. Belonging to the tradition of free churches surely implies a firm belief in the freedom of individuals to approach God without any mediator other than Christ, and this is exactly what this doctrine is sometimes reduced to. However, before I ponder its pertinence to preaching in greater detail, let me make a few initial remarks.

The very notion has its origins in a passage from 1 Pet 2:4–10 where the author explicitly identifies the people of God as a "holy priesthood" and a "royal priesthood" that is "to offer spiritual sacrifices acceptable to God through Jesus Christ" and to "declare the wonderful deeds of him who called you out of darkness into his marvellous light." Since this author remains secretive about the nature and quality of this priestly task, and since the only other book that openly identifies believers with "priests" is Revelation (Rev 1:6; 5:10; 20:6), the wealthiest source of material for the development of the doctrine remains the Epistle to the Hebrews. Although this book's primary theme is the high priesthood of Christ, the ministry of believers often emerges as a derivative topic discussed in cultic terminology related to the old covenant ritual system (Heb 4:10, 16; 7:19, 25; 10:19, 22; 11:6: 12:18–24; 13:13, 15–16, 21).[38] What do we learn from this teaching?

In a sense, the general idea of priesthood came to the Baptists as part of the Reformation heritage. The Reformers insisted on direct access to God through Christ alone as opposed to mediated access through clergy as a special priesthood. God's grace and forgiveness can (and should) be received by every believer by himself or herself. Traditionally, Baptists carried this belief over to their conviction that only an individual can respond to God's call and that each individual believer should accept the responsibility for all his or her personal actions and behaviour. On the other hand, a meticulous analysis of the New Testament writings (including an exegesis of the scriptural references mentioned above) with the purpose of establishing whether the church assumed the necessity of an ordained priesthood from its very beginnings, would likely yield a negative answer. For instance, Bulley, who writes about the rediscovery of the role of the laity and the tension between general and special priesthood, concludes: ". . . only Christ and Christians in general and individually are understood in priestly terms in the NT, and ideas are found there which undercut conceptions of a peculiarly priestly group within the church, except for the possibility of leaders representing the whole church's priestliness."[39] At the same time, though, the function of this general priesthood is very well documented in the writings of the early Church, not least in ideas such as "that Christ has offered the only effective sacrifice for sin so that the kinds of sacrifices which are now appropriate are those of people's lives and various aspects of those lives which are honouring to God. But these sacrifices are all such as can be, and are, offered by each Christian."[40] In his close exegetical reading of Hebrews, Garry Wills shows that the concept of "priest" is practically absent from the rest of the New Testament and employed in an innovative way within that book.[41] The evidence he collects throughout the book leads him to the conclusion that the idea of "priest" as visible in

---

38. The priesthood topic in Hebrews is extensively covered by scholars. A monograph exploring the priesthood of the epistle's readership is John Scholer, *Proleptic Priests: Priesthood in the Epistle to the Hebrews* (Sheffield: Sheffield Academic Press, 1991).

39. Bulley, *Priesthood of Some Believers*, 317.

40. Bulley, 48.

41. Wills, *Why Priests?*. Basically, he agrees with numerous Protestant scholars when he reports that priesthood is consummated in Jesus whose "onetime offering makes all other priesthoods obsolete."

the New Testament literature does not provide a support for the historical development of priestly roles within churches, especially hierarchical ones.

Furthermore, a number of authors remind us of the original Reformers' understanding of this doctrine and highlight its present-day misrepresentation. For example, Baptist theologian Timothy George quotes one of the most prominent experts on Luther's theology:

> Luther never understands the priesthood of all believers merely in the sense of the Christian's freedom to stand in a direct relationship to God without a human mediator. Rather he constantly emphasizes the Christian's evangelical authority to come before God on behalf of the brethren and also of the world. The universal priesthood expresses not religious individualism but its exact opposite, the reality of the congregation as a community.[42]

George believes that this crucial ecclesial dimension of the doctrine has been seriously obscured in contemporary Baptist congregations. Its very wording, "priesthood of all *believers*" (plural!), suggests a need to recover the authentic Reformation understanding of the doctrine. Instead of relying on the idea of royal priests as individual truth-seekers with their private judgements, which easily induces downright individualism or lax interpretations, he advises that we should perceive our priesthood as standing together before God and interceding for one another. In that light, priesthood of all believers is far more a matter of service than of a particular status, or as he puts it, ". . . it is a barometer of the quality of our life together in the Body of Christ and of the coherence of our witness in the world for which Christ died."[43]

So, if this priestly function implies responsibilities that surpass the freedom of the individual's direct access to God, then the real question is: *How do we give concrete expression to the doctrine of the general priesthood in this congregational context?* The answer may be partly related to the inner structure of the local congregation. Some ecclesiastical traditions, including many Baptist churches, organise themselves according to the principles of "democratic congregationalism." These are founded upon the New Testament testimony of a congregation's prominent role in appointing its leaders and

---

42. Althaus, *Theology of Martin Luther*, 314, in George, " Priesthood of All Believers," accessed 12 April 2018, <http://legacy.founders.org/main/wp-content/uploads/fj03.pdf>.

43. George, "Priesthood of All Believers."

officers, whom they entrust the entire congregation with final authority. Such a model is built on the expectation of the intentional participation of all members, not only in the decision-making process, but also in all other matters of congregational life and mission. This, then, leads to another piece of the puzzle: general priesthood requires the continuous setting in motion of everyone's spiritual gifts for the benefit of the whole (1 Cor 12:7; 1 Pet 4:10–11). There are no individual "royal priests," but there is a priestly body made up of all believers given access to God in order to corporately intercede, pray, and worship on behalf of each other. *Baptism, Eucharist and Ministry* (BEM), a well-known ecumenical document adopted by the members of the World Council of Churches, puts it this way: "The priesthood of Christ and the priesthood of the baptized have in their respective ways the function of sacrifice and intercession. As Christ has offered himself, Christians offer their whole being 'as a living sacrifice,'."[44] And even though this document is endorsed by numerous churches that uphold a distinct role for the ordained priesthood, its conclusion forthrightly spells out how decisive the role of the entire community is, that is, how pervasive its priestly function:

> Finally, the intimate relationship between the ordained ministry and the community should find expression in a communal dimension where the exercise of the ordained ministry is rooted in the life of the community and requires the community's effective participation in the discovery of God's will and the guidance of the Spirit.[45]

The priesthood of all believers, then, can be envisioned as the priestly identity of God's people that finds its proper expression only as a calling to all members of the church to share in Christ's priestly ministry, irrespective of their position in the church hierarchy or their gifts. Given the congregationalist outlook of Baptist churches, there is no reason why this calling should not be manifested within the community of believers as sacrificial efforts that exceed prayers and intercessions. And even if the legitimate locus

---

44. "Baptism, Eucharist and Ministry," 20, accessed 24 May 2018, <https://www.oikoumene.org/en/resources/documents/commissions/faith-and-order/i-unity-the-church-and-its-mission/baptism-eucharist-and-ministry-faith-and-order-paper-no-111-the-lima-text>.

45. "Baptism, Eucharist and Ministry," 23.

where this priestly calling is to be lived out is the local congregation, obedience to this calling, without doubt, possesses the potential to transform that congregation and shape its identity in ways that will not go unobserved by the surrounding culture.

In my understanding, the theological rationale for transforming preaching so the silent majority's voices can also be heard begins to emerge as soon as the congregational dimension of the priesthood of all believers is acknowledged. Since many Baptist congregations, at least in theory, adhere to congregationalism, they should not find it problematic to apply its principles to the practice of preaching practice as well. There is no reason why privileges and responsibilities tied to this democratic type of church governance should not be extended to the pivotal and defining practice of many Baptist congregations – preaching. For instance, just as the general expectation of these believers is that worship is not done by pastors or ministers *for* the people, but is open to everybody for the common benefit, why could that participatory approach not be transplanted to other elements of the church service, of which preaching is the most visible representative? If all believers are individually and corporately responsible for their congregation, why should they be exempted from both the benefits and duties of the preaching ministry that so many of them perceive as their key identity marker?

Wayne Grudem picks up the same problem from a different angle when he observes that the doctrine of the clarity of the Scripture paired with the doctrine of priesthood of all believers indicates that "all Christians have some ability to interpret the Scripture and some responsibility to seek God's wisdom in applying it to situations. All have access directly to God in order to seek to know his will."[46] If this is true, there is an enormous capacity buried behind those pews, waiting to be discovered. If the listeners can contribute to the understanding of the Scripture's meaning, then they are qualified to discern and spell out its bearing on their immediate context. In that case, their role should never again be reduced to that of passively receiving the message devised from the perspective of a single person, no matter how competent, benevolent, pious, or broad-minded their preacher is. I have mentioned how devastating the priesthood of all believers can be if it paves the way to individualism – and it seems to me that a preacher's solitary efforts in preparing

---

46. Grudem, *Systematic Theology*, 933.

and delivering sermon Sunday after Sunday can be found guilty of the same crime if they shut out every congregational input, preclude any participation, or present the listeners only with a "take-it-or-leave-it" choice.

Then, the findings of my study demonstrate the Croatian Baptists usually assign some special authority to their pastors and preachers. So, although these churches are governed in line with the congregationalist theory, there is nevertheless a distinction between "ordinary" believers and the ordained ministers (and preachers even if they are not officially ordained) in terms of their respective calling. When BEM discusses the calling of the whole people of God, they mention "diverse and complementary gifts" and specify some interesting couplets such as, "communicating the gospel in word and deed, . . . gifts of teaching and learning, . . . gifts of guiding and following . . ."[47] In each of these pairs the first gift seems more applicable to the ministers while the second one appears more fitting to the calling of the laity. Yet, I do not think it would be theologically unsound to add another couplet to the list: that of preaching and listening. More importantly, the borderline between them should not be drawn too strictly and crossing over to the other side should be encouraged in order to promote exchange between those gifts. Put simply, the listeners should be allowed to speak and say more, while preachers should be prompted to listen and hear more. By allowing the hearers to rediscover the gift of teaching others, and by letting preachers uncover the gift of learning by listening, the priesthood of all believers may be enlivened in previously unprecedented ways. At the same time, preaching could begin to be experienced as a truly life-changing practice, inconceivable without listening, a practice initiated and regularly brought to life by both preachers and listeners who are deeply aware of their interdependence.

10.2 Final Reflections . . .

Before I formulate specific proposals that might bring about positive developments in the preaching practice of Croatian Baptists, I must place the results of interpretation arrived at in chapter 9 within the theological framework declared in this chapter. That is, what happens when the specific hopes and expectations gathered in this study, understood and interpreted by means

---

47. "Baptism, Eucharist and Ministry," 17.

of disciplines such as rhetoric and congregational studies, are contemplated from a theological angle?

Undoubtedly, the participants in this study see the sermon as the very core of congregational life and as the default high point of a regular church service. So, it comes as no surprise there are some strong listeners' expectations attached both to the sermon and to the preacher. At the same time, the reality check of empirical study proves that these expectations are not always met. Consequently, listeners may feel excluded and frustrated because their growth is being hindered. Usually, they settle down by lowering their immediate expectations and by making some adjustments – one being their continuing to participate by complying with their relatively passive involvement in the preaching practice.

I believe, however, that the doctrine of the *imago Dei*, as exposed above, lends a full validation of the listeners' conviction that the purpose of preaching is to challenge them to change. Their longing to grow and to improve, prompted by preaching, perfectly accords with the emphasis on Christ as the supreme image of God to which all believers must conform. This expectation, then, is not fulfilled without sermons being designed and delivered with a clear intention to help them in the process of character formation. But this same doctrine also requires a proper appreciation of the believers' present state, made possible by God's act of creation, and of their individual experience of life as a result of this divine image still operating in them. Thus, the *imago Dei* endorses preaching that respects the hearers' experience and acknowledges their worlds as space where they, as bearers of the image of God, will most successfully co-create the meaning of sermons. Such preaching can respond to *their* genuine expectations and assist them on their way to taking the fullness of the image of God as seen in Christ.

On the other hand, reading this study's findings makes it impossible to overlook the compelling significance of the doctrine of the incarnation. Take, for instance, some of the respondents' specific expectations: they want the sermons to provide guidance for their everyday life, to help them get to know God better and to strengthen their private devotions, to charge their spiritual batteries. All of them reveal needs and profound desires that only the incarnation can adequately quench. In brief, they want to meet God and to be as close to him as possible. But they are not after a one-off meeting; rather, they want him by their side as they go through life. Is this not why the Son of God became human? And since preaching is strongly believed to communicate the word of that same God and to facilitate the encounter with the Divine, there are some telling implications. It cannot be coincidence that in the sermons these listeners find engaging they are able to recognise the preacher's solidarity with them, to feel her compassion with their troubles or circumstances of everyday life, and to respond to her act of identification with them (even if they are not able to remember the content of what was preached!) The kenotic approach of a preacher who does everything in and out of the pulpit to show his determination to expend himself for his listeners is also an incarnational feature of preaching, just as it is preaching not from a vantage point of a skilful, experienced pastor who "knows better," but of a fellow traveller who is one of them. All these qualities point to the focal reality of the incarnation – the messenger *is* the message – and this truth is readily observed or intuitively felt by many hearers and not only those who primarily listen to sermons by "hearing" the preacher's ethos. Preaching reinforced by the incarnation cannot but influence individual believers in a way that will shape them into a community of faith.

This congregational aspect of preaching is best disclosed when the concepts of passive and active responsibility are juxtaposed with the doctrine of the priesthood of all believers. As shown in the previous chapter, listeners' expectations can be backed up by their action of taking on responsibility for the preaching event. The more intentional this is, the higher will be the level of their participation. The higher the level of their participation, the more likely their expectations will be met. There is probably no better theological concept to feed this active involvement than the priesthood of all believers. It holds the capacity for activating a mutual accountability and transforming passive responsibility into a more proactive commitment. In the process, both congregants and their leaders may come to an understanding that the preaching practice is not so much a matter of style preferences, the choice of the method, the ideal duration of a sermon, or the content, as it is above everything else a matter of ecclesial identity. Holistically speaking, the notion of general priesthood teaches us that the role of listeners and their contribution (or its absence) to preaching in a given congregation reveals what kind of a congregation that church is. Or in more constructive terms, if one is to steer his or her community of faith toward a more participatory paradigm of being a church, then employing the priesthood of all believers in the practice of preaching is perhaps the best way to launch that initiative.

10.3 . . . and Some Personal Thoughts

Throughout this research, I pondered what would be the most arresting and accurate image of preaching as a practice with a monologic form and dialogical nature. Also, I wondered whether there were other biblical examples that could somehow confirm the matching value of both speech and silence, of speaking and listening, and indicate that these two are to the same extent part and parcel of every sermon. However, as this study began to end, I grew more confident that a painting and two scriptural motifs immensely helped to dispel my uncertainties on a personal level. Let me briefly describe them.

As Christians, we address God through prayer. This is a God who spoke to human beings first – he created our race by speaking out his word. He addressed us before we were able to address him. And yet, whenever we pray, it is we who are talking and he who is listening! If he was not to listen, who would listen to our prayers? At the very core of our faith, there is a seemingly simple but profound conviction – and it says that *God is one who both speaks and listens*. Without it, the belief that we can establish and maintain a relationship with a living God would be a wild fancy. By means of analogy, what right does the preacher have *not* to listen and to define preaching as a "talking matter" if God himself endorses listening as an invaluable component of his communication?

The second case in point can literally be called an argument from silence. The biblical narrative on the life of Jesus begins with his conception and birth, and with the exception of a brief episode in the Temple, the gospels tell us nothing about his life until his baptism and reveal close to nothing on the details of major milestones before the beginning of his ministry. Why? Is it because this period of Jesus's life is comparably irrelevant for the history of salvation and our daily spiritual wellbeing? From the incarnational perspective, I believe that the answer is just the opposite. This silence conceals a precious truth that preachers should note. The life of Jesus we know so little about must have been characterised by the silence of Jesus's preparation. As the Son of God, he took on human nature and set himself on learning and listening to his fellow humans before he would embark on his salvific mission.

And yet, he could not become ready at once. He needed a period of listening, and his being quietly immersed in the reality of human experience allowed him to become a Voice. Besides, the vocal period of his life was much shorter than the listening period. This complementarity of listening and speaking is a robust blueprint for a preaching practice that would be equally sensitive to both speech and silence.

And there is also a painting. I have quoted Jose Saramago's observation on eloquent silence and although it encapsulates my observations of all those sermons preached to the silenced majority, I have also remarked that there must be a more fertile and positive side to eloquent silence. The resolution of this suspense came during one of my study residencies, when I visited the Denver Art Museum to see an exhibition of Joan Miró's artworks from a later stage of his career. When I stood in front of his *Bird in Space* painting,[48] it struck me how just a few dots and a pale line on a relatively huge white canvas can evoke recognition of something so colourful, spirited, and mobile. As I continued to gaze at it, I gradually became aware that this is exactly how silence in the practice of preaching and listening can be. Something unremarkable, common and ordinary, and seemingly mute may, in fact, be the critical factor in generating its exact opposite. Back in the library, I did some research on Miró's life and came across a sentence that only deepened my impression that this is the piece of the puzzle I missed in understanding preaching as a give-and-take between speaking and listening: "What I am looking for . . . is an immobile movement, something that would be the equivalent of what we call the eloquence of silence – or what St John of the Cross, I believe, called soundless music."[49]

There is one remaining task to be dealt with: the task of offering pragmatic suggestions based on the collected data and the corresponding interpretation. I hope these tentative recommendations will blend the insights from homiletics, rhetoric, congregational studies, the existing empirical studies, the history of the Croatian Baptists, and my own field study in a useful manner.

---

48. Miro, *Oiseau Dans L'espace*.

49. *Joan Miró: Selected Writings & Interviews*, edited by Margit Rowell (Boston: Macmillan, 1986), 248.

CHAPTER 11

Suggestions for Improving the Practice of Preaching

As a rule, preaching has been preoccupied with the interpretation of biblical texts and proclamation based on that interpretation. Thus, preaching has been an intrinsically normative task. But the endorsement of the trend of turning to the listeners adds to the preaching a descriptive-empirical and interpretive task, too. To complete the process and to reinforce its normative task, I will close this exercise in practical theology and dedicate this chapter to the pragmatic task by asking: *What is the appropriate response and how can preaching be modified to bridge the gap between how it is done and how it should be done?*

Before I give specific suggestions, let me give two disclaimers and an explanation. First, the following suggestions are meant to build on the existing preaching practice that has brought benefits and blessings to many participants included in this study. They are not to be read as a call to abandon or discredit established homiletical methods and habits of preachers, some who have served their congregations for decades. Rather, they should be taken as an informed invitation to explore perhaps less-familiar dimensions of preaching that may open up new perspectives as preaching becomes a more collaborative practice. Secondly, these recommendations are not intended to function as ready-made or full-blown procedures. They are better envisaged as directions worth following, although several specific pointers will be presented as well. Moreover, they are related to the findings gathered in this study and consequently, they are expected to be relevant primarily in the context of Croatian Baptist congregations. While they are not universally applicable, my hope is that other faith communities might still find enough similarities to be able to identify with and become inspired to search for their own answers as they contemplate the suggestions presented here.

As for the explanation, I will produce two sets of suggestions, the first one relating to preachers while the other addresses listeners. This may sound incompatible with the emphasis on preaching as a congregational practice, and the larger quantity of suggestions to the preachers may seem contradictory to the plea for greater involvement of the listeners. However, this division has been introduced for the sake of clarity and by no means revokes the interconnectedness and mutual dependence of preachers and listeners. Also, within the present dispensation, the preachers are those who are more powerful and whose voices are louder. This is why their share of responsibility for the initiation of change must also be greater.

11.1 Suggestions to Preachers

11.1.1 Understand Your Expectations

Carrell's study reveals that at the root of many preaching-related problems is the mismatch of expectations perpetuated by the absence of meaningful and intentional dialogue about such expectations. But if anything is to be changed, the elementary precondition for all involved parties is to become aware of their expectations. Preachers, therefore, must start with themselves. If they preach regularly and if preparing and delivering sermons became a part of their weekly routine long ago, they might need to dig deeper to reach true answers. No matter how long their preaching experience is, they should stop wondering what their preaching *should* accomplish and what they themselves *should* be expecting to see as a result. Instead, they should be asking themselves what they truly anticipate each time they prepare and step up to preach. Do they just expect to get through another sermon? Do they think that this next sermon will make everyone in the congregation repentant, ready to get more involved, or enthusiastic about evangelism? Do they imagine that the believers will talk to them right after the sermon or bring up the sermon details during the mid-week pastoral visit? Do they believe preaching should edify their listeners through increasing their biblical knowledge? The answers may be different and change over time, but the vital objective is to honestly assess whether these expectations are being met and how they feel about it.

How do they bear unfulfilled expectations? Who do they blame them for? Do they change their expectations or adjust the ways of going about making those prospects come true?

Seeking to modify one's preaching practice without becoming sensitive to one's own expectations and the hearers' reactions to them is condemned to failure. It may be argued that this is an introductory step in building up a preacher's persona and an invisible yet precious brick in the construction of the preacher's overall ethos. Given how eagerly some hearers in this study point to the character of the preacher as one of the most influential features of engaging preaching, taking this step may pay dividends in the long run.

11.1.2 They Want to Hear – Help Them!

Preaching is a unique form of human communication, but it still shares some key characteristics with other types of verbal exchange. One is the active involvement of both sides. The responses of the interviewees demonstrate they are generally inclined to take their listening role more seriously. A closer reading of their answers shows that they sometimes (or perhaps, always) hear even more than their preachers assume they do! As human beings, they are capable of hearing behind and beyond spoken words, they instinctively create their own meanings, and they can read nonverbal levels of communication. Although this may be surprising, or even threatening, to some preachers, I believe this should serve as an encouragement. The participants in this study usually attend church services with a desire to listen and hear, and they, to a variable degree, feel responsible for the outcomes of the preaching. Preachers would do well to recognize and respond to this disposition and organise their preparation and delivery in ways that side with the hearers' willingness to hear. Preaching should be a joint venture and not a weekly burden for an exhausted preacher who feels he is the only one responsible for its success or failure. But his listeners will more readily accept their share of responsibility if they sense they are being helped to hear better. Chapters 8 and 9 present various experiences that participants identify as favourable to their listening engagement. I would suggest to any inquisitive preacher to use them as a point of departure for the analysis of their audience. It is not unlikely that the very shift in the preacher's perception of her listeners as believers who authentically seek to understand and hear the sermon might be sufficient to launch a series of small improvements that can lead to long-term progress in the preaching practice.

11.1.3 Never Underestimate their Commitment

One of the problems with preaching that reduces the believers to passive, silent listeners who are left with the "take it or leave it" option as their only choice, is that it makes it nearly impossible for the preachers to determine the level of their hearers' involvement or objectively assess the intensity of their commitment. This type of communication often does not allow for any meaningful or structured feedback channel that could provide preachers with reliable responses from their listeners and consequently, they are left to speculate about the hearers' dedication to listening to the sermon. In the long term, this guesswork can prove disastrous both for the preachers' motivation and for their approach to their listeners.

I believe this empirical study brings ample evidence for the claim that many congregants readily invest their commitment even though some of them have lowered their immediate expectations at some point. Their attendance sends to the preacher an unequivocal signal that they still cherish deep-seated hopes for preaching that have driven them to come to church once again. It is my impression that this is an easily overlooked truth, as preachers tend to take the congregants' attendance for granted (possibly until they stop coming). But on Sunday morning, although some believers may come out of habit or because of family reasons, a preacher should never underrate the fact that the people in the pews are there and not somewhere else (and for many of them, surely, there are many other tempting options). A simple exercise might be helpful here. Preachers could occasionally ask themselves: *If I knew these people would decide whether to keep coming to church based on my next sermon, how would that change my preaching?*

The same reality can be expressed by saying that by their presence attendees bring capital to the table (or to the pulpit) that no preacher, no matter how eloquent, devoted, or experienced, can. Regardless of how ignorant, simple, or biased they may be, every hearer contributes with his or her own confidence and anticipation, however restrained or latent they sometimes are. But their showing up is both an abundant resource and a genuine responsibility. The least any preacher can do in response is to keep ministering to them with a renewed awareness of their faith investments and to begin to shape her entire communication so that it reflects her respect for their having a stake in the sermon listening. This reflection need not be visible on a verbal level only, but if authentic, it will be intuitively acknowledged by alert listeners and will slowly find its way to the wearier ones. Finally, honouring their commitment can signify an occasion at which listeners may begin to feel like active companions and consider preaching as a practice they also may contribute to.

11.1.4 Appreciate the Diversity of the Audience

Alongside belonging to the same congregation, members also live in a contemporary society that is far more diversified than it was thirty or forty years ago. In the past, church communities were far more inwardly oriented, and many Baptists had limited social interaction with other groups and individuals. Often communication with the world outside of the church was discouraged or considered dangerous or sinful. The result was a relatively homogenous mindset, not particularly susceptible to different worldviews and influences.

Today, preachers should keep in mind their listeners inhabit numerous cultural worlds for most of the week and develop their convictions in a dialogue with believers from other traditions and in an exchange with people espousing various ideas. The omnipresence of mass media and online social networks facilitate the traffic of diverse ideas and increase their availability in unprecedented ways. Therefore, preachers simply cannot ignore the diversification of their audience and continue to preach as if all hearers belonged to the same imaginary group and share common expectations and beliefs. This study shows that different people from the same congregation can articulate different responses to preaching and that their propensity to hearing is affected by different qualities of preaching.

What can the preachers do? First, they should not quickly assume a correspondence between their own and the listeners' understanding of the biblical text and its message. They often come from diverse backgrounds, belong to different social classes, and are part of various age groups. There is no finding a way around their otherness; it bears upon the listening process and ignoring it will not make it disappear. Secondly, there is a need to discern the specific groups present in a particular congregation. What are their distinctive features or needs? Do they share some experiences other believers are unaware of? Are they easily offended by certain terminologies related to their past? In these interviews, I have discovered that in their assessment of personal sermon listening history first-generation Baptists use a different measuring mechanism than traditional Baptists. It directly impacts their level of satisfaction and can be used to predict the probability of their making a critical evaluation of the preacher's performance and capacity to preach well. The list of these groups can be long, but it is up to each preacher, and especially the pastoring preacher, to detect those groups and their particularities in his congregation. Thirdly, the recognition of diversity should transform the sermons in the sense that they should be deliberately designed to appeal to multiple groups and not to one general and unspecific group to which no one actually belongs. While no sermon can effectively address all groups at once, knowing her audience will enable the preacher to value its diversity by engaging all the existing groups over the course of time. And if the sermon material is prepared and delivered in a way that manages to absorb the attention of a particular group, it is more likely to also prompt the interest of those not belonging to it far more successfully than a sermon put together with no specific audience in mind.

11.1.5 If You Can't Listen, You Can't Preach – So Listen . . . and Repeat

If a single line can be isolated as the gist of this study, the one heading this section is the best candidate. Indeed, the last three suggestions are impossible to implement without the preacher accepting the necessity of understanding her listeners. More engaging sermons and preaching that is concerned with the hearers' real needs and expectations can come only from previously *listening to the listeners*. This is not to say that the preachers need to get to know their listeners so they can tickle their ears, as might be true if the preacher and listeners had totally opposite ideas on the purpose of preaching. Some might assume listeners just want to be entertained or patted on the back, but this is only an assumption unless it is tested with proper feedback. This study shows the problem is not that listeners have "wrong" expectations, but that preachers are typically ignorant of them. So, the more comprehensive their perception of the listeners' expectations, the more likely it is preachers will learn to appreciate the hearers' perspective and adapt their strategies and approach accordingly. Their investment in learning about and from their listeners increases the probability for successful communication and helps both preachers and listeners to grow in their understanding of preaching as a congregational practice shaped by the responsibilities taken on by various contributors.

Talking to my interviewees, I gradually reached the conviction that some pastors already spend a considerable amount of time listening to their congregants. Going about their pastoral duties and being immersed in shared experiences and occasions in the life of the congregation, they have many opportunities to get to know their believers. The next step to be taken is to allow the results of that listening to have an impact on their sermons. Just as it is possible to fix one's gaze on the sermon's notes or transcript and never lift eyes to meet one's listeners, so it is possible to be so taken up with the biblical text, its interpretation and application, that no room is left for the listeners and their voice. An ability to listen to the listeners and to incorporate their perspectives in the sermon will prevent the preacher from siding with the Bible against his hearers. Memories of sermons when preachers patronised or scolded their hearers mentioned in these interviews reveal that the trouble was not necessarily a faulty theology or an inaccurate reading of the Scriptures, but rather the inability to hear the listeners and the absence of imagination on the part of the preacher that would enable him to see through their eyes and to speak out with their voice.

Stated otherwise, congregants are usually able to tell whether they are *preached to* or *preached at*. Most of the time they look forward to the former and detest the latter, and what makes the difference is the preacher's ability to hear her listeners and to let that listening attitude saturate the sermon's content, inspire her gestures and motions at the pulpit, and energize her preaching ethos. To clarify the maxim from the subtitle: if a preacher cannot listen, she may still preach but how much of it will be heard is uncertain. If there is only one suggestion a preacher chooses to apply from this study, I would say this one is the best choice: Acknowledge *listening to the listeners* as an integral and vital part of faithful preaching and actively seek ways of melding their views and questions with biblical realities. If you are preaching to and for them, you must do everything possible to understand what "they" think, feel, and believe; only then should you stand up to preach.

11.1.6 Do Not Persuade – Identify with Them Instead

Throughout history, homiletics has taken its cue from rhetoric. At times, this threatened its justifiability as a distinct discipline. At other times, though, rhetoric helped homiletics to adapt and to survive. Perhaps in the twenty-first century homiletics has something to learn from rhetoric once again?

We discovered from the history of rhetoric that it developed as a highly contextual discipline, which is why it is no surprise that the concern for the audience in antiquity was not identical to the one advocated by proponents of conversational preaching today. The audience in the classical era was relatively homogenous, while contemporary audiences are usually far more diversified and thus more negotiation of meaning is required before any construction of meaning can happen. This explains why persuading the hearers is no longer the primary rhetorical goal and numerous contemporary rhetorical theories strive to provide some other dynamic equivalent to persuasion.

My suggestion here is therefore quite unpretentious. Instead of developing persuasive arguments to win over and convince the listeners, preachers should design their sermons around the concept of *identification*. Even though my study has a limited scope, there is a detectable tendency among its participants: whenever a particular sermon manages to initiate identification on their part, the probability of their engagement with the sermon increases. The more engaged they are, the more likely they will collaborate and claim the sermon's message. The higher the level of their engagement, the greater is the possibility of their establishing a connection between the meaning and their actual expectations. In this manner, identification functions as a prerequisite for a condition under which the listeners become willing to engage in a dialogue (with the preacher's input, the world of biblical texts, the tradition, theology, etc.) which in turn opens a way for their creation of meaning.

How can preachers turn this tendency to a common benefit for both sides? As they approach a biblical passage or topic, they would do well to think about its identification potential. Is there something there they themselves can identify with? Is there something that their audience or a particular group of hearers will readily recognize and establish an attachment to? Is it possible to create a story or evoke an experience familiar to their everyday life or current circumstances? How can a specific character, event, or emotion be depicted so that it authentically relates to the day-to-day realities as they live them out?

Again, this movement must be bidirectional. A preacher should start by asking what the point of identification is for herself, and only then move on to find potential areas where similar experience can be stimulated for her listeners. If hoping to encourage the hearers' identification with her experience, though, she must be careful not to impose herself or to present herself in a misleading light. The purpose is to motivate the people to come to grips with the challenge of the claims of the gospel and not to improve the public opinion of the preacher.

Also, sincere identification can happen only out of genuine respect for the other. McClure reminds us that a preacher should not assume a "symmetry of experiences" that would enforce the eradication of all differences. The diversity of backgrounds and experiences should be seen as a protection from the preacher's assuming an attitude of moral superiority that the participants in this study repeatedly identify as a sermon-killer. The otherness of the congregation should urge the preacher to take a humbler approach, not presuming from the start he knows where and how identification will take place but searching for opportunities in hope that it is possible. Giving up the ambition of persuading the listeners, a preacher provides a better chance for identification to take place, but also grants the congregation an opportunity to rediscover the doctrine of the priesthood of all believers and subtly supports their taking more and more responsibility for the preaching practice.

At this point, it should be clear that focus on identification as a key rhetorical category of preaching implies acceptance of the previous suggestions. And since preaching becomes much more effective insomuch as it insists on its contextual expression, I am not offering any detailed propositions on how to create identification opportunities in sermons. But I am positive that preachers can learn how to do this in their own contexts by engaging in open conversation with their audiences about their sermon listening experiences.

11.1.7 Actively Seek Critical Feedback

As has been shown, different authors have rightly located the absence of communication between preachers and their listeners as the origin of many difficulties. At this point, though, I want to underscore a need for preachers to learn not only about their listeners and their respective experiences and expectations, but also about their specific responses to the sermon they just heard. It is indispensable for the preachers to get direct feedback on their preaching from the people for whom these sermons are preached. They may be doing a good job in exegeting their audience and preparing their sermons in accordance with that knowledge, but they still need a response from real people to adjust their future preaching so that it better suits their needs.

Churches typically have no established mechanisms for providing this sort of feedback. In this study, there was only one congregation where there is a semi-formal opportunity for the members of an inner leadership circle to offer their feedback on the previous sermon. Usually, it all comes down to an occasional thank-you remark made on the way out of the church. Without questioning the honesty of those praises, I am convinced that every audience can provide more depth and variety of response if only given a proper chance. This is why I suggest it is the *preacher* who should take the initiative and set up a safe, dedicated environment where his congregants can express their reactions, comments, and observations after listening to the sermon. The purpose of such conversations would not be for a preacher to provide further explanations or to offer reasons for her choice of words, images, or rhetorical figures. Rather, this should be an occasion for the preacher to listen and learn how her preaching really correlates to the listeners' perceptions, ideas, and beliefs. In the process, some of her assumptions may be called into question and others may be shown as needing some accommodation.

Of course, this is only one of the immediate benefits. Regular feedback sessions can turn the preaching as a pivotal practice into a collaborative activity taking the Baptist congregationalist emphasis to the next level. At the same time, these sessions could inspire listeners to take active responsibility for their involvement in the preaching and listening practice and rouse interest among those who tend to be inert listeners. The preacher's work on his sermons based on listeners' feedback has the potential to gradually empower congregants and to disrupt the traditional model in which the preacher gives, and the listeners receive. Providing and accepting feedback teaches everyone the value of co-operation and acknowledges the multiplicity of gifts distributed to all believers.

To exploit the maximum potential of feedback sessions, preachers should make sure they welcome all feedback, including negative remarks. Probing the reasons and motives for making such comments can reveal more useful data for the improvement of preaching than simply collecting praises and positive experiences from listeners. Naturally, this would require a willingness to be exposed and subject to criticism as it could turn out to be an unpleasant experience for the preacher. However, preaching is not meant to be a homiletical extension of "happy-clappy" worship, but a crucial practice for the congregation, intended to benefit the spiritual development of all its members, preachers included. The preacher's courage to reveal such vulnerability may be rewarded by an increase of involvement and trust of those church members who used to be disappointed or who have grown disinterested. Yet a substantial requirement must be met for this to happen: access to the feedback sessions must be carefully and intentionally open to all hearers, not only to the most enthusiastic members, those with an excess of free time, or those who belong to the pastor's (or preacher's) "fan club." An equal opportunity to participate should be offered to everybody in the congregation, and the preacher should go the extra mile to include as many diverse listeners as possible.

11.1.8 Do Not Be Afraid of Losing Control

It is easy to imagine a preacher who would, after reading the previous suggestions, feel urged to object: "But wait, what happens with my authority? If I apply all of these, I will certainly lose all control!" There is a ring of truth about this objection. However, as various homiletical authorities point out and my study confirms, the preacher's authority is no longer something to be taken for granted. In fact, the preacher's authority should not be defended so much as it is earned. The redistribution of authority in contemporary society has affected churches as well, but that does not need to be bad news.

The gathered data demonstrate that Croatian Baptists still hold their preachers in relatively high esteem. They believe that preachers have been given a vital role and thus they have high expectations of them. And yet, many of them can register every shortcoming and intuitively realise whenever their preachers fall short of assumed standards. So, although some authority is given to preachers by their appointment to this ministry, they still need to attain and affirm that authority in front of the congregation not only by their preaching competence, but even more so by living in accordance with the ethical norms of the gospel. Their homiletical proficiency is never perceived and judged apart from their dealings with individual believers and their engagement in and for the congregation.

In that light, allowing listeners to influence the preaching practice cannot be seen as losing control or detracting from the authority of a preacher. Such a move has a strong biblical and theological backing and serves as a reinstitution of preaching understood in terms of the doctrines of the *Imago Dei*, the incarnation, and the priesthood of all believers. Creating opportunities for listeners to assume active responsibility and stimulating them to claim the practice of preaching as a focal point of dialogue and conversation within the congregation composed of various groups and individuals with equally valuable voices will eventually earn the preacher a lasting authority based not on clinging to his position, but on faithful preaching through his ethos.

Discussing the homiletical turn to the listener, Beverly Zink-Sawyer declares that it empowers preaching by adding to its communal and pneumatological dimension. That preachers can never ultimately know what is heard by their listeners (which also can cause feelings of insecurity and of losing control) can be turned into an act of recognition that "the task of preaching and the text from which we preach are not our own but are shared gifts given to the whole people of God." So, instead of seeing this as diminishing the preacher's authority, as if preaching were "some kind of 'zero-sum' game," it is far more beneficial to consider it as an invitation to the listeners to take on their share of responsibility for the sake of effective preaching accomplished through the work of the Holy Spirit.[1]

11.1.9 Go Slowly

Assuming there is a pastor or preacher who, after reading this research, becomes convinced that the preaching ministry of his congregation would benefit from implementing these suggestions, it is easy to imagine this person would be tempted to initiate changes as soon as possible. In that case, I have one more suggestion.

It is short and basic: *Go slowly*. Remember there are many believers for whom preaching is the most valuable part of the church service and possibly the most distinct element of your congregation's worship. Bear in mind that some of your congregants' expectations might be firmly related to maintaining the sense of belonging, to the consolidation of their identity as defined within the congregational network, and to reinforcing the atmosphere of security. Also, some are probably taking the approach of passive responsibility: the sermon is always the word of God, no matter how monological, communicationally ineffective, or plainly boring it is. In all these cases, introducing too many changes at once or launching them too early will likely be counterproductive. Causing strong opposition early in the process may mean

---

1. Zink-Sawyer, *Word Purely Preached*, 355–56.

that the door will get tightly closed and seriously obstruct the possibility of accomplishing the desired outcome.

Another reason for a cautious approach is the listeners' tendency to walk the well-trodden path of routine even when they are aware of the need for a change. In their answers, some respondents openly mentioned their laziness and indifference alongside their articulation that the purpose of preaching is to challenge the listeners and to dare them to change. Disturbing something that has been in place for a long time may mean one will face unexpected issues and will need to deal with them before turning to the original plans (and some of the early enthusiasm may wear down in the process).

In fact, the very process of introducing change needs to follow the same key rule: *listen to your listeners*. A preacher should start by inquiring how her hearers feel about the potential innovations and see what questions, hopes, and fears they have. Trying to identify those willing to get involved at the early stage would also be useful. A preliminary discussion on likely objections or undesired effects can help to avoid distractions. For instance, some believers may think that it is theologically wrong to question anything from the sermon because the sermon is a word from God. Therefore, they may refuse to participate in the feedback sessions where criticism of the latest sermon would be welcome. Or some may evade taking active responsibility for preaching by complaining that the preacher only shirked his duty by trying to get others involved.

A good rule of thumb is to introduce changes at the listeners' pace. Also, a preacher can always start with those amendments that are not immediately visible to the congregants – i.e., she can explore her expectations of the preaching practice first, begin to actively look for signs of the desire to hear, or invest more energy in efforts to understand the existing diversity in her congregation. Then some small-scale moves can be made: a sermon preached with a stronger awareness of the listeners' commitment to come and listen, or an informal discussion with a few church members about their best memories related to their sermon-listening experience. The next step may be something more daring and more official, but the progression should always be highly contextual and conditioned by the responses and needs of the congregation. My informed hunch is that along the way there will be some surprising blessings.

11.2 Suggestions to the Listeners

11.2.1 Come to Listen and Come to Hear

I am convinced that listeners themselves can greatly change the preaching practice in their congregation even if their preacher's contribution is at first minimal. There is at least one thing they can change without involving the other side, and the effect may be life changing. The study I conducted leaves no doubt that for some attendees, listening to the sermon has turned into a routine that they exercise without getting their hopes up. The gradual lowering of their expectations affects their level of attention and shrinks their reception capabilities. Their predefined anticipations ("the sermon will be boring," "the preacher will only repeat his pet phrases," "I won't hear anything new") petrify an attitude that functions as a self-fulfilling prophecy. In the end, they get into a downward spiral of listeners' depression and the prospects of reversing that state become less and less likely.

Therefore listeners need each other to break that spell and awaken from slumber. What they can do is ask questions such as: Why do I come to the church service? What do I *really* expect from a sermon? Is there anything that prevents me from being alert during the sermon? What would need to change in the preaching to make me more content with the listening experience? After answering these questions for themselves, the listeners could engage in a discussion with others – be it family members, co-members from different groups within the congregation, or other fellow believers – and help each other to understand their current thinking and feelings about the preaching. This exchange does not require an official occasion or a highly structured meeting; an informal conversation over a cup of coffee after the Sunday worship would be a more natural setting.

The next move could be to set for themselves a single listening goal for each upcoming sermon. For instance, a listener may decide to listen to a particular sermon with the intention of memorising a fact about the passage of Scripture. Or the purpose of listening could be to identify the preacher's main idea or argument and later to rephrase it to someone who has not heard the sermon. Another hearer may decide to look for the preacher's nonverbal gestures and communication beyond his verbal expression. Yet another possibility is to establish a link between a specific personal experience and a thought verbalised by the preacher.

The chief idea behind this exercise is that the listeners should retrain themselves: by becoming aware of their existing attitudes and expectations and by setting a clear listening goal, they are becoming attentive and focused on the moment. Over time, they will begin to listen expecting that there is something interesting to be heard, to inquire about what they can learn from others, and to allow preachers to express themselves without prematurely shutting their ears and minds. By doing so, they will cultivate listening skills that will foster their attempts to understand, remember, and examine even when they disagree with the preacher.

If listeners aim at hearing a sermon, they must come with the intention to listen. Some interviewees in this study have demonstrated an enviable degree of passive responsibility and rightly acknowledged that the capacity for hearing depends on and begins with their proper attitude. Such thoughtful concentration, though, rarely comes naturally and typically involves deliberate effort. The suggestions provided above can inspire listeners to set up and engage in such efforts within their respective preaching environment.

11.2.2 Become a Constructive Contributor

The study's data seem to verify the conclusion that whenever a conflict between the listeners' *expectations* and their listening *experience* arises, there is no established or applicable strategy for resolving the tension. The preacher simply continues to preach as she used to, and the listeners remain disappointed and unfulfilled. The problem is not that the listeners are unhappy with the sermons they hear; the problem is they are not given the opportunity to vent their dissatisfaction. Both my personal experience and these interviews appear to confirm Clyde Reid's observation that preaching is the Protestant "sacred cow,"[2] and therefore preaching-related problems are seldom openly addressed. On the surface, everything looks functional and people try to keep up appearances. But discontented hearers will quietly become frustrated and their irritation may, due to the special status of preaching, show up elsewhere. The resulting problem will not be easy to deal with because its origin is rooted in the lack of communication about the listeners' perspective on preaching.

However, the listeners' restlessness about preaching is not a symptom of spiritual disorder or indiscipline. On the contrary, it is a healthy indication

---

2. Reid, *Empty Pulpit*, 11.

of mature craving for a challenge to change. They expect preaching to provoke their positive transformation, but they feel the lack of impulse from the pulpit. It is crucial, then, not to permit this discrepancy to lead them to apathy, despondency, or aloofness. Their feeling of dissatisfaction needs to be redirected toward a constructive contribution. They could begin by trying to locate the sources of their disengagement with the preaching: What sorts of feelings does this create in me? Can I imagine using them toward a constructive goal instead of entertaining the sense of helplessness (because preaching is the preacher's job)?

Again, the contextually-given conditions and circumstances will determine what and how much can be done as a follow-up to these and other questions. It may be that congregants too often think their preacher would not be ready to hear their critical remarks. This may have to do with their past experiences or with their preacher's leadership style. Yet, using an inoffensive approach and focusing on their own perception of preaching, which does not directly question the preacher's performance, may open doors no one before dared to knock on. Also, it is not unlikely that the preacher would welcome input that may help him to orientate in the fog of ignorance about his hearers' real reception of the sermon. After all, both sides surely hold preaching in high esteem and wish its full potential to be unleashed for the sake of the entire congregation. By communicating their actual impressions and assessment of preaching, the hearers express that they care and are ready to offer their contribution to make it better instead of using their dissatisfaction to destructive ends (such as gossiping or negativism).

11.2.3 Take Your Share of Responsibility

All preaching is meant to benefit the congregation. I have demonstrated not only that it is highly contextual as practised within a particular congregation, but also that it finds its fullest expression in a congregationalist framework. From a purely theological perspective, it is paradoxical to observe congregations that traditionally keep preaching at the very centre of their ecclesial life while they comply with degrading almost the entire congregation (that is, everyone except one person – the preacher) to the role of recipients on the margins. This generates a forced imbalance of responsibility that is unfair both to the preacher and to the audience and becomes notably painful in situations when the majority feels that preaching no longer fulfils its purposes. Then the preacher may end up with too much responsibility, without substantial capacity to respond to the crisis, or without sufficiently strong support from the audience. On the other hand, the hearers may end up with almost no responsibility, but with a strong assumption that it is the preacher who needs to find a solution. With such realities in force, it is not always easy to improve preaching. But if preaching is to be a truly congregational practice, then the entire congregation must be more actively involved.

This is why I suggest listeners do not need to wait for the preacher to take responsibility. To begin, they could awaken themselves to the fact that preaching requires knowledge, energy, commitment, time, and continual improvement, to name only a few qualifications. In other words, an effective preacher must respond to great demands. His hearers can choose to share this burden and take on more responsibility by offering him their help and support, especially if he is their pastor, too. They can offer to help him out with administrative tasks to provide him with more time to spend in pastoral work or sermon preparation. Perhaps they can agree to meet with him after the Sunday service to provide immediate feedback to the sermon, thus helping him to gauge its impact on the congregation. A preacher may never ask for a comment or serious follow-up (the reasons can be manifold: insecurity, tradition, or something else) but could be nevertheless thrilled to hear it. Depending on the method of putting together a preaching plan, the listeners can also suggest topics or Bible books or passages to be covered in the future. Discussing their choice may improve the preacher's understanding of their needs and interests. If the preacher is a pastor who is used to do one-on-one counselling, perhaps she will accept a suggestion from an engaged hearer to privately examine her sermon and hear his or her questions and suggestions. (I am aware that some of those suggestions may not work in some congregations and some of them may take a lot of time to become viable within a given context.)

These proposals all have the same intention: to highlight the essential truth that listeners can take the initiative and transform the nature of the relationship between preacher and audience. By establishing different proportions of involvement of preachers and listeners and by better redistributing the responsibility, preaching can be reclaimed by the entire congregation. A preacher may be too exhausted or busy to even think about changes in that direction. Yet, those hearers who take this advice to heart could discover they are able to influence both the sermon and the pastor. And by assuming an active responsibility for preaching, they will make it easier for their preacher to join them, and their communal preaching practice can become a vivid expression of the priesthood of all believers.

Eventually, my hope is that both listeners and preachers in the Croatian Baptist churches might be intrigued enough by this study to start exploring how the silent majority and its eloquent silence can contribute to, transform, and promote preaching in such a way that the traditional speaking and listening roles be reshuffled for the sake of faithfulness to the gospel, and that the gap between the preacher and her hearers will be closed in order to build a long-lasting partnership.

CHAPTER 12

Conclusion

There are several substantial concerns to deal with in this closing chapter. First, I will pinpoint the methodological limitations of my study in order to situate my contribution claims within the appropriate context. Also, I will note those aspects of my research that, in hindsight, I would do differently. Secondly, I intend to review my research question and objectives and compare them with my findings and ensuing conclusions. Following that, I will specify the contributions of this work to the knowledge about the topic in question proceeding from my research. Finally, I will provide some recommendations for further research and some broad guidelines on how to build on the evidence of this present study.

12.1 Limitations

My hope is that the previous chapters were successful in pointing out the value of the research results and subsequent recommendations. However, any trustworthy evaluation must also include an identification of the inherent limitations of the research. Some of these are essentially methodological limitations of the field study while others are related to the scope of the literature review.

To begin with, a phenomenological approach paired with the choice of a semi-structured interview clearly seeks to apprehend the respondents' experience of listening to sermons. As such, it attempts to isolate their subjective perceptions and the meanings they construct as they participate in the phenomenon of sermon listening. It acknowledges the existence of multiple realities and strives to depict the listeners' experience from their own perspective as exhaustively as possible. However, there is an intrinsic limitation here; answering questions about sermon listening may still differ from the actual engagement in the practice that is the central subject matter of the interviews.

Secondly, this study is based on the data collected through a single method. Certainly, a multiple-method approach would have provided a welcome opportunity to compare different data sources and improve the data's accuracy and appropriateness. For instance, a triangulation consisting of organising several focus groups and subsequent individual interviews designed in keeping with the findings of these group interviews would have likely overcome the limitations typical of a single method. Also, implementing such a research design would have permitted me to explore and identify the prevailing trends in sermon listening in each congregation included in the research (and not only the experiences of individual believers). The dynamics of focus group discussions may would have revealed something of a congregational identity being formed and re-formed through sermon listening. In any case, restrictions in time and resources have determined the structure of this study and affected the choice of data collection method.

Thirdly, there is the interviewer effect. As in any qualitative analysis, the interviewees responded depending on their perception of the person asking the questions. The identity of the interviewer has been pertinent to the supply of information that the respondents provided. Indeed, the fact that many respondents heard the interviewer's sermon prior to the interview could mean that it not only helped them shape their judgement of his character, but also that the listening experience affected their assumptions on what was expected of them, thus impelling or influencing their answers. However, the interviewer consciously invested every effort in making both his sermon and his general appearance and performance as conducive to their honest and uninhibited participation as possible.

Fourthly, although it may sound like a self-evident fact, I should emphasise that this qualitative research with a relatively small sample does not produce fully generalizable results. What it does seek to provide, however, is a rich description of the sermon-listening practice within a specific context, namely that of individuals in their respective congregations. The study was not designed to focus on a sample representative of the wider population, but rather to examine thoroughly some specific situations. In other words, I have no grounds for predicting how likely my findings are to occur on other occasions, or for claiming that *all* Croatian Baptists have the same expectations and convictions concerning preaching. Nevertheless, I have tried to structure my findings in a way that suggests their "transferability."[1] This includes providing enough detail about the participants and their immediate contexts so the reader may infer the possible applicability of these findings. The idea has been to make the reader reach the point where he or she decides to ask to what extent these findings could be transferred to other contexts.[2] Another way of expressing this aim is to use Swinton and Mowatt's concept of identification and resonance. In their view, good qualitative research will create a resonance ". . . with the experiences of others in similar circumstances," which in turn invokes "a sense of identification with those who share something of the experience."[3] My claim, then, is that those uninvolved in these immediate congregational situations who also experience the phenomena of sermon listening in other contexts may discover that these results reveal similarities sufficient to create a certain level of resonance with a transforming potential.

Fifthly, my original research design included conducting twenty interviews. However, two distinct determinants altered this intention. At some time during the last three or four interviews, I reached the point where new data seemed merely to confirm the previously amassed insights and the collected feedback only reinforced the existing codes and concepts. Recognising this saturation coincided with the fact that several potential respondents within the sample who had expressed interest in taking part were repeatedly unable to come to the arranged interview appointment. Since this stage of research had already spanned more than three months, I decided to conclude it after completing eighteen interviews.

In addition, although the topic of this thesis is, strictly speaking, a homiletical one, my literature review extended across several disciplines. Five distinct chapters dedicated to the turn toward the listener in homiletical theory, the connection between rhetoric and homiletics, congregational studies, existing empirical studies in preaching, and the history of Croatian Baptists and their

---

1. The term has been originally used in Yvonna S. Lincoln and Egon G. Guba, *Naturalistic Inquiry* (London: SAGE, 1985).
2. Denscombe, *Good Research Guide*, 301.
3. Swinton and Mowatt, *Practical Theology*, 47.

preaching practice enabled me to build a broad stage for my own qualitative study and to present a solid justification of the need to conduct it. On the other hand, this breadth prevented me from exploring more material in each of these fields and from using more diverse interpretive tools in my analysis section.[4] Following those leads would have inevitably taken me beyond the scope of this study.

In retrospect, if done differently, several aspects might have contributed to the research in a more useful fashion. For one, during the interviews, I should have asked more probing questions. As I analysed my transcripts, I realised that insisting on such questions would have brought about a deeper understanding of the interviewees' experience. To be more specific, I assume that probing for their emotions and their attitudes (e.g., on the role that the Bible has or should have in preaching) would have resulted in more nuanced and diverse insights. Another thing that I discovered during my fieldwork, especially when visiting churches outside my place of residence, was that conducting more than two interviews within the same day presents an overwhelming workload, which easily diminishes the quality of the interviewer's performance. This effect was particularly noticeable in my moderately reduced ability to write substantial field notes due to the weakened focus and

---

4. For instance, the work of modern rhetoricians such as Kenneth Burke are an excellent framework for further development of the argument that identification may be a supplement to (possibly even a replacement of) persuasion as a goal of the rhetorical (preaching) act. Also, Wayne Booth's notion of "listening rhetoric," according to which discovery of new, shared truths surpasses persuasion as the ultimate goal of rhetoric, could be fruitfully utilised to evaluate sermon-listening as a congregational practice with a strong unifying potential based on preaching as a process of co-creating meaning between the preacher and the audience. See Burke, *A Rhetoric of Motives*; Wayne C. Booth, "Rhetoric and Religion: Are They Essentially Wedded?," in *Radical Pluralism and Truth: David Tracy and the Hermeneutics of Religion*, edited by Werner G. Jeanrond and Jennifer L. Rike (New York: Crossroad, 1991), 62–80, Wayne C. Booth, *The Rhetoric of RHETORIC: The Quest for Effective Communication* (Oxford: Blackwell, 2004), 39–54, 153–70.

Also, there are other phenomenological studies of listening to preaching worthy of more investigation. Their perspectives would, without doubt, be a dynamic contribution and correlative to my own study. A good example is Theo Pleizer's research (*Religious Involvement*) that discusses the listener's function within the preaching event and puts together a rich description of the listening process. Gaarden and Lorensen have conducted an empirical study to understand how listeners receive and appropriate sermons and concluded that their construction of meaning happens in at least three modes and therefore has a far more active role in the preaching event than usually assumed by more traditional homiletical theories. Gaarden and Lorensen, "Listeners as Authors in Preaching – Empirical and Theoretical Perspectives," *Homiletic* 38, no. 1 (2013), accessed 23 October 2015, <http://www.homiletic.net/index.php/homiletic/article/view/3832>.

powers of retention. The last research component to be addressed in this section is the quality of audio recording. All the interviews were recorded with nonprofessional equipment and the results are accordingly less than perfect. There were a few instances when small parts of the interview had to be repeated, but the biggest issue was related to transcribing the data from these audio files because of the noise, which at times considerably slowed the process. In any case, these are the explicit lessons I have learned by engaging in fieldwork of qualitative research, and they will be a valuable experience to build on in my future projects.

12.2 Research Objectives

The final assessment of this research requires a final revisit of the research question: What are the real expectations and receptiveness of the Croatian Baptists as sermon listeners, and how can these findings be utilised to improve the quality of preaching? A search for answers to this question necessitated setting up the following objectives:

1. to identify the hearers' actual expectations directing their listening participation;
2. to understand what are the engaging or disengaging factors that considerably influence their reception of the sermon; and
3. to formulate constructive suggestions for the transformation of the preaching practice based on the study's findings and reinforced by insights from disciplines and similar studies covered in my literature review section.

The rest of this section will be dedicated to the recapitulation of the accomplished results.

12.2.1 Expectations

This research reveals a variety of profound expectations pertinent to sermon listening which sometimes are all pervaded by a striking tension between the listeners' high hopes in preaching and the realities of their listening history. Additionally, these expectations are typically grounded in a variety of convictions revealed as the participants discussed their sermon listening experiences. More specifically, the high view of preaching, based on understanding the sermon as the proclaimed word of God, the assumption that preaching is a central element of church life, and the belief in the prominent role of the preacher and her authority are the most prominent convictions.

Consequently, there is no doubt these congregants consider preaching a highlight of church worship and the fullest expression of their congregational identity; and yet, many of them claim their expectations are not being met. This experience often leads them to lower their immediate expectations, making them more passive. The noteworthy detail is that the probability of expressing their discontent increases with those interviewees who belong to the traditional Baptists with more "years of service" in church. However, the study also confirms that this discrepancy does not extinguish the dormant hope that preaching is still capable of meeting the presumed higher standards.

When it comes to specific expectations concerning the purpose of preaching, my research demonstrates several trends. Some listeners want sermons to teach them more about the Bible and make it closer to their life. The underlying goal of this process, however, is a provision of direction in their everyday living. Starting from the Bible, a sermon is to show them the next step on their journey. Secondly, there is a link between the expectation to meet God during the sermon and the anticipation of preaching as enhancing the devotional reading of the Bible. There are hearers who feel that a sermon is purposeful when it helps them encounter God as they listen and reflect on the preacher's words. Such an experience certainly stimulates their individual edification, usually practised through regular Bible reading. Thirdly, several respondents offered answers that can be interpreted as expressing hope that listening to a sermon will recharge their spiritual batteries. By their commitment to come and listen repeatedly, they signify their willingness to invest their faith and seek confirmation of their sense of identity and belonging. Finally, the interviews indicate that for some hearers a sermon must question their status quo and challenge them to change. For them, preaching should address their life situation with specific proposals and urge them to take practical actions in response to what they heard.

12.2.2. (Dis)engaging Factors

Not all participants shared the same eagerness for pointing out those elements of preaching that cause them to withdraw from listening to the sermon, but their feedback still provides enough information to reach certain conclusions.

Their hearing is hindered when preachers underperform by using excessive repetition, generic illustrations, clichés, or Christian jargon. Poorly arranged preaching material, too much content, and unfocused messages have the same effect. Similarly, an overly long sermon easily revokes a positive listening experience.

Some congregants, particularly traditional Baptists, also mention the preacher's incapacity as an important obstacle to their engagement with the sermon. Their sense of disconnection can be additionally intensified by preaching that allows no differing views and enforces uniformity. A number of interviewed listeners remember sermons preached with a judgemental attitude. They felt such preachers have assumed a morally superior position and this, they agree, destroys their receptivity.

On the other hand, the participants were explicit in naming those features that contribute to their listening. Broadly speaking, their sense of involvement is tightly related to their perception that the preacher manages to establish a connection between the biblical text or message and their life situation. This connection is felt each time there is some correspondence to their real-life experiences or an impression that the preacher's words are an expression of his authentic engagement with the Bible and loaded with his own personal experience. Such type of recognition triggers their identification: either with the preacher's position, that is, with his embodiment of the message, or with specific elements of the message, considered to be relevant to their experience. The correlated quality is the preacher's vulnerability and willingness to be transparent in her preaching. Other preaching features that stimulate the listeners' engagement belong to the categories of style and delivery – use of plain language rich in evocative imagery, easily remembered introductions, poignant catchphrases, and humour.

12.3 Contribution to Knowledge

Before this research, there was no empirical attempt to explore the practice of preaching among Croatian Baptists (or any other Christian church in the country) from the listeners' perspective. As a matter of fact, given the reality of preaching as the most treasured aspect of their denominational identity, this absence of any structured effort to understand and evaluate it is even more critical. In this respect, my research may be regarded as a pioneering project and serve as a reference point for future studies. I am convinced that it effectively illustrates the benefits of empirical investigation of a particular practice and presents a case for the development of that practice through a dialogue with various disciplines and theological reflection on its findings.

Allow me to spell out the specifics of my study's contribution. First, I have presented a brief history of the Croatian Baptists from the perspective of their homiletical practice. Preaching has been a distinguishing part of the Baptist identity for decades, but one of the consequences is that it so easily slips under the radar and remains uncritically taken for granted. Throughout the denomination's history sermons have circulated and many of them are preserved and available today, but very little or no attention has been given to issues such as *Why are these sermons preached in this particular way? What can be done to adjust the sermons so that they fit their audience better?* or *How receptive are the hearers and why?* After juxtaposing this brief historical account and the overview of contemporary homiletical literature with its "turn to the listener," the report on how rhetoric and preaching coexisted over the centuries, the developments facilitated by the congregational studies, and the existing empirical studies exploring the listeners' role in preaching, I believe there is a full justification for the conclusion that an empirical exploration of the listeners' reception of and engagement in the preaching practice is not only beneficial, but also an urgent exercise that may have a valuable effect on the future of Croatian Baptist congregations.

Secondly, I situated my qualitative study and its results among other, similar studies. By doing that, I discovered several striking correlations and overlaps as well as some original findings. For instance, this study confirmed that Carrell's judgement about the listeners' thoughts being undiscoverable in the usual routine of preaching practice is valid for the Croatian Baptists' context, too. It also identified the "cycle of low expectations" as the real experience of some listeners who continuously have their expectations betrayed. Likewise, it proved that the "dominant listening setting," as described in *Listening to Listeners*, is a feasible concept. At the same time, the influence of other settings reveals a diversity that translates itself into a spectrum of expectations that cannot be easily classified – and yet, some of the expectations typical for those three settings (ethos, logos, and pathos) show up in my study as well. Furthermore, considering van der Geest's study, it is easy to notice that his dimension of security finds its counterpart in an expectation of spiritual battery-charging and identity affirmation. His dimension of deliverance roughly matches the challenge to change from my study, and the desire to get to know God better and to understand the Bible more profoundly through sermon listening in order to make sense out of life can be correlated to his dimension of understanding. At the same time, focusing on the twelve specific expectations pointed out by the researchers behind *Listening to Listeners* also resembles the results of this study.

In addition, both van der Geest and *Listening to Listeners* point to the underlying expectancy as to the preacher's life of integrity and a close correspondence between her preaching and living. My results accordingly disclose it as crucially important, since to be persuaded these listeners need to be able to identify with the preacher or with his situation. Identification often functions as the gateway to engagement with the sermon and increases the likeliness of having their expectations addressed. In that respect, there is also agreement about the preacher's role being decisive. It is to be defined through his relationship with the listeners and incorporate not only his different attitude during preaching, but also, in Carrell's words, "studying the text of his listeners."

These findings, however, lay bare an additional dimension of sermon listening, which is not fully accounted for in other studies. In a nutshell, the interviews tell us that simply bringing the listeners' expectations into focus is not sufficient. Insisting on expectations without backing them up with taking certain responsibilities only perpetuates their subdued and detached involvement in preaching. For the listeners to claim preaching as something that belongs to them as well, something they help shape and direct, they must understand their share of responsibility and begin to act upon it. The participants in this study have indeed shown that they possess a spark of awareness that such responsibility is necessary. Some of them have also exhibited readiness to put this awareness into practice. But there is a crucial distinction to be stressed: a majority have manifested passive responsibility, which is remarkably different from active responsibility. Taken to its extreme, passive responsibility becomes self-destructive for listeners and keeps them isolated from the preacher. The hearer and the preacher, each with their own concerns, remain on different sides of the gap. On the other hand, active responsibility translates to a constructive enterprise that unifies their efforts and bridges the gap. Only then can preaching turn into a truly congregational practice and an authentic centre of worship and ecclesial life for all believers. To accomplish this transformation, the initiative must come from the listeners themselves. And yet, the current balance in Croatian Baptist congregations suggests that the onus is on the preachers, who should do everything they can to stimulate their listeners to take this initiative on their own account.

Thirdly, I have offered a theologically sustainable warrant for the transformation of the practice of preaching through a stronger involvement of the listeners as well as a theological reflection on the key findings of this study. Focusing on three potent doctrines – *imago Dei*, the incarnation, and the priesthood of all believers – I have developed a proposal for similar attempts at a re-evaluation of preaching, providing a validation for empowering silenced majorities and giving voice to their eloquent silence. At the same time, I have shown that a revised preaching practice contains the potential for character formation, building a community of faith, and relating communal identity to the wider society, thus turning preaching and listening into a genuinely congregational practice based on reciprocity and shared responsibility. Put briefly: listening to the listeners not only changes preaching and worship, but also irreversibly alters the nature of the congregation and transforms its self-perception as a Christian church.

Fourthly, I began this study with a firm conviction that the final product would remain deficient if left without a pragmatic and practical element that puts forward tentative ideas on how this practice can be improved. So, my distinct contribution consists of contextually driven recommendations to both preachers and listeners belonging to Croatian Baptist churches. Moreover, these guidelines are not an offshoot of a purely theoretical treatment of homiletical literature, since they also proceed from raw empirical data, provided by those involved in sermon listening at the most fundamental level: those who are usually the silenced majority. Furthermore, they are also informed by proposals from other homileticians, such as Lucy Atkinson Rose and John S. McClure, and filtered through theological reflection aided by my insider's perspective and contextual awareness. Hence, I hope this original contribution to knowledge will also be applicable in real-life settings.

Finally, I believe that specifically Baptist homiletics would ensue from the appropriation of these practical suggestions and the reassessment of current preaching practice informed by a fresh reading of classical doctrines from the perspective of practical theology. In a sense, the basic historical principles of Baptist identity – the autonomy of a local, gathered church, the diversity of gifts distributed across the congregation, the clarity of Scripture, the individual responsibility of every believer, and the understanding of ministry as servanthood – simply need to be allowed to find their authentic expression in the ministry of preaching. A solid lead in that respect could be found, for instance, in Paul Fiddes's elucidation of the Baptist understanding of ministry as based not on the delegation of authority (either "from above" or "from below"), but on servanthood that creates trust and on "the self-giving humility of God."[5] Under such an economy of power, there is a dynamic distribution of authority that attributes responsibility for overseeing each other to *all* members. There is no connection between spiritual gifts and authority, and therefore no need to uphold the hierarchy of submission to those who "possess" gifts. Hence the distinction between the clergy and the laity should be seen as two different "ways of being," which should by no means imply a difference in rank. Fiddes rightfully reminds us that the concept of royal priesthood belongs to the entire church and not exclusively to any individual believer or any particular ministry. In light of this research, his warning can be read in terms of not allowing the same concept to be reserved for the preacher or preaching alone.

At the same time, it is worth remembering that the participants' feedback in this study implies the existence of a deep-seated theology (or theologies) of preaching and juxtaposes this reality to Christopher Ellis' reminder that "worship is embodied theology."[6] This should encourage congregations to reexamine whether they can see their preaching not only as the sacrosanct and essential reason for their regular coming together (while other elements are only, in Ellis's words, "preliminaries"), but as a part of the more comprehensive purpose of their being a church. Ellis also suggests that "worship is the place where the Church is gathered by God and becomes *ekklesia*."[7] The main purpose of worship, thus, is for people to encounter one another and to meet God. In a way, holding a too high view of preaching can threaten to overshadow the rest of theology and render other practices as secondary. But if preaching is an integral part of worship, if worship always embodies

---

5. Fiddes, *Tracks and Traces*, 83–106.
6. Ellis, *Gathering*, 2.
7. Ellis, 5.

communal and individual theological convictions, and if there is no worship unless the congregants take an active part in it, then preaching in future should necessarily seek to devise new ways of stronger participation of all those gathered to hear the word of God. Theologically speaking, the imminent challenge for Baptists might be to align their homiletics with their ecclesiology.

To accomplish that, the operative theology of preaching should undergo a series of transformations, among which a move of the listeners' responsibility from passive to active might be most important. Such empowerment of the hearers for participating in a practice that so distinctively shapes the Baptist identity may pave the way for the development of a highly contextual Baptist homiletical ecclesiology. Perhaps this development could be aided by Fiddes' proposal; when discussing the church as a temple inhabited by the Spirit of God, he says: "the same Spirit who indwelt the body of the earthly Jesus like a temple, and gave him power for ministry, now indwells his body the church. In this sense, the church might be called an 'extension of the incarnation.'"[8] It is my hope that the reader of this work will see such a development as a conceivable and natural next step to be taken in this context and imagine a comparable theological and practical progression in his or her specific circumstances.

12.4 Further Research Suggestions

During the research, I gradually discovered a number of areas deserving further study. Naturally, this present study, being determined by the limitations described above, could not follow their lead and investigate them properly. However, not mentioning them would be negligent, and they need to at least be identified for the sake of other researchers who might consider related issues in the future.

12.4.1 Preachers' Perspective

Throughout this study, I tried to show there were observable reasons why every effort to empirically understand the practice of preaching should begin with listening to the listeners and letting them articulate their perceptions,

---

8. Fiddes, *Tracks and Traces*, 68 (italics mine).

experiences, and questions. Nonetheless, to gain even more comprehensive knowledge of what really happens in preaching and to inspect the depth of the gap between listeners and preachers, it might be mandatory to hear the preachers' story, too. What are their *actual* expectations of preaching, of their listeners, and of themselves? How do those expectations overlap or conflict with those of the listeners? Is the preacher's function a desolate position where preachers find it hard to authentically express themselves even though they occupy an office of authority and power? Do they feel they are expected to preach the Word, but not expected to come out with their real perception of that responsibility? Can the preaching practice lead to an alienation between the pastor and her congregation if preaching is mainly conceived as done by one active and another passive party? Consequently, do preachers believe that preaching should be more of a joint effort? These are some of the questions worth asking, and answers to them could open new horizons in our appreciation of preaching and its effects on Christian congregations.

12.4.2 Female Listeners' Perspective

Typically, a Croatian Baptist church is attended by more female than male believers. Women, thus, represent most of the silenced majority in the listening process. Yet, there are no female pastors and women preach only occasionally (and some congregations decidedly believe such practice to be contrary to the Bible and sound theology). In light of this, at the moment there is no reliable way of discovering any specifically female perspectives on preaching. Do they perceive the purpose of preaching differently than their brothers in Christ? Are there some specific expectations, possibly neglected by male preachers but closely related to their female identity? Do they, as listeners, feel they should be allowed to articulate their concerns and asked to participate in more active ways, or do they agree with their role as simply recipients of the message? Again, these and similar questions could initiate some valuable explorations.

12.4.3 Perceptions from the Margin

One of the evident limitations of this study is its focus on believers who regularly listen to sermons. Therefore, the participants were individuals with a positive attitude toward preaching. Their general inclination usually makes them benevolent to preaching and preachers. Their feedback also reveals their strong feeling of belonging to their respective congregations and of involvement in various activities of their local churches. However, finding out about the attitudes and perceptions of occasional listeners and irregular church service attenders , of those who linger on the margins of the congregation, could significantly add to our understanding not only of the attractive sides and relevance of preaching in the eyes and ears of those who do not identify as full members of a particular church, but also of the ecclesiological context of a specific congregation as observed by those from the outside. Such research may disclose how receptive this church is at its boundaries and help us rethink its attitude to those from the outside. Surely, in that case, the recruiting process may be more demanding, but the long-term rewards may easily compensate for these methodological difficulties.

12.4.4 Passive Responsibility and Cultural Conditioning

Another intriguing question to be considered in some future study is a possible connection between the passive responsibility of listeners and factors other than Baptist local theology and tradition. Are there influences from the wider culture that effectively sway Croatian Baptist hearers towards passive responsibility even if there are no theological or biblical obstacles to their more active involvement with the preaching practice? Could it be that this denomination, with its history as a religious minority since its very beginnings, developed specific behavioural patterns conditioned by the pervading forces coming from the realities of social and political systems around them? For instance, in his D. Min. thesis, Dražen Glavaš explored the faith and work gap in the Croatian culture.[9] His surveys, conducted among the general population (of which over 90 percent consider themselves Christians), reveal three main reasons for the current situation of "economic and social crisis, unemployment, high debt, brain drain, loss of values and trust." These are corruption, inefficient leadership (both in politics and economy), and a negative attitude toward work (laziness, nepotism, irresponsibility).[10] I believe that asking whether this general and dominant distrust in leaders, and negativism about the prospects of work being properly appreciated and rewarded, might

---

9. Glavaš, "Christian on Sunday."
10. Glavaš, 14.

be somehow projected on the believers' preferences in relation to preaching and may unveil some far-ranging insights.

12.4.5 Identification Techniques and Strategies

The participants in this study have undeniably exhibited susceptibility to sermons that foster their process of identification. In fact, identification is perhaps the most prominent rhetorical feature that intensifies the hearers' engagement with the sermon and paves the ways to their actual expectations being met. The data gathered also indicate that there are various levels at which this process takes place: sometimes listeners identify with the preacher's experience or a particular life situation, sometimes they connect with her personality or a specific emotion, and sometimes they can relate to the world of biblical characters. It would be highly beneficial to plumb the depths of techniques and strategies of these and other variants of identification.[11] Burke is known for his remark on identification: "Only those voices from without are effective which can speak in the language of a voice within."[12] Taking this cue, a study could be done based on exploring how much identification depends on the purposed use of appropriate language. What elements of delivery are particularly of service in creating such an intense connection with the hearers? What are the most effective procedures for allowing congregants to identify with the preacher's ethos in order to increase their receptivity to the experience of sermon listening? My expectation is that both Burke's notion of identification and Booth's concept of listening rhetoric could be especially helpful companions in investigating those mechanisms.[13]

---

11. Such a strand of research should also include an inquiry into the complexity of identification dynamics. For instance, McClure's concept of otherness warns against dissolving the asymmetry of relationships by seeking for "some kind of consensual intimacy." McClure, "Conversation and Proclamation," 2–3. Thus, identification must presuppose and respect the otherness of others. Similarly, Michael Brothers shows that the principle of distance must be applied in both biblical interpretation and sermon construction, by paying deliberate attention to the distance between the hearers and the sermon, between the hearers and the preacher, and between the hearers and the biblical text. Brothers, *Distance in Preaching*.

12. Burke, *Rhetoric of Motives*, 69.

13. In particular, see Booth, *Rhetoric of RHETORIC*, 55–83.

12.5 "Amen to That!"

At the end of the day, my learning process is not over, and this previous section should serve as a case in point. Still, I have reached some valuable convictions that will necessarily feed my future thinking and praxis. This study has taught me that the complexity and depth of the preaching practice cannot be expended by reduction to one of the rival constituents. Preaching is not a choice – *either* speech *or* silence. Preaching should not be viewed as *either* a domination of talking *or* a primacy of listening. The purpose of preaching is not to be lowered to the matter of preference for *either* persuasion *or* identification. And authority in preaching should not be perceived as assigned *either* to the preacher *or* to the congregation. Arguably, preaching is at its best whenever it sways between these poles, exercising its inclusive and unifying forces.

Looking back to the enigma expressed at the very beginning of this work, I am a little bit more confident of the possibility of finding a solution. And though this attempt at pronouncing this solution and closing my thesis in a single sentence may risk of sounding like a somewhat heedless simplification, here I will declare it nevertheless: Listening better means better preaching and preaching better means better listening!

APPENDIX

Interview Questions

Ethos-Related

1. Tell me about your becoming a member of this particular congregation.

2. What is the most important thing that takes place in this congregation?

3. Describe a typical Sunday morning service.

4. In this congregation, what is accomplished only through preaching?

5. What would be missing if there were no sermons?

6. Tell me how preaching shapes your church as a community.

7. Share about your experience of listening to sermons. What were the best moments? And the worst? Have you ever almost decided to leave the building?

8. Describe your relationships with pastors and preachers.

9. Tell me more about the pastor who was (or still is) a good preacher. What do you like about that person?

Logos-Related

1. What do you think pastor does when he or she is preaching?

2. Describe a particular sermon that you found truly interesting.

3. What was in that sermon that you found attractive or inspiring?

4. Tell me about a sermon that did not interest you or left you cold.

5. What was it about that sermon that left you indifferent or put you off?

6. What role does or should the Bible have in preaching?

7. When is the sermon authoritative for you?

8. What do you most want to find about God when listening to preaching?

9. How does God work during the sermon?

10. I assume you heard a sermon that made you change a certain conviction or behaviour. Tell me more about that sermon.

11. What did the pastor say or do to motivate you to act differently?

Pathos-Related

1. When a preacher stands behind the pulpit, what do you expect will happen as a result of listening to that sermon?

2. Can you describe a sermon that stirred your emotions?

3. What was it about that sermon that moved you?

4. Now, can you describe a sermon that seemed to move the congregation as a whole, as a community?

5. What was it about that sermon that moved the congregation?

6. Tell me about the situation when the sermon stirred some emotions you were not comfortable with.

7. What happens after the service during which a sermon stirred some emotions?

8. Do you think there are some issues or topics that are too dangerous to be dealt with from the pulpit? Can you name some of those issues and explain why do you think they are too dangerous or too sensitive?

Closing Question

If you had an opportunity to communicate to the preachers one or two things that would help them to motivate you for listening to sermons, what would they be?

Bibliography

The Academy of Homiletics. *Papers of the Annual Meeting,1965–2001: 36th Meeting Theme: Teaching Preaching.* St. Louis: The Academy of Homiletics, 2001.
Agnew, Lois. "The Classical Period." In *The Present State of Scholarship in the History of Rhetoric: A Twenty-First Century Guide*, edited by Lynée Lewis Gaillet and Winifred Bryan Horner, 7–41. Columbia: University of Missouri Press, 2010.
Allen, O. Wesley. *The Homiletic of All Believers: A Conversational Approach to Proclamation and Preaching.* Louisville: Westminster John Knox Press, 2005.
———. *The Renewed Homiletic.* Minneapolis: Fortress Press, 2010.
Allen, Ronald J. *Hearing the Sermon: Relationship, Content, Feeling.* Channels of Listening Series. St. Louis: Chalice Press, 2004.
———. *Interpreting the Gospel: An Introduction to Preaching.* St. Louis: Chalice Press, 1998.
———. *Preaching: An Essential Guide.* Nashville: Abingdon, 2002.
———. "Preaching as Mutual Critical Correlation through Conversation." In *Purposes of Preaching*, edited by Jana Childers, 1–22. St. Louis: Chalice Press, 2004.
———. "The Turn to the Listener: A Selective Review of a Recent Trend in Preaching." *Encounter* 64 (2003): 167–96.
Althaus, Paul. *The Theology of Martin Luther.* Minneapolis: Fortress, 1966.
Ammerman, Nancy. *Congregation and Community.* New Brunswick: Rutgers University Press, 1996.
Ammerman, Nancy, Carl S. Dudley, Jackson W. Carroll, and William McKinney, eds. *Studying Congregations: A New Handbook.* Nashville: Abingdon, 1998.
Aristotle. *On Rhetoric: A Theory of Civic Discourse.* Oxford: Oxford University Press, 1991.
Bailey, Raymond. "Proclamation as a Rhetorical Art." *Review & Expositor* 84, no. 1 (1987): 7–21. doi:10.1177/003463738708400102.

Ballard, Paul H., and John Pritchard. *Practical Theology in Action: Christian Thinking in the Service of Church and Society*. London: SPCK, 2006.
Barr, Browne. *Parish Back Talk*. New York: Abingdon, 1964.
Barth, Karl. *Church Dogmatics*, 2nd ed., 14 vols. Peabody: Hendrickson, 2010.
———. *Homiletics*. Louisville: Westminster John Knox Press, 1991.
———. *The Preaching of the Gospel*. Philadelphia: Westminster Press, 1963.
Bartlett, Gene E. *The Audacity of Preaching: The Lyman Beecher Lectures*. New York: Harper & Brothers, 1962.
Bartow, Charles L. *The Preaching Moment: A Guide to Sermon Delivery*. Dubuque: Kendall Hunt, 1995.
Bass, Dorothy C., and Craig Dykstra, eds. *For Life Abundant: Practical Theology, Theological Education, and Christian Ministry*. Grand Rapids: Eerdmans, 2008.
Beardslee, William A. "Incarnation." In *The Oxford Companion to the Bible*. Oxford University Press, 1993. Accessed 24 April 2018. http://www.oxfordreference.com/view/10.1093/acref/9780195046458.001.0001/acref-9780195046458-e-0344.
Belenky, Mary Field, Blythe Mcvicker Clinchy, Nancy Rule Goldberger, and Jill Mattuck Tarule. *Women's Ways of Knowing: The Development of Self, Voice, and Mind*, 10th Anniversary Edition. New York: Basic Books, 1997.
Bender, John, and David E. Wellbery. "Rhetoricality: On the Modernist Return to Rhetoric." In *The Ends of Rhetoric: History, Theory, Practice*, edited by John B. Bender and David E. Wellbery, 3–39. Stanford: Stanford University Press, 1990.
Bhatti, Deborah, Catherine Duce, James Sweeney, and Clare Watkins. *Talking about God in Practice: Theological Action Research and Practical Theology*. London: SCM Press, 2010.
Birviš, Aleksandar. "Dopuna knjizi 'Ludost propovedanja.'" *Teološki časopis* 7 (2007): 21–24.
Booth, Wayne C. "Rhetoric and Religion: Are They Essentially Wedded?" In *Radical Pluralism and Truth: David Tracy and the Hermeneutics of Religion*. Edited by Werner G. Jeanrond and Jennifer L. Rike, 62–80. New York: Crossroad, 1991.
———. *The Rhetoric of RHETORIC: The Quest for Effective Communication*. Oxford: Blackwell, 2004.
Braudrick, Michael Wayne. "Closed-Loop Preaching: Enhancing Preaching Using Lay Feedback." Unpublished doctoral thesis, Middlesex University, 2004. Accessed 8 April 2016. http://eprints.mdx.ac.uk/2658/.
Broadus, John A. *On the Preparation and Delivery of Sermons*. 4th ed. San Francisco: HarperOne, 1979.

———. *A Treatise on the Preparation and Delivery of Sermons*, ed. by Edwin Charles Dargan. New York: A. C. Armstrong & Son, 1898. Accessed 25 February 2015. http://archive.org/details/treatiseonprepar1898broa.

Brothers, Michael. *Distance in Preaching: Room to Speak, Space to Listen*. Grand Rapids: Eerdmans, 2014.

Brown Taylor, Barbara. "Preaching the Body." In *Listening to the Word: Studies in Honor of Fred B. Craddock*, edited by Gail R. O'Day and Thomas G. Long, 207–21. Nashville: Abingdon, 1993.

Browning, Don S. *A Fundamental Practical Theology: Descriptive and Strategic Proposals*. Minneapolis: Fortress Press, 1991.

Browning, W. R. F. "Incarnation." *A Dictionary of the Bible*. Oxford: Oxford University Press, 2009. Accessed 26 April 2018. http://www.oxfordreference.com/view/10.1093/acref/9780199543984.001.0001/acref-9780199543984-e-935.

Brueggemann, Walter. "The Preacher, the Text, and the People." *Theology Today* 47, no. 3 (1990): 237–47. doi:10.1177/004057369004700302.

———. *The Word Militant: Preaching a Decentering Word*. Minneapolis: Fortress, 2010.

Bulley, Colin J. *The Priesthood of Some Believers: Developments from the General to the Special Priesthood in the Christian Literature of the First Three Centuries*. Carlisle: Paternoster Press, 2000.

Bullinger, E. W. *Figures of Speech Used in the Bible*. New York: Cosimo, 2012.

Burke, Kenneth. *Counter-Statement*. Berkeley: University of California Press, 1968.

———. *Permanence and Change: An Anatomy of Purpose*. Berkeley: University of California Press, 1984.

———. *A Rhetoric of Motives*. Berkeley: University of California Press, 1969.

Buttrick, David G. *Homiletic: Moves and Structures*. Philadelphia: Fortress Press, 1987.

Byker, Donald. *Communication as Identification: An Introductory View*. New York: Harper & Row, 1975.

Cahalan, Kathleen A., and James R. Nieman. "Mapping the Field of Practical Theology." In *For Life Abundant: Practical Theology, Theological Education, and Christian Ministry*, edited by Dorothy C. Bass and Craig Dykstra, 62–90. Grand Rapids: Eerdmans, 2008.

Calvin, Jean. *Institutes of the Christian Religion*. Peabody, MA: Hendrickson, 2008.

Cameron, Helen, and Catherine Duce. *Researching Practice in Mission and Ministry: A Companion*. London: SCM Press, 2013.

Cameron, Helen, and Philip Richter. *Studying Local Churches: A Handbook*. London: SCM Press, 2005.

Carrell, Lori. *The Great American Sermon Survey*. Wheaton, IL: Mainstay Church Resources, 2000.

Carroll, Jackson W., and Carl S. Dudley. *Handbook for Congregational Studies.* Nashville: Abingdon, 1986.

Chopp, Rebecca. "Theological Persuasion: Rhetoric, Warrants, and Suffering." In *Worldviews and Warrants: Plurality and Authority in Theology*, edited by William Schweiker and Per M. Anderson, 17–31. Lanham, MD: University Press of America, 1987.

Cicero, Marcus Tullius. *Cicero in Twenty-Eight Volumes: De Oratore, Books 1–2.* Translated by E. W. Sutton. Cambridge, MA: Harvard University Press, 1967.

———. *The Orations of Marcus Tullius Cicero*, trans. by C. D. Yonge, 4 vols. London: G. Bell and Sons, 1913–1921. Accessed 25 April 2016. https://oll.libertyfund.org/titles/1736.

Coakley, Sarah. "Kenosis: Theological Meanings and Gender Connotations." In *The Work of Love: Creation as Kenosis*, 192–10. Grand Rapids: Eerdmans, 2001.

———. *Powers and Submissions: Spirituality, Philosophy and Gender.* Oxford: Blackwell, 2002. doi:10.1002/9780470693407.

Combrink, H. J. Bernard. "The Rhetoric of Sacred Scripture." In *Rhetoric, Scripture and Theology: Essays from the 1994 Pretoria Conference*, edited by Stanley E. Porter and Thomas H. Olbricht, 102–23. Sheffield: Sheffield Academic Press, 1996.

Compier, Don H. *What Is Rhetorical Theology?: Textual Practice and Public Discourse.* Harrisburg, PA: Trinity Press, 1999.

Congar, Yves Marie Joseph. *Lay People in the Church: A Study for a Theology of Laity.* Revised Edition. London: Westminster Christian Classics, 1985.

Cosgrove, Charles H., and W. Dow Edgerton. *In Other Words: Incarnational Translation for Preaching.* Grand Rapids: Eerdmans, 2007.

Counted, Victor. "Understanding God Images and God Concepts: Towards a Pastoral Hermeneutics of the God Attachment Experience." *Verbum et Ecclesia: Pretoria* 36 (2015): 1–14. doi:10.4102/ve.v36i1.1389.

Craddock, Fred B. *As One without Authority.* Nashville: Abingdon, 1979.

———. *First and Second Peter, and Jude.* Louisville: Westminster John Knox, 1995.

———. "Is There Still Room for Rhetoric?" In *Preaching on the Brink: The Future of Homiletics: In Honor of Henry H. Mitchell*, edited by Henry H. Mitchell and Martha J. Simmons, 66–74. Nashville: Abingdon, 1997.

———. *Preaching.* Nashville: Abingdon, 1985.

———. *Propovijedanje. Umijeće navještaja riječi danas*, Priručnici. Zagreb: Kršćanska sadašnjost, 2009.

Creswell, John W. *Qualitative Inquiry and Research Design: Choosing among Five Approaches.* 2nd ed. Thousand Oaks, CA: SAGE, 2007.

Cross, Frank Leslie, and Elizabeth A. Livingstone. *The Oxford Dictionary of the Christian Church.* 3rd ed. Oxford: Oxford University Press, 1997.

Davis, H. Grady. *Design for Preaching.* Minneapolis: Fortress, 2003.

De Koster, Lester. "The Preacher as Rhetorician." In *The Preacher and Preaching: Reviving the Art in the Twentieth Century*, edited by Samuel T. Logan, 303–30. Phillipsburg, NJ: P&R, 2011.

Denscombe, Martyn. *The Good Research Guide: For Small-Scale Social Research Projects*. 4th ed. Maidenhead: McGraw-Hill, 2010.

Dingemans, Gijsbert D. J. "A Hearer in the Pew: Homiletical Reflections and Suggestion." In *Preaching as a Theological Task: World, Gospel, Scripture: In Honor of David Buttrick*, edited by Thomas G. Long and Edward Farley, 38–49. Louisville: Westminster John Knox Press, 1996.

Dover, Greg. "Every Member a Minister? (Re)Claiming the Priesthood of All Believers." DMin diss., Drew University, 2015. Accessed 13 June 2018. https://search.proquest.com/docview/1680274232/abstract/280D5C26D1D0411APQ/1.

Dudley, Carl S. *Building Effective Ministry: Theory and Practice in the Local Church*. San Francisco: HarperCollins, 1983.

———. "Giving Voice to Local Churches: New Congregational Studies." *Christian Century (Chicago, Ill.)* 109 (1992): 742–6.

Dykstra, Craig R. "The Formative Power of the Congregation." *Religious Education* 82, no. 4 (1987): 530–46. doi:10.1080/0034408870820403.

Edwards, O. C. *A History of Preaching*. Nashville: Abingdon, 2004.

Ellis, Christopher J. *Gathering: A Theology and Spirituality of Worship in Free Church Tradition*. London: SCM Press, 2004.

Eslinger, Richard L. *A New Hearing: Living Options in Homiletic Method*. Nashville: Abingdon, 1987.

———. *Pitfalls in Preaching*. Grand Rapids: Eerdmans, 1996.

Fantham, Elaine. *The Roman World of Cicero's De Oratore*. Oxford: Oxford University Press, 2007.

Fiddes, Paul S. *Tracks and Traces: Baptist Identity in Church and Theology*. Eugene: Wipf & Stock, 2007.

Fox, Mark, Gill Green, and Peter J. Martin. *Doing Practitioner Research*. London: SAGE, 2007. Accessed 18 September 2013. http://public.eblib.com/EBLPublic/PublicView.do?ptiID=354878. doi:10.4135/9781849208994.

Frank, Thomas Edward. *The Soul of the Congregation: An Invitation to Congregational Reflection*. Nashville: Abingdon Press, 2000.

Freeman, Curtis W. *Contesting Catholicity: Theology for Other Baptists*. Baylor University Press, 2014.

Gaarden, Marianne. *The Third Room of Preaching: The Sermon, the Listener, and the Creation of Meaning*. Louisville: Westminster John Knox, 2017.

Gaarden, Marianne, and Marlene Ringgaard Lorensen. "Listeners as Authors in Preaching – Empirical and Theoretical Perspectives." *Homiletic* 38 (2013). Accessed 23 October 2015. doi:10.15695/hmltc.v38i1.3832.

Gaillet, Lynée Lewis, and Winifred Bryan Horner, eds. *The Present State of Scholarship in the History of Rhetoric: A Twenty-First Century Guide.* Columbia, MO: University of Missouri Press, 2010.

Garsten, Bryan. *Saving Persuasion: A Defense of Rhetoric and Judgment.* Cambridge, MA: Harvard University Press, 2009.

Geertz, Clifford. *The Interpretation of Cultures: Selected Essays.* New York: Basic Books, 1973.

George, Timothy. "The Priesthood of All Believers and the Quest for Theological Integrity." Accessed 12 April 2018. http://legacy.founders.org/main/wp-content/uploads/fj03.pdf.

Glavaš, Dražen. "Christian on Sunday and Atheist on Monday: Bridging the Faith and Work Gap in Croatian Culture." PhD diss., Gordon-Conwell Theological Seminary, 2016.

Graham, Elaine. "Practical Theology as Transforming Practice." In *The Blackwell Reader in Pastoral and Practical Theology,* edited by James Woodward and Stephen Pattison, 104–17. Oxford: Wiley, 2000.

Graham, Elaine L., Heather Walton, and Frances Ward. *Theological Reflection: Methods.* London: SCM Press, 2005.

Graves, Mike. "Deeply Dialogical: Rethinking the Conversation Called Preaching." *Journal for Preachers* 32 (2009): 24–31.

Green, Joel B. *1 Peter.* Grand Rapids: Eerdmans, 2007.

Greenhaw, David M., and Ronald J. Allen, eds. *Preaching in the Context of Worship.* St. Louis: Chalice Press, 2000.

Greggs, Tom. "The Priesthood of No Believer: On the Priesthood of Christ and His Church." *International Journal of Systematic Theology* 17, no. 4 (2015): 374–98. doi:10.1111/ijst.12122.

Grenz, Stanley J. *The Baptist Congregation: A Guide to Baptist Belief and Practice.* Vancouver: Regent College Publishing, 2002.

———. *Theology for the Community of God.* Carlisle: Paternoster, 1994.

Grlj, Giorgio. "Bogoslužbeni red baptističkih crkava." Unpublished document. Rijeka: Savez Baptističkih crkava, 1998.

———. "Propovijedi." *Pen de Gio.* Accessed 14 July 2015. https://pendegio.wordpress.com/propovijedi/.

Grudem, Wayne A. *Systematic Theology: An Introduction to Biblical Doctrine.* Leicester: Inter-Varsity Press, 1994.

Guest, Mathew, Karin Tusting, and Linda Woodhead. "Congregational Studies: Taking Stock." In *Congregational Studies in the UK: Christianity in a Post-Christian Context,* edited by Mathew Guest, Karin Tusting, and Linda Woodhead, 1–24. Ashgate: Routledge, 2004.

Hampson, Margaret Daphne. "On Power and Gender." *Modern Theology* 4, no. 3 (1988): 234–50. doi:10.1111/j.1468-0025.1988.tb00168.x.

———. *Swallowing a Fishbone?: Feminist Theologians Debate Christianity.* London: SPCK, 1996.

Hauerwas, Stanley. *A Cross-Shattered Church: Reclaiming the Theological Heart of Preaching.* Grand Rapids: Brazos Press, 2009.

Haymes, Brian. "Towards a Sacramental Understanding of Preaching." In *Baptist Sacramentalism*, edited by Anthony R. Cross and Philip E. Thompson, 263–70. Eugene: Wipf & Stock, 2006.

Heitink, Gerben. *Practical Theology: History, Theory, Action Domains: Manual for Practical Theology.* Grand Rapids: Eerdmans, 1999.

Herbert, T. D. *Kenosis and Priesthood: Towards a Protestant Re-Evaluation of the Ordained Ministry.* Eugene: Wipf & Stock, 2009.

Hesse-Biber, Sharlene Nagy, and Patricia L. Leavy. *The Practice of Qualitative Research.* Thousand Oaks, CA: SAGE, 2006.

Hilkert, Mary Catherine. *Naming Grace: Preaching and the Sacramental Imagination.* New York: Continuum, 1997.

Hinze, Bradford E. "Reclaiming Rhetoric in the Christian Tradition." *Theological Studies* 57, no. 3 (1996): 481–99. doi:10.1177/004056399605700305.

Hogan, Lucy Lind. "Rethinking Persuasion: Developing an Incarnational Theology of Preaching." *Homiletic* 24 (1999): 1–12.

Hogan, Lucy Lind, and Robert Reid. *Connecting with the Congregation: Rhetoric and the Art of Preaching.* Nashville: Abingdon, 1999.

Hopewell, James F. *Congregation: Stories and Structures.* London: SCM Press, 1988.

Horak, Josip. *Baptisti: povijest i načela vjerovanja.* Zagreb: Duhovna stvarnost, 1989.

Horton, Harold. *Propovijedanje i homiletika.* Trans. by Boris Arapović. Zagreb: Kristova Pentekostna crkva u SFRJ, 1967.

Howe, Reuel L. *Partners in Preaching: Clergy and Laity in Dialogue.* New York: Seabury Press, 1967.

Hustler, Jonathan. *Making the Words Acceptable: The Shape of the Sermon in Christian History.* London: SCM Press, 2009.

Jeter, Joseph J., and Ronald J. Allen. *One Gospel, Many Ears: Preaching for Different Listeners in the Congregation.* St. Louis: Chalice Press, 2002.

Jost, Walter, and Wendy Olmsted, eds. *A Companion to Rhetoric and Rhetorical Criticism.* Malden: Blackwell, 2008.

Keifert, Patrick, and Craig Van Gelder. *Testing the Spirits: How Theology Informs the Study of Congregations.* Grand Rapids: Eerdmans, 2009.

Kennedy, George A. "Historical Survey of Rhetoric." In *Handbook of Classical Rhetoric in the Hellenistic Period, 330 B.C.–A.D. 400*, edited by Stanley E. Porter, 3–42. Boston: Brill, 2001.

Kerr, Peter. "Listening to the Listeners." In *A Preacher's Companion: Essays from the College of Preachers*, edited by Geoffrey Hunter, Gethin Thomas, and Stephen I. Wright, 147–52. Oxford: Bible Reading Fellowship, 2004.

Kim, Eunjoo Mary. *Preaching in an Age of Globalization*. Louisville, KY: Westminster John Knox Press, 2010.

Kinast, Robert L. *What Are They Saying about Theological Reflection?* New York: Paulist Press, 2000.

Knežević, Ruben. "Baptist History in Croatia." In *A Dictionary of European Baptist Life and Thought*, edited by John H. Y. Briggs, 130–31. Studies in Baptist History and Thought, Vol. 33. Eugene: Wipf & Stock, 2009.

———. *Pregled povijesti baptizma na hrvatskom prostoru*. Osijek: Savez Baptističkih crkava u Republici Hrvatskoj – Baptistički institut, 2001.

Knowles, Michael P., ed. *The Folly of Preaching: Models and Methods*. Grand Rapids: Eerdmans, 2007.

Kolarić, Juraj. *Ekumenska trilogija: Istočni kršćani, pravoslavni, protestanti*. Zagreb: Prometej, 2005.

Lehotsky, Adolf. *Kratke upute za propovedanje*. Novi Sad: n.p., 1961.

Lincoln, Yvonna S., and Egon G. Guba. *Naturalistic Inquiry*. London: SAGE, 1985. doi:10.1016/0147-1767(85)90062-8.

Lischer, Richard. "Why I Am Not Persuasive." *Homiletic* 24 (1999): 13–16.

Lischer, Richard, and William H. Willimon. "Interview with Richard Lischer and William Willimon." *Homiletic* 20 (1995): 15–21.

Livingstone, E. A. "Image of God." In *The Concise Oxford Dictionary of the Christian Church*, edited by E. A. Livingstone. Oxford University Press, 2014. Accessed 5 April 2018. http://www.oxfordreference.com/view/10.1093/acref/9780199659623.001.0001/acref-9780199659623-e-2897.

———. "Incarnation." In *The Concise Oxford Dictionary of the Christian Church*, edited by E. A. Livingstone. Oxford University Press, 2014. Accessed 26 April 2018. http://www.oxfordreference.com/view/10.1093/acref/9780199659623.001.0001/acref-9780199659623-e-2919.

Llewellyn, Dawn, and Elaine Graham. "Theology & Religious Studies: Dawn Llewellyn & Elaine Graham Presentation." Accessed 12 March 2017. https://vimeo.com/130438142.

Long, Thomas G. "And How Shall They Hear? The Listener in Contemporary Preaching." In *Listening to the Word: Studies in Honor of Fred B. Craddock*, edited by Gail R. O'Day and Thomas G. Long, 167–88. Nashville: Abingdon, 1993.

———. *The Witness of Preaching*. 2nd ed. Louisville: Westminster John Knox, 2005.

Lorensen, Marlene Ringgaard. *Dialogical Preaching: Bakhtin, Otherness and Homiletics*. Göttingen: Vandenhoeck & Ruprecht, 2013. doi:10.13109/9783666624247.

Loscalzo, Craig A. *Preaching Sermons That Connect: Effective Communication through Identification*. Downers Grove, IL: InterVarsity Press, 1992.

Lundin, Roger. *Beginning with the Word: Modern Literature and the Question of Belief*. Grand Rapids: Baker Academic, 2014.

Lyons, Mary E. "Homiletics and Rhetoric: Recognizing an Ancient Alliance." *Homiletic* 12 (1987): 1–4.

MacBride, Tim. *Preaching the New Testament as Rhetoric: The Promise of Rhetorical Criticism for Expository Preaching*. Eugene: Wipf & Stock, 2014.

MacKenzie, Peter Donald. *Propovijedi o izgubljenom sinu*, Propovijedi pastora Pere. Zagreb: STEPress, 2009.

Maroney, Eric Kane. "Conflict, Change, and Conversion: Four Decades of Conversion among Baptists in Croatia 1970–2010." PhD diss., The Southern Baptist Theological Seminary, 2015. Accessed 28 May 2017. https://search.proquest.com/docview/1757267797/abstract/792786A1B59E40A3PQ/1.

Martin, John M. "Preaching for the Listener: Does Vineville Baptist Church in Macon, Georgia, Prefer Logos, Pathos, or Ethos in Connecting with Sermons?" DMin Thesis, Mercer University, 2011. Accessed 20 November 2015. http://search.proquest.com/pqdt/docview/864740931/abstract/CEA9F964C1C24725PQ/1.

Marty, Martin E. "Preaching Rhetorically." In *The Folly of Preaching: Models and Methods*, edited by Michael P. Knowles, 98–112. Grand Rapids: Eerdmans, 2007.

McClure, John S. "Conversation and Proclamation: Resources and Issues." *Homiletic* 22 (1997): 1–13.

———. *The Four Codes of Preaching: Rhetorical Strategies*. Louisville: Westminster John Knox, 2003.

———. *Other-Wise Preaching: A Postmodern Ethic for Homiletics*. St. Louis: Chalice Press, 2001.

———. "The Practice of Sermon Listening." *Congregations* 32 (2006): 6–9.

———. *Preaching Words: 144 Key Terms in Homiletics*. Louisville: Westminster John Knox, 2007.

———. *The Roundtable Pulpit: Where Leadership and Preaching Meet*. Nashville: Abingdon, 1995.

———, ed. *Best Advice for Preaching*. Minneapolis: Fortress Press, 1998.

McClure, John S., L. Susan Bond, Dan P. Moseley, G. Lee Ramsey, Ronald J. Allen, and Dale P. Andrews. *Listening to Listeners: Homiletical Case Studies*, Channels of Listening Series. St. Louis: Chalice Press, 2004.

McGrath, Alister E. *Christian History*. Malden: John Wiley & Sons, 2013.

———. *The Landscape of Faith: An Explorer's Guide to The Christian Creeds*. London: SPCK, 2018.

McKenzie, Alyce M. *Hear and Be Wise: Becoming a Preacher and Teacher of Wisdom*. Nashville: Abingdon, 2004.

McLaughlin, Raymond W. "The Ethics of Persuasive Preaching." *Journal of the Evangelical Theological Society* 15 (1972): 93–106.

Menzel, Kent E., and Lori J. Carrell. "The Relationship between Preparation and Performance in Public Speaking." *Communication Education* 43, no. 1 (1994): 17–26. doi:10.1080/03634529409378958.

Mercedes, Anna. "Christ as Chrism, Christ Given Away." *Dialog: A Journal of Theology* 53, no. 3 (2014): 233–39. Accessed 3 September 2019. doi:10.1111/dial.12120.

———. *Power for: Feminism and Christ's Self-Giving*. London: T & T Clark, 2011.

Meyers, Robin Rex. *With Ears to Hear: Preaching as Self-Persuasion*. Cleveland: Pilgrim Press, 1993.

Michaels, J. Ramsey. *1 Peter*. Word Biblical Commentary 49. Grand Rapids: Zondervan, 2018.

Migliore, Daniel L. *Faith Seeking Understanding: An Introduction to Christian Theology*. 3rd edition. Grand Rapids: Eerdmans, 2014.

Miro, Joan. *Oiseau Dans L'espace*, 17 July 1976, Centro de Arte Reina Sofía: "Miró en las colecciones del Estado." Accessed 1 August 2018. http://www.museoreinasofia.es/sites/default/files/obras/AS08874_0.jpg.

Moltmann, Jurgen. *God in Creation*. Minneapolis: Fortress, 1993.

Mulligan, Mary Alice, Diane Turner-Sharazz, and Dawn Ottoni Wilhelm. *Believing in Preaching: What Listeners Hear in Sermons*. Channels of Listening Series. St. Louis: Chalice Press, 2005.

Mulligan, Mary Alice, and Ronald J. Allen. *Make the Word Come Alive: Lessons from Laity*. Channels of Listening Series. St. Louis: Chalice Press, 2005.

Murphy, Nancey C. *Reasoning and Rhetoric in Religion*. Eugene: Wipf & Stock, 2001.

Nawrocki, Suzanne Scheiber. "Every Body Helps the Preacher: The Impact of Embodied Communication." PhD diss., Aquinas Institute of Theology, 2013. Accessed 10 September 2017. https://search.proquest.com/docview/1426182389/abstract/9F020DB466814AB9PQ/1.

Nedjeljne propovijedi – Baptistička crkva Rijeka. Accessed 12 January 2016. https://drive.google.com/folderview?ddrp=1&id=0B0lz01Z7YoZgSFdYTjQ4RVpma2c#.

Nieman, James R. *Knowing the Context: Frames, Tools, and Signs for Preaching*. Minneapolis: Fortress, 2008.

Nieman, James R., and Thomas G. Rogers. *Preaching to Every Pew: Cross-Cultural Strategies*. Minneapolis: Fortress, 2001.

Norrington, David C., Timothy L. Price, and Jon H. Zens. *To Preach or Not to Preach: The Church's Urgent Question*. Omaha: Quoir, 2013.

Old, Hughes Oliphant. *The Medieval Church*. Vol. 3, *The Reading and Preaching of the Scriptures in the Worship of the Christian Church*. Grand Rapids: Eerdmans, 1999.

Orčić, Stjepan, *Ludost propovedanja: predavanja o propovedništvu*. Novi Sad: MBM plas - Savez baptističkih crkava u Srbiji, 2007.

Osmer, Richard R. *Practical Theology: An Introduction*. Grand Rapids: Eerdmans, 2008.

Pagitt, Doug. *Preaching Re-Imagined: The Role of the Sermon in Communities of Faith*. Grand Rapids: Zondervan, 2009.

Pannenberg, Wolfhart. *Systematic Theology*, 3 vols. Grand Rapids: Eerdmans, 1994.

Pattison, Stephen. "Some Straw for Bricks: A Basic Introduction to Theological Reflection." In *The Blackwell Reader in Pastoral and Practical Theology*, edited by James Woodward and Stephen Pattison, 135–45. Oxford: Blackwell, 2000.

Peterlin, Davorin. "The Baptist Church in Zagreb: Early Years, 1921–1927." *Journal of Contemporary History* 40 (2008): 455–87.

———. "Počeci Baptističke crkve u Zagrebu 1870–1921." *Journal of Contemporary History* 38 (2006): 523–48.

———. "'Tabitha': The First Baptist Women's Association in Zagreb." *Kairos: Evangelical Journal of Theology* 1 (2007): 247–292.

———. "Theological Education among Croatian Baptists to 2000: A Socio-Historical Survey." *Baptist Quarterly* 38, no. 5 (2000): 239–59. doi:10.1080/0005576X.2000.11752098.

Pew Research Center. "Religious Belief and National Belonging in Central and Eastern Europe, 2017." Accessed 9 January 2019. http://www.pewforum.org/2017/05/10/religious-belief-and-national-belonging-in-central-and-eastern-europe/.

Plantinga, Richard J., Thomas R. Thompson, and Matthew D. Lundberg. *An Introduction to Christian Theology*. Cambridge: Cambridge University Press, 2010. doi:10.1017/CBO9780511800856.

Plato. *Gorgias*. Edited by C. J. Emlyn-Jones, translated by Walter Hamilton. Harmondsworth: Penguin Books, 2004.

Pleizier, Theo. *Religious Involvement in Hearing Sermons: A Grounded Theory Study in Empirical Theology and Homiletics*. Delft: Eburon Academic Publishers, 2010.

"Protestant Heritage, The." *Encyclopedia Britannica*. Accessed 22 March 2018. https://www.britannica.com/topic/The-Protestant-Heritage-1354359.

Purdy, Michael. "Listening, Culture and Structures of Consciousness: Ways of Studying Listening." *International Journal of Listening* 14, no. 1 (2000): 47–68. Accessed 12 November 2017. doi:10.1080/10904018.2000.10499035.

Quintilian, Marcus Fabius. *Institutio Oratoria*. Translated by Harold Edgeworth Butler. Cambridge, MA: Harvard University Press, 1920. Accessed 3 December 2013. http://penelope.uchicago.edu/Thayer/E/Roman/Texts/Quintilian/Institutio_Oratoria/home.html.

Randolph, David James. *The Renewal of Preaching*. Philadelphia: Fortress Press, 1969.

———. *The Renewal of Preaching in the Twenty-First Century: The Next Homiletics*. 2nd ed. Eugene: Wipf & Stock, 2008.

Rapp, Christof. "Aristotle's Rhetoric." In *The Stanford Encyclopedia of Philosophy*, edited by Edward N. Zalta, Spring 2010. Accessed 30 October 2014. http://plato.stanford.edu/archives/spr2010/entries/aristotle-rhetoric/.

Ratcliffe, Krista. "The Twentieth and Twenty-First Centuries." In *The Present State of Scholarship in the History of Rhetoric: A Twenty-First Century Guide*. Edited by Lynée Lewis Gaillet and Winifred Bryan Horner, 185–236. Columbia: University of Missouri Press, 2010.

Reid, Clyde H. *The Empty Pulpit: A Study in Preaching as Communication*. New York: Harper & Row, 1967.

Resner, André. *Preacher and Cross: Person and Message in Theology and Rhetoric*. Grand Rapids: Eerdmans, 1999.

Riegert, Eduard R. "What Is Authoritative for the 'Post-Modern' Listener." *Currents in Theology and Mission* 25 (1998): 5–14.

Rietveld, David. "A Survey of the Phenomenological Research of Listening to Preaching." *Homiletic* 38, no. 2 (2013). Accessed 14 March 2015. doi:10.15695/hmltc.v38i2.3867.

Ritchie, Jane, and Jane Lewis, eds. *Qualitative Research Practice*. London: Sage, 2013.

Ritschl, Dietrich. *A Theology of Proclamation*. Richmond, VA: John Knox Press, 1963.

Roen, William H. *The Inward Ear: A Sermon Evaluation Method for Preachers and Hearers of the Word*. Durham, NC: Alban Institute, 1989.

Rose, Lucy A. "Conversational Preaching: A Proposal." *Journal for Preachers* 19 (1995): 26–30.

———. *Sharing the Word: Preaching in the Roundtable Church*. Louisville, KY: Westminster John Knox, 1997.

Rowell, Margit, ed. *Joan Miro: Selected Writings & Interviews*. Boston: Macmillan, 1986.

Saint Augustine. *On Christian Teaching*. Edited and translated by R. P. H. Green. Oxford: Oxford University Press, 1997.

Saramago, José. *The Cave*. Translated by Margaret Jull Costa. Orlando, FL: Harcourt, 2002.

Schlafer, David J. *Surviving the Sermon: A Guide to Preaching for Those Who Have to Listen.* Cambridge, MA: Cowley Publications, 1992.

Scholer, John. *Proleptic Priests: Priesthood in the Epistle to the Hebrews.* Sheffield: JSOT Press, 1991.

Schultze, Quentin J. *An Essential Guide to Public Speaking: Serving Your Audience with Faith, Skill, and Virtue.* Grand Rapids: Baker Academic, 2006.

Schumacher, Karl Peter. "A Functional Holistic View of Man as the Image of God and Its Implications for Environmentalism." DMin diss., The Southern Baptist Theological Seminary, 2010. https://search.proquest.com/docview/883384803/abstract/4FD21336951C47FDPQ/1.

Schweiker, William, and Per M. Anderson, eds. *Worldviews and Warrants: Plurality and Authority in Theology.* Lanham, MD: University Press of America, 1987. Accessed 20 April 2018. http://catalog.hathitrust.org/api/volumes/oclc/16277809.html.

Selak, Annie. "Orthodoxy, Orthopraxis, and Orthopathy: Evaluating the Feminist Kenosis Debate." *Modern Theology* 33, no. 4 (2017): 529–48. Accessed 3 September 2019. doi:10.1111/moth.12354.

Silverman, David. *Doing Qualitative Research: A Comprehensive Guide.* Los Angeles: SAGE, 2008.

Smit, Dirk J. "Theology as Rhetoric? Or: Guess Who's Coming to Dinner." In *Rhetoric, Scripture and Theology: Essays from the 1994 Pretoria Conference*, edited by Stanley E. Porter and Thomas H. Olbricht, 393–422. Sheffield: Sheffield Academic Press, 1996.

Smith, Mary J. *Persuasion and Human Action: A Review and Critique of Social Influence Theories.* Belmont: Wadsworth, 1985.

Smyth, Charles. "The Art of Preaching: A Practical Survey of Preaching." In *The Church of England, 747–1939.* London: SPCK, 1953.

Sperdžen, Čarls H. *Pouke propovednicima*, trans. by Jovan Vlašić. Veternik: LDIJ, 2000.

Spurdžon, Čarls Hedon. *Dobri saveti propovednicima Jevanđelja*, trans. by Mih. Popović. Beograd: Knjižara S. B. Cvijanovića, 1909.

Spurgeon, Charles H. *Tako je govorio Spurgeon*, trans. by Gabrijel Jonke and Mirjana Lovrec. Zagreb: Branko Lovrec, 1971.

Standing, Roger. *Preaching for the Unchurched.* Cambridge: Grove Books, 2002.

"Statut mjesne baptističke crkve." Savez Baptističkih crkava u Republici Hrvatskoj, 1997. Accessed 26 September 2015. http://www.baptist.hr/dokumenti-saveza/59-dokumenti/83-statut-mjesne-baptistike-crkve.

"Statut Saveza baptističkih crkava u Republici Hrvatskoj." Savez Baptističkih crkava u Republici Hrvatskoj, 1991. Accessed 29 July 2015. http://www.baptist.hr/slube-u-savezu7/159-sbc/dokumenti/81-statut-saveza-baptistiki-crkava-u-republici-hrvatskojj.

"Statut Saveza baptističkih crkava u Republici Hrvatskoj." Savez Baptističkih crkava u Republici Hrvatskoj, 2015. Accessed 20 October 2015. http://baptist.hr/images/stories/pdf/Statut_SBC_u_RH.pdf.

Stokes, Allison, and David A. Roozen. "The Unfolding Story of Congregational Studies." In *Carriers of Faith: Lessons from Congregational Studies*, edited by Carl S. Dudley, Jackson W. Carroll, and James P. Wind, 183–92. Louisville, KY: Westminster John Knox, 1991.

"Strategija SBC u RH 2020." Savez Baptističkih crkava u Republici Hrvatskoj.

Swinton, John, and Harriet Mowatt. *Practical Theology and Qualitative Research*. London: SCM Press, 2006.

Tannen, Deborah. *You Just Don't Understand: Women and Men in Conversation*. New York: William Morrow Paperbacks, 2007.

Tillich, Paul. *Systematic Theology: Existence and the Christ*. Chicago: University of Chicago Press, 1957.

Tisdale, Leonora Tubbs. "Exegeting the Congregation." In *Teaching Preaching as a Christian Practice: A New Approach to Homiletical Pedagogy*, edited by Thomas G. Long and Leonora Tubbs Tisdale, 75–89. Louisville: Westminster John Knox, 2008.

———. *Preaching as Local Theology and Folk Art*. Minneapolis: Fortress, 1997.

Torrance, Thomas F. *Royal Priesthood: A Theology of Ordained Ministry*. London: A&C Black, 1993. doi:10.5040/9780567690852.

"Treatise on Rhetorical Invention." In *The Orations of Marcus Tullius Cicero*, trans. by C. D. Yonge, 4 vols. London: George Bell & Sons, 1888. Accessed 20 January 2015. http://www.classicpersuasion.org/pw/cicero/dnvindex.htm.

"Ugovor s Vladom RH," 2005. Accessed 21 July 2015. http://baptist.hr/images/stories/pdf/Ugovor%20s%20Vladom%20RH.pdf.

Van der Geest, Hans. *Presence in the Pulpit: The Impact of Personality in Preaching*. Atlanta: John Knox, 1981.

Van Harn, Roger E. *Preacher, Can You Hear Us Listening?* Grand Rapids: Eerdmans, 2005.

Warner, Martin, ed. *The Bible as Rhetoric: Studies in Biblical Persuasion and Credibility*. Warwick Studies in Philosophy and Literature. London: Routledge, 1990.

Webb, Stephen H. "Reviving the Rhetorical Heritage of Protestant Theology." In *A Companion to Rhetoric and Rhetorical Criticism*, edited by Walter Jost and Wendy Olmsted, 409–24. Oxford: Wiley, 2004. doi:10.1002/9780470999851.ch26.

Welker, Michael. *God the Revealed: Christology*. Grand Rapids: Eerdmans, 2013.

Welz, Claudia. "Imago Dei." *Studia Theologica* 65, no. 1 (2011): 74–91. Accessed 12 May 2018. doi:10.1080/0039338X.2011.578372.

Willimon, William H., and Richard Lischer, eds. "Rhetoric." In *Concise Encyclopedia of Preaching*, 409–16. Louisville: Westminster John Knox, 1995.

Wills, Garry. *Why Priests?: A Failed Tradition*. New York: Penguin, 2013.

Wilson, Paul Scott. *Broken Words: Reflections on the Craft of Preaching*. Nashville: Abingdon, 2004.

———. "Learning from Classical Rhetoric." In *Broken Words: Reflections on the Craft of Preaching*, 125–34. Nashville: Abingdon, 2004.

———. *The Practice of Preaching*. Rev. ed. Grand Rapids: Abingdon, 2012.

World Council of Churches. "Baptism, Eucharist and Ministry." Faith and Order Paper No. 111, the "Lima Text", 15 January 1982. Accessed 24 May 2018. https://www.oikoumene.org/en/resources/documents/commissions/faith-and-order/i-unity-the-church-and-its-mission/baptism-eucharist-and-ministry-faith-and-order-paper-no-111-the-lima-text.

Wright, Christopher J. H. *Old Testament Ethics for the People of God*. Downers Grove, IL: InterVarsity Press, 2004.

Wright, Stephen I. *Alive to the Word: A Practical Theology of Preaching for the Whole Church*. London: SCM Press, 2010.

Zink-Sawyer, Beverly. "The Word Purely Preached and Heard." *Interpretation: A Journal of Bible & Theology* 51 (1997): 342–57. doi:10.1177/002096439605100402.

Zulick, Margaret D. "The Active Force of Hearing: The Ancient Hebrew Language of Persuasion." *Rhetorica* 10, no. 4 (1992): 367–80. Accessed 3 December 2015. doi:10.1525/rh.1992.10.4.367.

Langham Literature, with its publishing work, is a ministry of Langham Partnership.

Langham Partnership is a global fellowship working in pursuit of the vision God entrusted to its founder John Stott –

> *to facilitate the growth of the church in maturity and Christ-likeness through raising the standards of biblical preaching and teaching.*

Our vision is to see churches in the Majority World equipped for mission and growing to maturity in Christ through the ministry of pastors and leaders who believe, teach and live by the word of God.

Our mission is to strengthen the ministry of the word of God through:
- nurturing national movements for biblical preaching
- fostering the creation and distribution of evangelical literature
- enhancing evangelical theological education

especially in countries where churches are under-resourced.

Our ministry

Langham Preaching partners with national leaders to nurture indigenous biblical preaching movements for pastors and lay preachers all around the world. With the support of a team of trainers from many countries, a multi-level programme of seminars provides practical training, and is followed by a programme for training local facilitators. Local preachers' groups and national and regional networks ensure continuity and ongoing development, seeking to build vigorous movements committed to Bible exposition.

Langham Literature provides Majority World preachers, scholars and seminary libraries with evangelical books and electronic resources through publishing and distribution, grants and discounts. The programme also fosters the creation of indigenous evangelical books in many languages, through writer's grants, strengthening local evangelical publishing houses, and investment in major regional literature projects, such as one volume Bible commentaries like the *Africa Bible Commentary* and the *South Asia Bible Commentary*.

Langham Scholars provides financial support for evangelical doctoral students from the Majority World so that, when they return home, they may train pastors and other Christian leaders with sound, biblical and theological teaching. This programme equips those who equip others. Langham Scholars also works in partnership with Majority World seminaries in strengthening evangelical theological education. A growing number of Langham Scholars study in high quality doctoral programmes in the Majority World itself. As well as teaching the next generation of pastors, graduated Langham Scholars exercise significant influence through their writing and leadership.

To learn more about Langham Partnership and the work we do visit **langham.org**

www.ingramcontent.com/pod-product-compliance
Lightning Source LLC
Chambersburg PA
CBHW070235240426
43673CB00044B/1798